EXPAND 3

STUDENT'S BOOK & WORKBOOK

Carla Maurício Vianna
Luciana Santos Pinheiro

Pearson

Pearson

Head of Product - Pearson Brasil	Juliano de Melo Costa
Product Manager - Pearson Brasil	Marjorie Robles
Product Coordinator - ELT	Mônica Bicalho
Authors	Carla Maurício Vianna
Teacher's Guide	Carla Maurício Vianna
Workbook	Luciana Santos Pinheiro (Allya Assessoria Linguística)
Extra content	Carla Maurício Vianna Luciana Santos Pinheiro (Allya Assessoria Linguística)
Editors - ELT	Gisele Aga Renata S. C. Victor Simara H. Dal'Alba (Allya Assessoria Linguística)
Editors (Teacher's Book)	Gisele Aga Simara H. Dal'Alba (Allya Assessoria Linguística)
Proofreader (English)	Silva Serviços de Educação
Proofreader (Portuguese)	Fernanda R. Braga Simon
Copyeditor	Maria Estela Alcântara
Pedagogical Reviewer	Najin Lima
Quality Control	Viviane Kirmeliene
Art and Design Coordinator	Rafael Lino
Art Editor - ELT	Emily Andrade
Acquisitions and permissions Manager	Maiti Salla
Acquisitions and permissions team	Andrea Bolanho Cristiane Gameiro Heraldo Colon Maricy Queiroz Paula Quirino Sandra Sebastião Shirlei Sebastião
Graphic design	Mirella Della Maggiore Armentano MRS Consultoria Editorial
Graphic design (cover)	Mirella Della Maggiore Armentano MRS Consultoria Editorial
Media Development	Estação Gráfica
Audio	Maximal Studio
Audiovisual Editor	Tatiane Almeida
Audiovisual	Desenrolados

The publisher would like to thank the following for their kind permission to reproduce their photographs:

Alamy Stock: p. 24, 40, 46. **Always/ Leo Burnett**: p. 12. **Cartoonstock**: p.48. **Getty Images**: p. 43. **iStock**: capa, p. 9, 17, 18, 24, 27, 34, 38, 45, 53, 63, 64, 68, 71, 72, 79. **Jennifer Siebel Newsom**: p. 16. **King Vidor (Warner Home Video)**: p. 16. **Los Angeles Times**: p. 32. **Mark Andrews (Pixar Animation Studios)**: p. 16. **Shutterstock**: p. 35, 41, 52, 57, 70, 73. **Sustain**: p. 43. **The Penguin Press**: p. 28.

Every effort has been made to trace the copyright holders and we apologize in advance for any unintentional omissions. We would be pleased to insert the appropriate acknowledgement in any subsequent edition of this publication.

Dados Internacionais de Catalogação na Publicação (CIP)
(Câmara Brasileira do Livro, SP, Brasil)

Expand 3: Student's Book / Carla Maurício Vianna, Luciana Santos Pinheiro. -- São Paulo:
Pearson Education do Brasil, 2019.

ISBN 978-65-50110-36-9

1. Inglês (Ensino Médio) I. Pinheiro, Luciana Santos. II. Título.

19-25487   CDD-420.7

Índices para catálogo sistemático:
1. Inglês: Ensino Médio 420.7
Maria Alice Ferreira - Bibliotecária - CRB-8/7964

ISBN 978-65-50110-36-9 (Student's Book & Workbook)
ISBN 978-65-50110-37-6 (Teacher's Book)

EXPAND 3

❯ Unit 1	9
❯ Unit 2	17
❯ Review 1	25
❯ Unit 3	27
❯ Unit 4	35
❯ Review 2	43
❯ Unit 5	45
❯ Unit 6	53
❯ Review 3	61
❯ Unit 7	63
❯ Unit 8	71
❯ Review 4	79
Grammar Overview	81
Language Reference	85
Reading Strategies	93
Irregular Verbs	94
Common Mistakes	96
False Friends	98
Glossary	99
Workbook	103
Audio Scripts	136

CONTENTS

	READING	VOCABULARY IN USE	LANGUAGE IN USE 1	EXPAND YOUR READING	LANGUAGE IN USE 2	LISTENING COMPREHENSION
UNIT 1 Gender Equality is for Everybody » page 9	Research article: Working women: Key facts and trends in female labor force participation	Expressions for gender parity and inequality	Present perfect continuous	Position article: Boys do cry: one man's experience of depression	Present perfect simple vs. present perfect continuous	A talk about an interview with a documentary director
UNIT 2 Technology in the School Curriculum » page 17	Informative article: Coding In Education: Why It's Important & How It's Being Implemented	Coding language	Subject-verb agreement	Curriculum: Junior Computer Curriculum	Compound adjectives	An interview with students who built a robot

Review 1 (Units 1-2)
» Page 25

	READING	VOCABULARY IN USE	LANGUAGE IN USE 1	EXPAND YOUR READING	LANGUAGE IN USE 2	LISTENING COMPREHENSION
UNIT 3 Can We Eat with a Clear Conscience? » page 27	Book excerpt: Omnivore's dilemma	Words derived from Latin	Second conditional	Book review: No Accounting for Mouthfeel	Zero, first, and second conditionals	A lecture about agriculture and the environment
UNIT 4 Extreme Weather Events Affecting the Planet » page 35	News stories: 4 People Who Faced Disaster – And How They Made It out Alive	Weather-related phrasal verbs and idioms	Past perfect	Expository essay: Widespread impacts	Adverbs of degree	A testimonial about being caught in an avalanche

Review 2 (Units 3-4)
» Page 43

Grammar Review	Language Reference	Reading Strategies	Irregular Verbs
» page 81	» page 85	» page 93	» page 94

	READING	VOCABULARY IN USE	LANGUAGE IN USE 1	EXPAND YOUR READING	LANGUAGE IN USE 2	LISTENING COMPREHENSION
UNIT 5 **In the Limelight** page 45	Entertainment news: What would have happened next if these TV characters hadn't died?	Homonyms, homophones, and homographs	Third conditional	List: TV Shows You Wish You Were a Character On	*Wish*	Results of research on binge-watching TV shows
UNIT 6 **Uncovering Blockchain and the Dark Web** page 53	Opinion article: Forget Bitcoin, It's All About The Blockchain	Technology and financial nouns and phrasal verbs	*Some, any, no, every*	Information report: The dark web and how to access it	Direct and indirect speech	A talk about Bitcoin and the Dark Web

Review 3 (Units 5-6)
Page 61

UNIT 7 **Digital Influencing** page 63	Blog post: Under the Influence: The Power of Social Media Influencers	Adjectives ending in *-ed* and *–ing*	Modal verbs for assumption: *must* and *can*	Guide: How to make it as an Instagram influencer	Passive voice	A talk about what makes a real influencer
UNIT 8 **The End of a Journey** page 71	News article: Too many graduates are mismatched to their jobs. What's going wrong?	Collocations with *have* and *take*	Future continuous and future perfect	Advice letter: How do I deal with the post-university blues?	Verb tense review	A graduation speech

Review 4 (Units 7-8)
page 79

Common Mistakes page 96

False Friends page 98

Glossary page 99

Workbook page 103

Audio Scripts page 136

PRESENTATION

STUDENT'S BOOK

Welcome to the *Expand* collection! *Expand* prepares students for the English part of Brazilian exams ENEM and vestibular, which are aimed at testing students' ability to read a wide variety of authentic texts of different genres. *Expand* provides students with listening, speaking, and writing activities that help them to develop their overall knowledge of the language. Each thematic unit contains two reading sections that introduce grammar and vocabulary topics, as well as listening comprehension activities that give students contact with oral text genres.

OPENING PAGE

Each unit starts with an opening page containing:

IN THIS UNIT YOU WILL…

This shows the main objectives for the unit.

> **▶ IN THIS UNIT YOU WILL…**
> - take part in discussions about coding in education;
> - talk about a technology curriculum and robotics;
> - learn about subject-verb agreement;
> - identify and use compound adjectives.

LEAD OFF

This section presents three to four questions for content contextualization.

LEAD OFF
- What situation does the picture represent? Are you familiar with that situation?
- Do you know what *coding* means? Explain.
- What do you think about the integration of technological projects in school curriculums?

READING PAGES

This two-page section contains the first reading text and activities of the unit. It develops reading strategies and is subdivided into the following stages:

BEFORE READING

This section contains one or two activities that help students to prepare for the text topic, which is presented in the section WHILE READING.

> **READING**
> **▶▶ BEFORE READING**
> You are going to read a text about the implementation of computer programming in education. Is this a reality in your country or school? How do you think students could benefit from having computer programming lessons? Exchange ideas with your classmates.

WHILE READING

In this section students read a text and answer a question related to it. Texts are in a variety of different genres and aimed at developing several reading strategies.

> **▶▶ WHILE READING** | Selecting a good title
>
> Read the whole text and check (✓) the best title for it.
> a. ( ) The YouTube Phenomenon: a disruptive force
> b. ( ) Globalization: Concepts, Causes, and Consequences
> c. ( ) Under the Influence: The Power of Social Media Influencers

Selecting a good title

AFTER READING

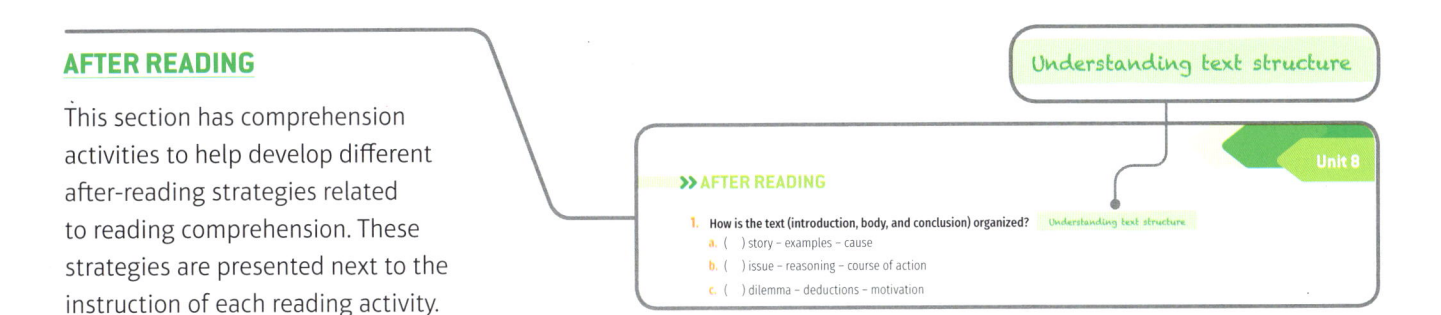

This section has comprehension activities to help develop different after-reading strategies related to reading comprehension. These strategies are presented next to the instruction of each reading activity.

VOCABULARY PAGES

This stage develops students' vocabulary through activities containing vocabulary from the text and related to the topic of the unit.

EXPAND YOUR VOCABULARY

This section contains one to three activities related to the vocabulary presented in the text. It also prompts students to engage in conversational topics based on the text students have read.

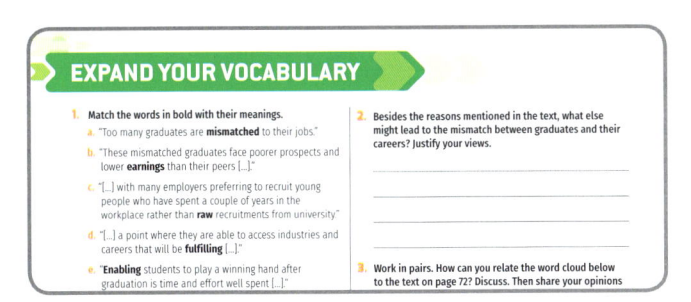

VOCABULARY IN USE

Here students are presented with an example of the target vocabulary taken from the main reading text and do activities to develop their vocabulary knowledge.

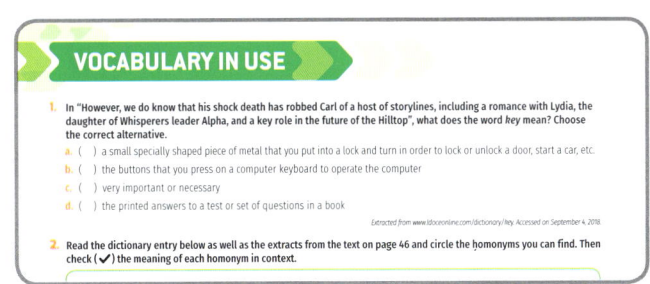

LANGUAGE IN USE 1

This page shows the first grammar topic of the unit. It contains examples from the text and activities that develop students' grammar knowledge in the target language.

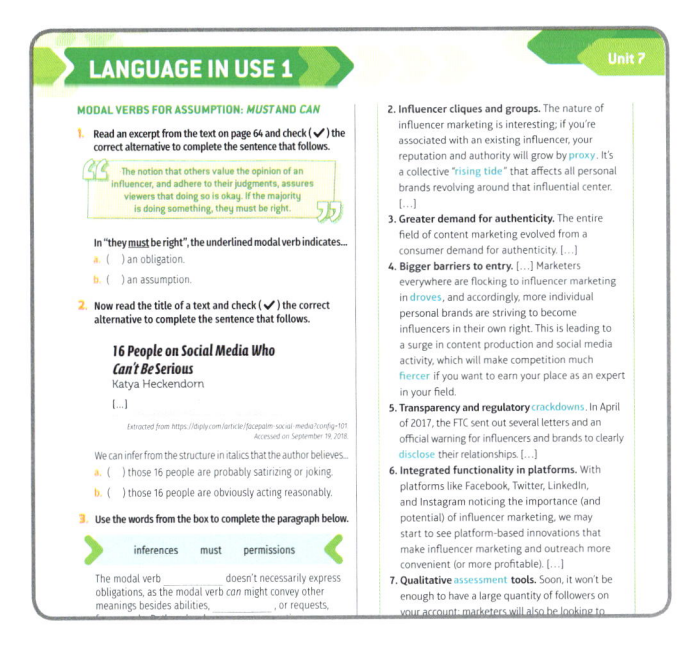

EXPAND YOUR READING

This section contains another text for students to work on both the text genre and comprehension.

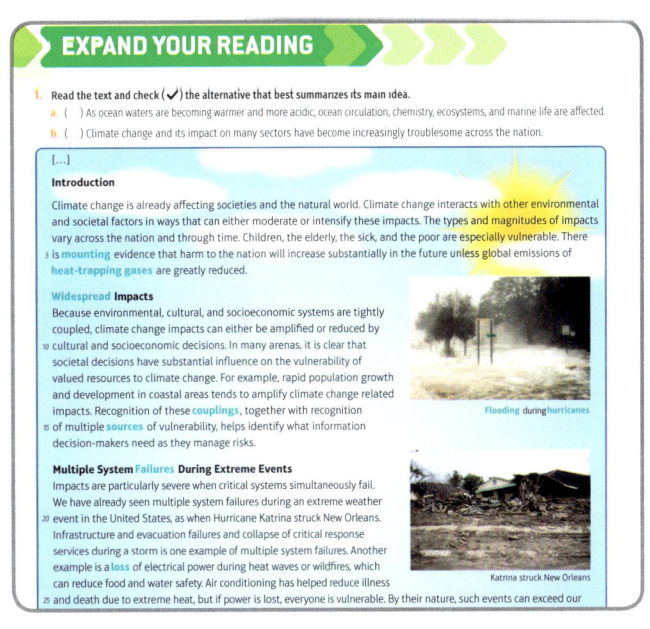

PRESENTATION

LANGUAGE IN USE 2

This page shows the second grammar topic of the unit. It contains examples from the text in *Expand your reading* and activities that develop students' grammar knowledge in the target language.

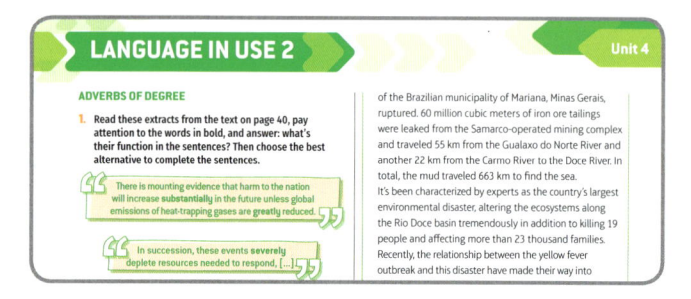

LISTENING COMPREHENSION

This section contains listening activities with authentic texts aimed at developing students' listening skills.

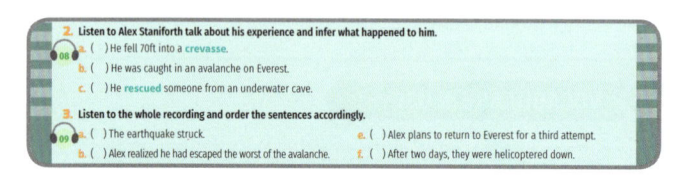

EXPAND YOUR HORIZONS

In this end-of-unit section students are presented with three statements that allow them to discuss the topic in the listening comprehension section and think critically about it while using the target language.

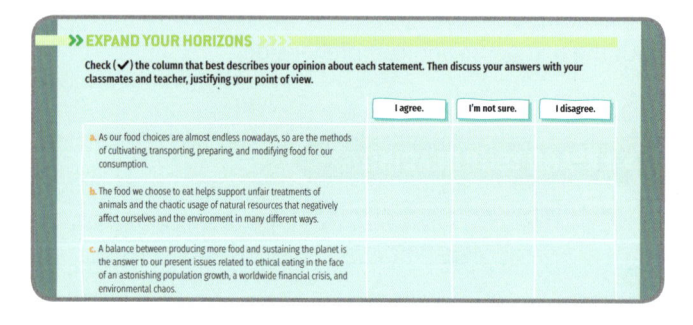

REVIEW

After every two units there is a two-page section for students to review and practice the language they have learned so far.

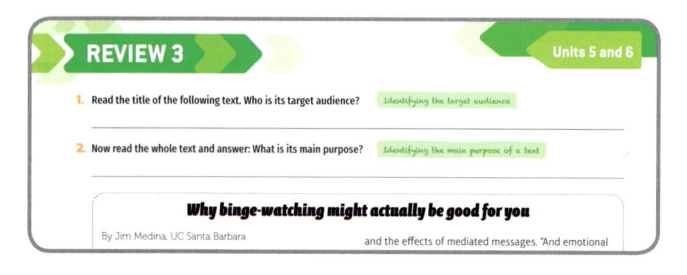

WORKBOOK

Each unit has four pages of reading, vocabulary, and grammar activities. It also has an ENEM or vestibular question in the section AN EYE ON ENEM / VESTIBULAR.

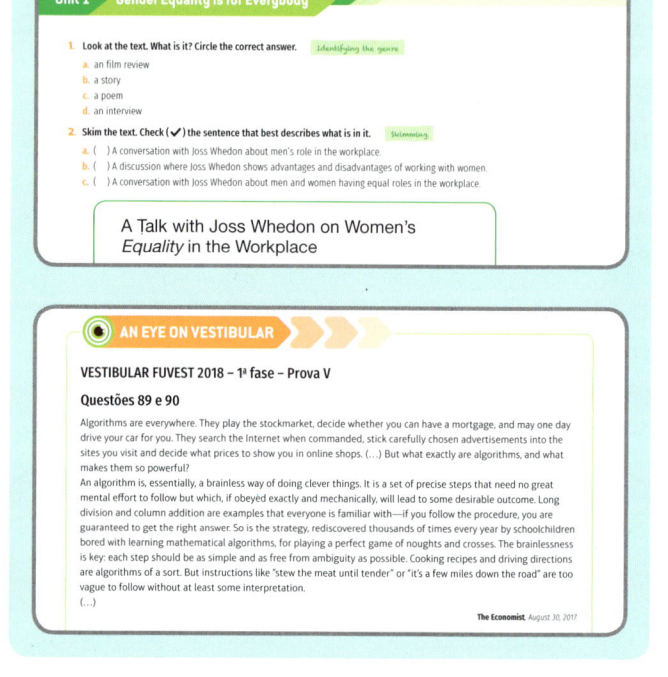

DIGITAL COMPONENTS

Video lessons for all *Language in Use* and *Vocabulary in Use* sections and for exam practice.

Mock test generator with major Brazilian *Vestibular* and ENEM questions to prepare students for these exams.

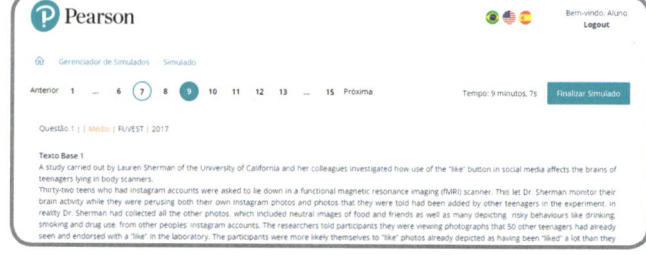

UNIT 1
Gender Equality is for Everybody

▶ IN THIS UNIT YOU WILL...
- reflect on gender equality;
- talk about gender stereotypes and modern masculinity;
- learn how to use the present perfect continuous for actions or states that started in the past and are still going on in the present;
- compare the uses of the present perfect simple and the present perfect continuous.

LEAD OFF

- Do you agree with the title of this unit? How can you relate it to the picture?
- Do women and men have equal opportunities in Brazil? What about in other parts of the world?
- What are some stereotypes about men and women? Do you think that any of them are true?

READING

▶▶ BEFORE READING

Work in pairs. What do you understand from the quotes below? *Bridging and relating to the topic*

> My message to girls everywhere in this world: believe in yourself and trust yourself, because if you don't believe in yourself, no one else will.
> (Marta Vieira da Silva, Brazilian – FIFA Women's World Player of the Year 2006, 2010, and 2018)

> Speak without shame and stand up with love for women's equality, and bring about the change we all want to see.
> (Ram Devineni, Indian-American – co-creator of comic book superhero Priya, who fights gender-based violence)

Extracted from www.unwomen.org. Accessed on January 27, 2019.

▶▶ WHILE READING

Skim the text. What is it about? *Skimming to identify the main topic*

Working women: Key facts and trends in female labor force participation

In almost every country in the world, men are more likely to participate in labor markets than women. However, these gender differences in participation rates have been narrowing substantially in recent decades. […]
- All over the world, labor force participation among women of working age increased substantially in the last century.
- In some parts of the world, the historical increase in female labor force participation has slowed down or even regressed slightly in recent years.
- Women all over the world allocate a substantial amount of time to activities that are not typically recorded as "economic activities". **Hence**, female participation in labor markets tends to increase when the time-cost of unpaid care work is reduced, shared equally with men, and/or made more compatible with market work.

[…]
The following visualization provides a picture of how men and women compare today in terms of participation in labor markets, country by country. Shown is the female-to-male **ratio** in labor force participation rates (expressed in percent). These **figures** show estimates from the International Labor Organization (ILO). These are "modelled estimates" in the sense that the ILO produces them after harmonizing various data sources to improve comparability across countries.

As we can see, the numbers for most countries are well below 100%, which means that the participation of women tends to be lower than that of men. Yet differences are **outstanding**: in countries such as Syria or Algeria, the ratio is below 25%. In contrast, in Laos, Mozambique, Rwanda, Malawi, and Togo, the relationship is close to, or even slightly above 100% (i.e. there is gender parity in labor force participation or even a higher share of women participating in the labor market than men).
[…]

Ratio of female to male labor force participation rates (%), 2015

Our World in Data

The female-to-male ratio of labor force participation rates is calculated by dividing the labor force participation rate among women, by the corresponding rate for men. The labor force participation rate is defined as the proportion of the population ages 15+ that is economically active. All figures correspond to 'modeled ILO estimates' (see source for details).

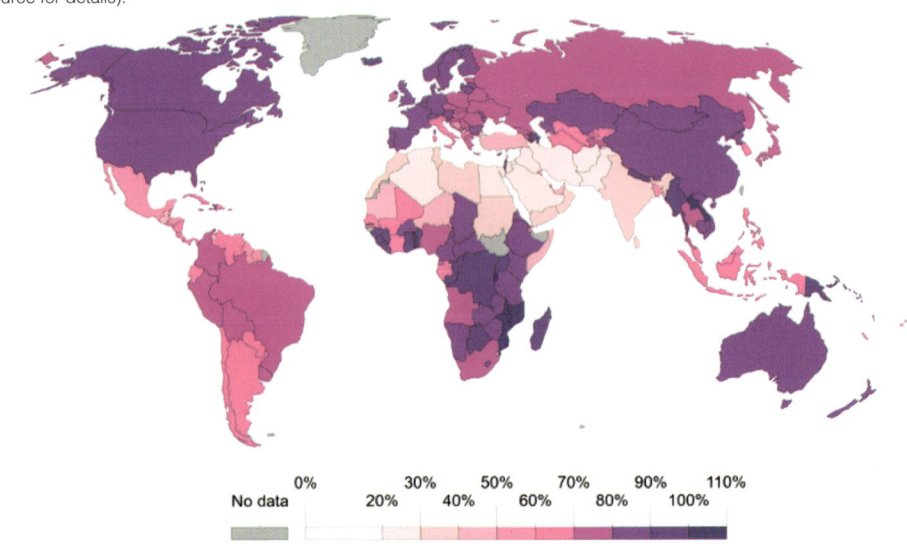

Source: World Bank - WDI

Extracted from https://ourworldindata.org/female-labor-force-participation-key-facts. Accessed on August 7, 2018.

Unit 1

» AFTER READING

1. Check (✓) the statement that best summarizes the text. *Summarizing*
   a. ( ) Men and women participate equally in labor markets around the world.
   b. ( ) In most countries men tend to take part in job markets more than women.
   c. ( ) All around the world, women participate in job markets more than men.

2. Decide if the sentences are true (T) or false (F). Use fragments from the text to correct the false ones. *Understanding details*
   a. ( ) Women's participation in the job market has declined around the world in this century.
   _____
   _____

   b. ( ) The ratio of female to male labor force participation is similar in Syria and Mozambique.
   _____
   _____

   c. ( ) All over the world, some activities performed by women are not considered economic activities.
   _____
   _____

EXPAND YOUR VOCABULARY

1. Refer to the text on page 10 to infer the meaning of these words and match the columns to find their synonyms. Then use some of them to complete the headlines that follow.

   a. parity   ( ) assign
   b. labor   ( ) equality
   c. slow down   ( ) work
   d. allocate   ( ) portion
   e. share   ( ) reduce

   a.
   "In many countries, at least four-in-ten in the _____ force are women"

   Extracted from www.pewresearch.org
   Accessed on August 8, 2018.

   b.
   "Gender _____ in the Workplace Is Possible. We Did It; You Can, Too"

   Extracted from www.workforce.com
   Accessed on August 8, 2018.

   c.
   Women make up nearly half of the labor force; _____ will remain steady in coming decades

   Extracted from www.pewresearch.org
   Accessed on August 8, 2018.

2. Work in pairs. Discuss the headlines from activity 1. Relate them to the text on page 10 and to your previous knowledge on the subject. Then answer the question: What does women's labor force participation actually tell us about gender equality?
_____
_____
_____

VOCABULARY IN USE

1. Read an extract from the text on page 10 and pay attention to the part in bold. Then use other expressions from the same word group to complete the diagrams below. Use the suggestions from the box.

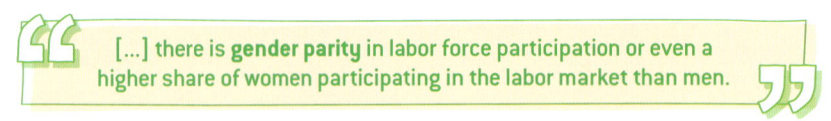

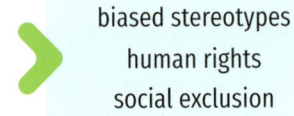

> [...] there is **gender parity** in labor force participation or even a higher share of women participating in the labor market than men.

biased stereotypes	call for change	diversity appreciation	equal pay
human rights	imbalance of power	sexual harassment	social awareness
social exclusion	unequal salaries	women's empowerment	workplace discrimination

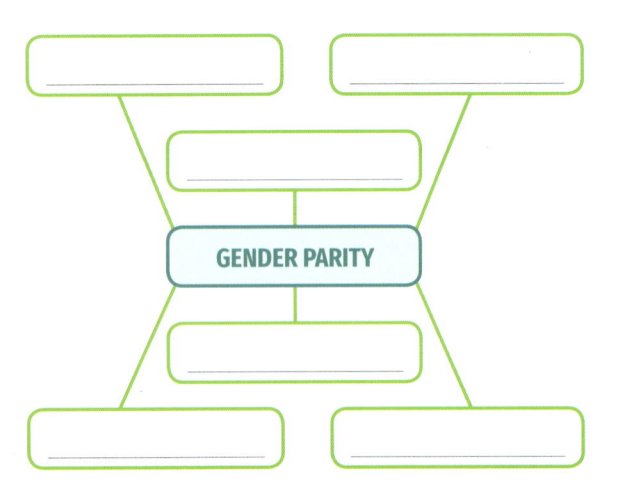

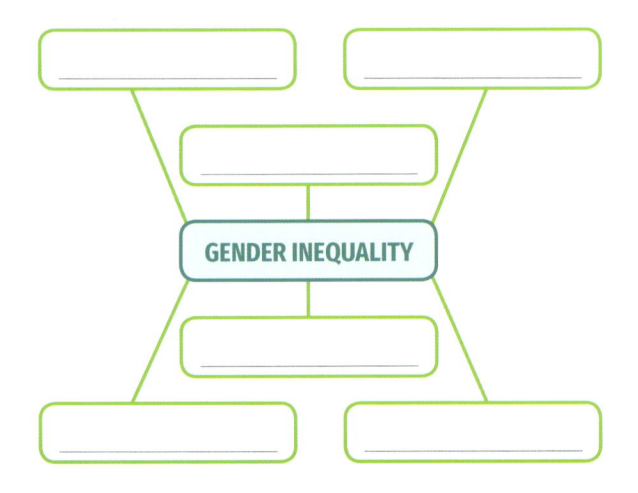

GENDER PARITY

GENDER INEQUALITY

2. The campaign ad below is part of the feminine hygiene products line Always initiative "#LikeAGirl", which aims at ensuring girls' self-confidence by showing them that doing things like a girl is great. Exchange ideas about it with your classmates.

3. Look at the ad again and answer: What is the function of the hashtag in this context?
   a. ( ) It expresses humor by referring to a famous internet meme.
   b. ( ) It encourages people to share and support the campaign.

4. Match the hashtags with the corresponding initiatives.
   a. #GeenaOnGender   b. #ItsOnUs   c. #girlsCHARGE

   ( ) To back the movement to abolish sexual assault on college campuses, saying that all of us have the responsibility to stop it.

   ( ) Created by Geena Davis, it aims to modify how women and girls are portrayed in media, film, and entertainment.

   ( ) To promote the effort to safely educate and raise ambition for more girls globally.

Based on https://mashable.com/2014/10/01/women-hashtags/#ol0EvZdAysqp. Accessed on August 8, 2018.

LANGUAGE IN USE 1

Unit 1

PRESENT PERFECT CONTINUOUS

1. The excerpt below was extracted from the text on page 10. Read it, pay special attention to the part in bold, and answer the questions.

> However, these gender differences in participation rates **have been narrowing** substantially in recent decades.

a. When did gender differences start narrowing?
_____

b. Are they still narrowing nowadays?
_____

2. Considering the extract and your answers in activity 1, check (✓) the correct alternatives to complete the sentences below.

a. The structure *have been narrowing* was used to
   ( ) talk about an action that was in progress in the past.
   ( ) talk about an action that started in the past and is still in progress.

b. The verb tense used in the structure is the present perfect continuous. It is formed by
   ( ) have/has + been + verb + *-ing*.
   ( ) have/has + been + verb in the past participle.

3. Use the verbs *consider*, *fight*, and *go* in the present perfect continuous to complete the text fragments that follow.

a. How the Fight for Gender Equality Is Changing in 2018

> [...]
> Women _____ for equal rights for generations, for the right to vote, the right to control our bodies, and the right to equality in the workplace. And these battles have been hard fought, but we still have a long way to go, and our victories are under threat. Equality in the workplace – women in a **range** of fields from domestic work to the entertainment industry can tell you – it's still just a dream.
> [...]
> The message is loud and clear: We'll take over from here, thanks. The rate things _____, we're certain we'll do a better job. When Lev Grossman wrote the feature for TIME's Person of the Year in 2006, he said, "It's

about the many **wresting** power from the few and helping one another for nothing and how that will not only change the world, but also change the way the world changes." The same is true of the power shift we are witnessing with women.
[...]

Extracted from http://time.com/5191419/women-leading-fight-equality-sexual-harassment. Accessed on August 9, 2018.

b. Eurimages and gender equality

> Since 2012, Eurimages _____ the issue of gender equality in the film industry.
> A Gender Equality Working Group composed of representatives from a number of member states has been set up and meets quarterly, with the aim of:
> • studying the current situation of the presence of women in the cinema sector at national and international level in co-operation with other national and international bodies;
> • analyzing the current situation of Eurimages with regards to gender equality in the selection of projects;
> [...]

Adapted from www.coe.int/en/web/eurimages/gender-equality. Accessed on August 9, 2018.

4. Work in pairs and answer these questions. If possible, use the present perfect continuous in your answers. Then report your opinions to the class.

a. What other aspects concerning gender equality have we been neglecting nowadays?
_____
_____

b. Have gender stereotypes been showing boys and girls in your country what the culture expects?
_____
_____

c. Have gender roles been changing in your community? Provide examples.
_____
_____

13

EXPAND YOUR READING

1. **Read the text and check (✓) the correct alternative to answer the question: What's the author's purpose?**
   a. ( ) To teach or provide information.
   b. ( ) To tell his story and convince the reader that his position is valid.
   c. ( ) To hold the attention of the reader through entertainment.

Men do cry: one man's experience of depression

By Matt Heig - Canongate Books

I can remember the day the old me died. It started with a thought. Something was going wrong. That was the start. Before I realized what it was. And then, a second or so later, there was a strange sensation inside my head. Some biological activity in the rear of my skull, not far above my neck. The cerebellum. A pulsing or intense flickering, as though a butterfly was trapped inside, and a tingling sensation. I did not yet know of the strange physical effects depression and anxiety would create.

[...]

Anyway, I was 24. I was living in Spain – in one of the more sedate and beautiful corners of the island of Ibiza. It was September. Within a fortnight, I would have to return to London, and reality. After six years of student life and summer jobs. I had put off being an adult for as long as I could, and it had loomed like a cloud. A cloud that was now breaking and raining down on me. [...] I didn't want to die. Death was something that scared me. And death only happens to people who have been living. [...]

When you are trapped inside something that feels so unreal, you look for anything that can give you a sense of your bearings. I craved knowledge. I craved facts.

A lot of people still believe that depression is about chemical imbalance. "Incipient insanity was mainly a matter of chemicals," wrote Kurt Vonnegut, in Breakfast of Champions. "Dwayne Hoover's body was manufacturing certain chemicals which unbalanced his mind." It is an attractive idea. And one that has, over the years, been supported by numerous scientific studies. A lot of research into the scientific causes of depression has focused on chemicals such as dopamine and, more often, serotonin. Serotonin is a neurotransmitter, a type of chemical that sends signals from one area of the brain to the other. The theory goes that an imbalance in serotonin levels – caused by low brain cell production of serotonin – equates to depression. So it is no surprise that some of the most common antidepressants, from Prozac down, are SSRIs – selective serotonin reuptake inhibitors – which raise serotonin levels in your brain.

However, the serotonin theory of depression looks a bit wobbly. The problem has been highlighted by the emergence of antidepressants that have no effect on serotonin, and some that do the exact opposite of an SSRI (namely, selective serotonin reuptake enhancers, such as tianeptine) which have been shown to be as effective at treating depression. Add to this the fact that serotonin in an active living human brain is a hard thing to measure and you have a very inconclusive picture indeed.

[...]

For me, the moment of recovery came in April 2000. It was totally inconsequential. In fact, there is not much to write about. That was the whole point. It was a moment of nothingness, of absent-mindedness, of spending almost 10 seconds awake but not actively thinking of my depression or anxiety. I was thinking about work. About trying to get an article published in a newspaper. It wasn't a happy thought, but a neutral one. But it was a break in the clouds, a sign that the sun was still there, somewhere. It was over not much after it began, but when those clouds came back there was hope. There would be a time when those painless seconds would become minutes and hours and maybe even days.

[...]

So what should we do? Talk. Listen. Encourage talking. Encourage listening. Keep adding to the conversation. Stay on the lookout for those wanting to join in the conversation. Keep reiterating, again and again, that depression is not something you "admit to", it is not something you have to blush about, it is a human experience. It is not you. It is simply something that happens to you. And something that can often be eased by talking. Words. Comfort. Support. It took me more than a decade to be able to talk openly, properly, to everyone, about my experience. I soon discovered the act of talking is in itself a therapy. Where talk exists, so does hope.

Adapted from www.theguardian.com/society/2015/feb/22/men-do-cry-depression-matt-haig-reasons-to-stay-alive. Accessed on February 5, 2019.

2. **What is the author's assumed position in the article?**

   _____

3. **Underline the correct statements about position articles such as the one above.**
   a. They focus on topics that need or call for discussion or reconsideration.
   b. They shouldn't report a clear position on the target topic.
   c. They should suggest a call for action or a proposal regarding the target topic.
   d. They present a balanced and logical view of an issue.
   e. They are short pieces of fiction that present the following parts: introduction, rising action, climax, falling action, and resolution.

LANGUAGE IN USE 2

Unit 1

PRESENT PERFECT SIMPLE vs. PRESENT PERFECT CONTINUOUS

1. Read the extracts from the text on page 14 and choose the correct words in parentheses to complete the information about the present perfect simple and the present perfect continuous.

> And death only happens to people who **have been living**.

> A lot of research into the scientific causes of depression **has focused** on chemicals such as dopamine [...].

a. Both the present perfect simple and the present perfect continuous are used to indicate that an action started in the past and is _____ (not / still) going on or has just finished.

b. In some cases, both tenses are correct, but there is often a difference in meaning. Besides meaning that an action is still in progress in the present, we use the present perfect simple mainly to emphasize the _____ (completion / progress) or the result of an action and the present perfect continuous focuses on the _____ (conclusion / duration) or continuous course of an action.

2. Refer back to the extracts in activity 1 and complete the chart below with the structures in bold.

Focus on the result or completion	Focus on the duration

3. Use the verb forms from the box to complete the text.

| has been | has found | have captured |
| have changed | 've been trying | |

Modern masculinity: Are we in crisis? 06 March 2017

In recent years, female **empowerment** _____ a hot topic in marketing and broader culture – from the 3% Conference (and their mission to support female creative **leadership** in agencies) to the lyrics of Beyoncé. But while we _____ to address female stereotypes, have we been blind to the stereotypes around masculinity? Our view on what it is to be 'a man' still remains limited. [...]

In just three generations, our ideas about masculinity _____ dramatically. A recent UK YouGov survey highlighted this divide, with 56% of 65+ men describing themselves as 'completely masculine', opposed to only 2% of 18-24s. [...]

The psychologist Geert Hofstede applied 'masculine' and 'feminine' traits to countries, examining how a society's culture influenced its values and behavior. More 'masculine' countries favor ambition, wealth, and differentiated gender roles, while more 'feminine' countries **overlap** gender roles, and place value on things like modesty and quality of life. In Mexico, a machismo culture is associated with masculine **pride** and power. This _____ negative expression in sexual violence and abuse, to the point that many women and men have tired of this norm and are protesting against it in an effort to promote change.

By contrast, in South Korea, many men use **skincare** products and makeup as a part of their daily routine. The perfectly **kohl-lined eyes** of the country's **K-Pop bands** _____ the hearts of fans worldwide.
[...]

Adapted from www.iris-worldwide.com/news/modern-masculinity-are-we-in-crisis. Accessed on August 9, 2018.

4. Discuss the quote below in small groups. Then come up with your own definition of gender injustice.

> Gender injustice is a social impairment and therefore has to be corrected in social attitudes and behavior.
> (Mohammad Hamid Ansari)

Extracted from www.brainyquote.com/quotes Accessed on August 9, 2018.

_____
_____
_____
_____
_____

15

LISTENING COMPREHENSION

1. What do you think the movies in these posters have in common?

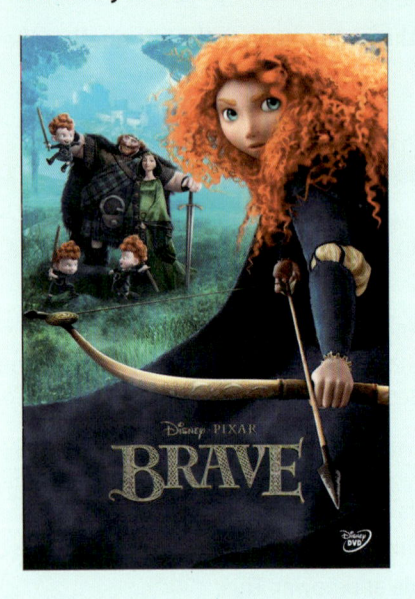

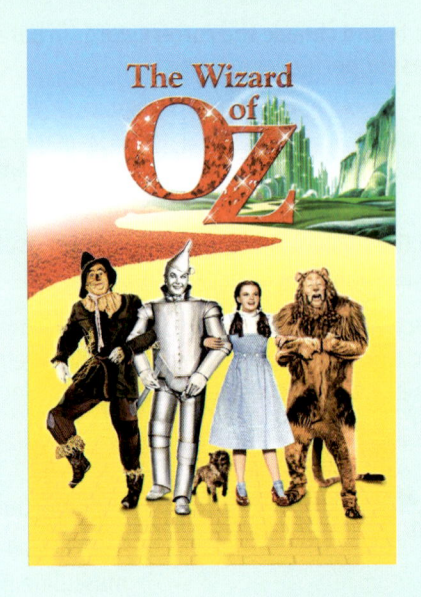

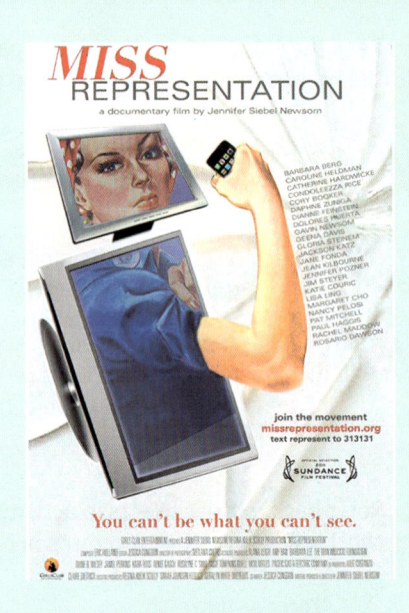

2. Listen to part of a talk on an interview with Jennifer Siebel Newsom. Which movie listed in activity 1 is it about?

02 _____

3. Listen to another part of the talk that explains what the movie is about and fill in the blanks.

03

[…]
Her film was originally shown at Sundance and broadcast in the US in 2011. It features an impressive line-up of _____ women, including Nancy Pelosi, Condoleezza Rice, Katie Couric, and Gloria Steinem, as well as academics and activists who all flesh out the idea that the demeaning and _____ representation of women in the media is a significant contributor in holding women back from positions of power. This, in turn, _____ the lives of all women, from the _____ pay gap and career opportunities after _____, to mental health issues and the rise of cosmetic surgery.
[…]

Extracted from www.theguardian.com/lifeandstyle/2014/mar/03/feminist-film-maker-taking-on-hollywood. Accessed on October 4, 2018.

4. Work with a partner. Refer to the texts you have read in this unit and to the transcript on page 136. Then answer: How has the way media portrays women and men been changing over the past years? What other changes do you think should happen in the future? Share your opinions and experiences with the class.

>> EXPAND YOUR HORIZONS >>>

Check (✔) the column that best describes your opinion about each statement. Then discuss your answers with your classmates and teacher, justifying your point of view.

	I agree.	I'm not sure.	I disagree.
a. The growth of the number of women in the workforce is unquestionably the most significant change in the economy in the past century.			
b. Gender stereotypes sustain gender-specific behaviors that can harm everybody.			
c. Gender roles and expectations are still deep-rooted into our culture although a lot of progress has been made towards gender equality.			

UNIT 2
Technology in the School Curriculum

▶ IN THIS UNIT YOU WILL...

- take part in discussions about coding in education;
- talk about a technology curriculum and robotics;
- learn about subject-verb agreement;
- identify and use compound adjectives.

LEAD OFF

- What situation does the picture represent? Are you familiar with that situation?
- Do you know what *coding* means? If so, explain.
- What do you think about the integration of technological projects into school curriculums?

READING

›› BEFORE READING

You are going to read a text about the implementation of computer programming in education. Is this a reality in your country or school? How do you think students could benefit from having computer programming lessons? Exchange ideas with your classmates.

Contextualizing

›› WHILE READING

Look at the picture and read the title of the text. Then write down two reasons for coding in education that you think will be mentioned in the text. Finally, read the whole text.

Predicting

_____

_____

Coding In Education: Why It's Important & How It's Being Implemented

By Marianne Stenger

Although computer *programming* was once seen as a skill reserved for geeks and computer nerds, it's now regarded as an essential ability for 21st century learners and is becoming a key component of many curriculums, even in elementary schools. So, what's the benefit of teaching kids as young as five years old how to code?

For starters, basic coding courses in schools provide students with the know-how to develop their own websites, apps, and computer software.

LinkedIn data shows that skills like mobile development and user interface design will be in high demand in the coming years, and a 2016 Gallup report found that 40% of American schools now offer coding classes, compared to just 25% a few years ago.

In Australia, the government has been investing in STEM initiatives in recent years, and coding classes will soon be mandatory in Queensland schools. Meanwhile in the UK, kids aged five and over have been learning the fundamentals of coding since 2014.

But coding education can also be beneficial for students who aren't necessarily interested in pursuing computer programming, but would like to gain a better understanding of technology and how it's shaping our world.

At its most basic, learning how to code is learning to tell machines what to do. But this requires the mastery of a problem-solving skill known as computational *thinking*, which involves breaking larger tasks into a logical sequence of smaller steps, diagnosing errors, and coming up with new approaches when necessary.

So, what exactly does coding look like in schools and learning institutions throughout the world and why does it matter? We talked to a few teachers and EdTech experts about some of the ways coding is being implemented in education.

Coding Bootcamps

[…]

Coding to Transition into the Workforce

[…]

Coding For Cyber Security

[…]

Coding to Build Logic and Persistence

[…]

Coding For Early *Literacy* Development

[…]

An Informal Approach to Learning How to Code

Former software engineer and co-founder of the Holberton School of *Software* Engineering Sylvain Kalache says coding is important because it's all around us.

"From the smartphone in our pocket, to the smartwatch on our wrist, it's also launching rockets in space or controlling our fridge," says Kalache. "All industries are disrupted by software and even if not all of us will become Software Engineers, all of us will be interacting with it, so it's important to understand the foundations of it."

[…]

Adapted from www.opencolleges.edu.au/informed/features/coding-education-important-implemented. Accessed on August 11, 2018.

AFTER READING

1. Go back to the text and underline the reasons why coding is important. Do the reasons mentioned match the ones you wrote down in the While Reading task? *Scanning to check predictions*

2. What's the main purpose of the text? Use your own words to state it. *Stating the main purpose of the text*

_____

_____

3. Underline the correct statements about the text. *Understanding details*
   a. Computer programming is still considered a skill reserved for computer experts.
   b. The number of schools using coding in their curriculum in North America has increased by 15% in the last few years.
   c. The introduction of coding in classrooms prepares students for real-life situations such as entering the job market.
   d. Computational thinking is the ability to master the concepts to work with word processing and spreadsheets.

EXPAND YOUR VOCABULARY

1. Use the words in italics in the text on page 18 to complete the text below.

> _____ in Coding is an advantage in this technology-driven economy.
> [...]
> _____ and computers are taking over the world. Almost everything we do requires some form of programming and almost every student has access to computers, tablets, and smart cell phones. Are we doing enough in our schools to encourage computer science and prepare our students for this future? More than half of projected STEM (science, technology, engineering, and mathematic) jobs are in computing occupations. There is more demand for people who can write computer programs than there is supply.
> In the United States, there will be 1.4 million jobs in computer science over the next 10 years but only 400,000 will qualify for it.
> Coding is the new **buzz language** of today's **tech-savvy** world. No matter what the occupation is, it would surely **coincide** with using technology, and those who know how to code, which is the basis of computer science _____ language, would surely be at an advantage.
> Computer science develops students' computational and critical thinking skills and shows them how to create, and not simply use, new technologies.
> This fundamental knowledge is needed to prepare students for the 21st century. Perhaps incorporating computer science studies in lessons will help improve the desired critical _____ in our students.
> [...]

Adapted from https://bambooinnovator.com/2013/11/30/steve-jobs-everybody-in-this-country-should-learn-to-program-a-computer-because-it-teaches-you-how-to-think. Accessed on August 11, 2018.

2. Discuss the quote below in small groups. Refer to the texts you have read and to your own experience and expectations. If possible, use some of the words and expressions from activity 1 to develop your arguments.

> "I think everybody in this country should learn how to program a computer, should learn a computer language, because it teaches you how to think. I view computer science as a liberal art. It should be something that everyone takes."
> (Steve Jobs, American entrepreneur)

Extracted from https://bambooinnovator.com/2013/11/30/steve-jobs-everybody-in-this-country-should-learn-to-program-a-computer-because-it-teaches-you-how-to-think. Accessed on August 11, 2018.

VOCABULARY IN USE

1. Read an extract from the text on page 18 and check (✔) the statement that mentions probable aims of basic coding courses.

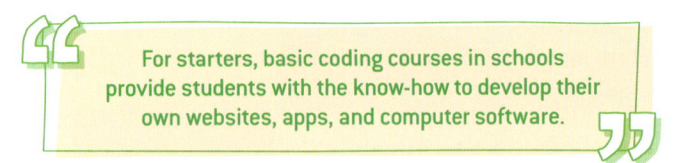

> For starters, basic coding courses in schools provide students with the know-how to develop their own websites, apps, and computer software.

a. (   ) To master dynamic programming and to start diving into understanding algorithms.

b. (   ) To learn common terminology, working practices, and software tools.

2. When a person sets out to learn the science and art of computer programming, he/she is learning a whole new language to write the code in. Some basic coding language is listed below. Match the words or expressions with their definitions.

> algorithm   compiler   GUI   Iteration   JSON   loop
> markup language   run time   sandbox   variable

a. _____: a program which takes the code you have written and translates it into the binary ones and zeros of actual machine code

b. _____: a set of logical or mathematical procedures to solve a problem

c. _____: a piece of code which keeps running until a certain condition is fulfilled, or isn't fulfilled in the case of an 'infinite loop', which will crash the system running it

d. _____: a way to store a piece of data which can then be modified at any time

e. _____: a place to run a program for testing, and for experimenting

f. _____: the time during which a program is running

g. _____: a relatively simple language used to format pages, such as HTML

h. _____: General User Interface, refers to the "front end" of a piece of software which the end user actually sees and interacts with

i. _____: a sequence of instructions which are repeated

j. _____: a format for transmitting information between locations which is based on JavaScript

Adapted from https://owlcation.com/stem/Programming-Basics-for-Beginners. Accessed on August 11, 2018.

3. Work in pairs. Read the infographic below and discuss whether you agree or not with the reasons mentioned to teach coding. Justify your answer.

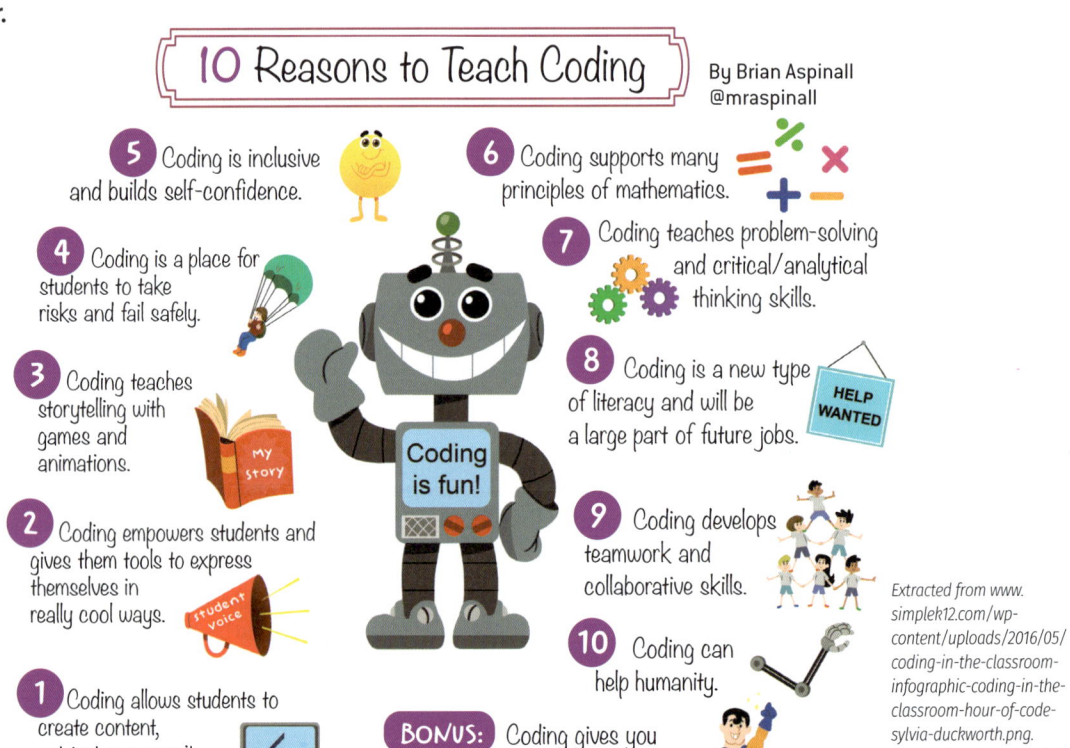

10 Reasons to Teach Coding
By Brian Aspinall @mraspinall

1. Coding allows students to create content, not just consume it.
2. Coding empowers students and gives them tools to express themselves in really cool ways.
3. Coding teaches storytelling with games and animations.
4. Coding is a place for students to take risks and fail safely.
5. Coding is inclusive and builds self-confidence.
6. Coding supports many principles of mathematics.
7. Coding teaches problem-solving and critical/analytical thinking skills.
8. Coding is a new type of literacy and will be a large part of future jobs.
9. Coding develops teamwork and collaborative skills.
10. Coding can help humanity.

BONUS: Coding gives you SUPER POWERS!

Extracted from www.simplek12.com/wp-content/uploads/2016/05/coding-in-the-classroom-infographic-coding-in-the-classroom-hour-of-code-sylvia-duckworth.png. Accessed on August 12, 2018.

LANGUAGE IN USE 1

Unit 2

SUBJECT-VERB AGREEMENT

1. The excerpts below were extracted from the text on page 18. Underline the subjects and circle the verbs. Then complete the sentences.

> I. For starters, basic coding courses in schools provide students with the know-how to develop their own websites, apps, and computer software.

> II. In Australia, the government has been investing in STEM initiatives in recent years.

> III. Meanwhile in the UK, kids aged five and over have been learning the fundamentals of coding since 2014.

a. In extracts _____ and _____, plural subjects agree with plural verbs and in extract _____, a singular verb agrees with a singular noun.

b. If you have a noun phrase, such as "basic coding courses in schools" in extract I, the verb agrees with the head of the noun, which is *courses*. As *courses* is a plural subject, it agrees with a plural verb. In extract III, the head of the noun phrase is _____.

2. Read other extracts from the texts on pages 18 and 19 and pay attention to the parts in bold to complete the explanations.

> I. "More than **half** of projected STEM… jobs are in computing occupations."

> II. "[…] a 2016 Gallup report found that **40%** of American schools now offer coding classes."

a. When noun or pronoun subjects indicate parts of a whole such as _____, *all, the majority, none,* and *more,* followed by a prepositional phrase such as _____ in extract I, verbs agree with the object of the preposition.

b. Percentages and fractions require a plural verb form when the object of the preposition is plural, such as _____ in extract II, and a singular verb form when the object of the preposition is singular.

3. Check (✓) the statement that explains the subject-verb agreement in the following quotes.

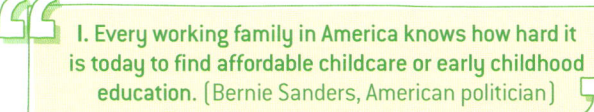

> I. Every working family in America knows how hard it is today to find affordable childcare or early childhood education. (Bernie Sanders, American politician)

Extracted from www.brainyquote.com/quotes/bernie_sanders_714833. Accessed on September 3, 2018.

> II. Each country thinks its school is in a specific crisis, without ever linking the school's crisis to that of the society around it. (Daniel Pennac, French writer)

Extracted from www.brainyquote.com/quotes/daniel_pennac_522388. Accessed on September 3, 2018.

a. ( ) When words such as *every* and *each* are used as subjects, they take plural verb forms.

b. ( ) When words such as *every* and *each* are used as subjects, they take singular verb forms.

4. Choose between the singular or plural verb forms in parentheses to fill in the blanks.

Why are there so few girls in computer science? And how can we change that?

In September 2015, New York City Mayor Bill de Blasio announced that within 10 years every child in the city would be able to study computer science in a public school. The **decree** came as no surprise. Nationwide, educators _____ (is coming / are coming) to the consensus that computer science literacy _____ (is / are) beneficial – even necessary – for students to succeed in a digitized world. Writer Alison Derbenwick Miller on the technology blog TechCrunch: "With the shift to data-based decision-making for everything from traditional business marketing to local government and health care, a basic understanding of how computers work and process information, as well as a basic literacy in computer programming and data analysis, _____ rapidly _____ (is… becoming / are… becoming) workplace essentials."

Unfortunately, these essentials _____ (is / are) harder to come by for some students than for others. Low-income communities are more likely to be technology deserts, **disproportionately** leaving behind students of color and English language learners. And, **despite** the growing number of computer science programs in public schools (including traditional classes and coding "boot camps"), another group of students _____ (is / are) **conspicuously** absent: girls.

The disconnect between girls and computer science _____ (doesn't improve / don't improve) after high school. In the last two decades, the percentage of U.S. computer science bachelor's degrees awarded to women has fallen from 28 to just 18. According to the National Science Foundation, only 25 percent of computer and math scientists _____ (is / are) women. […]

Extracted from www.tolerance.org/magazine/spring-2016/cracking-the-code. Accessed on August 12, 2018.

21

EXPAND YOUR READING

1. Read part of a curriculum and check (✓) the correct alternative. A curriculum refers to...
   a. (   ) the days and times of classes taught in a school or in a specific course or program.
   b. (   ) the subjects that are taught by a school, college, etc., or the things that are studied in a particular subject.

Junior Computer Curriculum

Project-Based Learning and Elementary Students

TechnoKids Junior Computer Curriculum is a collection of technology projects. Each project includes a teacher guide, workbook, and customizable resource files. Computer lessons are project based and have students apply technology to make learning meaningful.

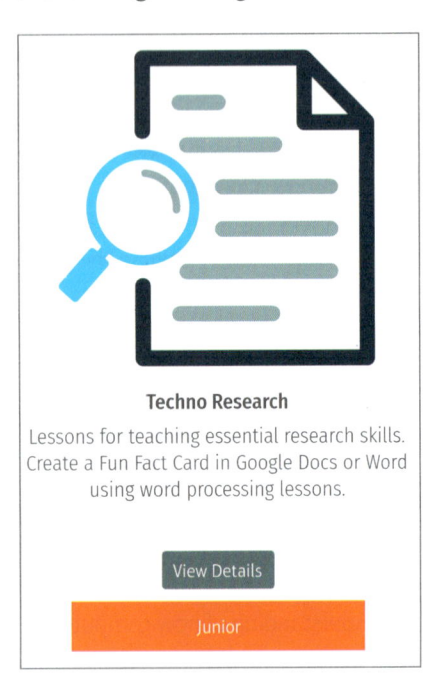

Techno Research
Lessons for teaching essential research skills. Create a Fun Fact Card in Google Docs or Word using word processing lessons.

Techno Toon
Create a graphic story that looks like a cartoon or animated comic strip using Google Slides or PowerPoint. Integrate creative writing with technology using digital storytelling lessons.

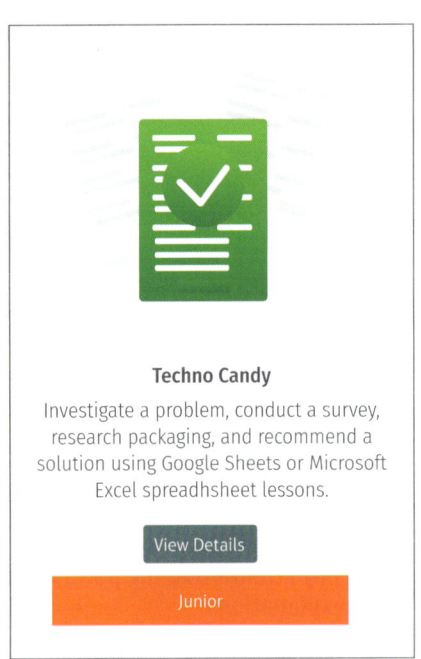

Techno Candy
Investigate a problem, conduct a survey, research packaging, and recommend a solution using Google Sheets or Microsoft Excel spreadsheet lessons.

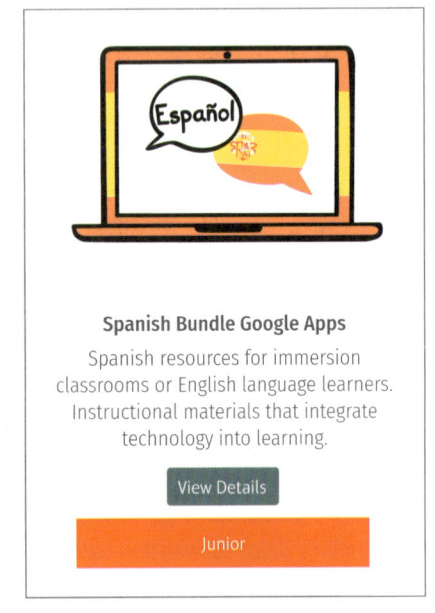

Spanish Bundle Google Apps
Spanish resources for immersion classrooms or English language learners. Instructional materials that integrate technology into learning.

Junior Computer Curriculum Set
Student-centered lessons promote the practical application of technology. Teach the fundamentals with engaging activities.

Techno Internet
Lessons provide a thorough introduction to the Internet. Studentes apply search strategies, access digital resources, practice Internet safety, and communicate electronically.

Extracted from www.technokids.com/computer-curriculum/junior.aspx. Accessed on August 12, 2018.

2. Cross out the item that is <u>not</u> part of the curriculum in activity 1.
   a. web protection tools
   b. word processing software
   c. nanotechnology
   d. animated stories
   e. instructional materials

LANGUAGE IN USE 2

Unit 2

COMPOUND ADJECTIVES

1. Read these extracts from the texts on pages 22 and 18, paying attention to the parts in bold, and answer: What's their function in the sentences? Then check (✔) the correct alternative to complete the paragraph.

_____

> "**Student-centered** lessons promote the practical application of technology."

> "But this requires the mastery of a **problem-solving** skill known as computational thinking."

The adjectives *student-centered* and *problem-solving* are called _____ adjectives because they are formed by two or more words. They can be formed by different word classes such as _____, verbs, nouns, and adverbs, for example. A _____ is often used between the words to indicate they act as a single idea.

a. ( ) defining – articles – apostrophe
b. ( ) compound – adjectives – hyphen

2. Use the two compound adjectives from the extracts above and others from the box to complete the chart. Then read the sentences and fill in the blanks with some of them.

bottom-left	old-fashioned
good-looking	real-life
highly-respected	smoke-free

adjective + adjective	
adjective + noun	
adjective + verb + -ing	
adjective + verb (past participle)	
verb + adjective	
noun + verb + -ing	
noun + verb (past participle)	
adverb + verb (past participle)	

a. Unfortunately, most students found the computing course material boring and _____.
b. Computer programming tutorials are likely to be devoted to _____ skills.
c. Carnegie-Mellon University is one of the most _____ universities in the USA due to their Robotics Systems Development program.
d. Coding classes are mainly _____ as the focus of instruction is on the student.

3. Finish the paragraph below. Use at least one compound adjective in your answer.

In my opinion, the biggest challenges of implementing a technology curriculum in schools throughout Brazil is…

_____
_____
_____

4. Now read the definitions below and match them with a compound adjective from the box. There is an extra option which you will not use. Then look up the other compound adjective and write a definition for it.

well-known	narrow-minded
absent-minded	five-star
kind-hearted	well-behaved
hard-working	open-minded

a. _____: someone who performs a task with a lot of effort
b. _____: notorious, known by a lot of people
c. _____: likely to forget things, especially because you are thinking about something else
d. _____: the characteristic of a place that has been judged to be of the highest standard
e. _____: generous
f. _____: willing to consider and accept other people's ideas and opinions
g. _____: not being rude or violent

Based on www.ldoceonline.com. Accessed on October 22, 2018.

_____
_____
_____

LISTENING COMPREHENSION

1. **Read the dictionary entry and discuss the questions below.**

   > **robotics**
   > ro-bo-tics /rəʊˈbɒtɪks $ ˈroʊbɑː-/
   > **noun [uncountable]**
   > the study of how robots are made and used

   Extracted from www.ldoceonline.com/dictionary/robotics. Accessed on August 13, 2018.

   a. What is the connection between robotics and coding?
   b. How is robotics used nowadays?
   c. What might be the downsides of robotics?
   d. How can robotics be useful in education?

2. **You are going to learn about a robot built by ten students from Berwick Lodge, Glendal, and Mount View elementary schools in Australia. Listen to the first part of the recording, pay attention to what that robot can do, and check (✓) the picture that illustrates it.**

   a. (   )

   Extracted from www.pocket-lint.com/gadgets/news/134820-real-life-robots-that-will-make-you-think-the-future-is-now. Accessed on August 13, 2018.

   b. (   )

   Extracted from http://education.abc.net.au. Accessed on August 13, 2018.

3. **Now listen to the whole recording and answer the questions.**

   a. What's the name of the robot?
   _____
   b. According to the reporter, why isn't robotics popular in many Australian schools?
   _____
   c. What's stopping the students from competing at the World Robotics Championships in Spain?
   _____
   d. What institutions have approved the initiative?
   _____

4. **What kind of robot could help you with your studies? Talk to a classmate and justify your answer.**

›› EXPAND YOUR HORIZONS ›››

Check (✓) the column that best describes your opinion about each statement. Then discuss your answers with your classmates and teacher, justifying your point of view.

	I agree.	I'm not sure.	I disagree.
a. The benefits of learning to code aren't limited to knowing how to create an app or develop a website, for example. They involve skills that can be applied to different areas of our lives.			
b. We use coding skills every day when we program our microwave oven, our phones, our TVs, etc.			
c. The advantages of robotics in our lives are unquestionable, but there may also be downsides to it. The more prepared we are to deal with both the advantages and disadvantages, the more we'll be able to integrate robotics successfully into our everyday lives.			

REVIEW 1

Units 1 and 2

1. Skim the text. What is it about? *Skimming*

INTERNATIONAL EDUCATION

Adding Coding to the Curriculum

By Beth Gardiner

March 23, 2014

LONDON — Estonia is teaching first graders how to create their own computer games and offering scholarships to **entice** more **undergraduates** into technology-driven disciplines. In England, an updated national curriculum will soon expose every child in the public school system to computer programming, starting at age five. The American "Hour of Code" effort says it has already **persuaded** 28 million people to give programming a try.

5 Around the world, students from elementary school to PhD. level are increasingly getting **acquainted** with the basics of coding, as computer programming is also known. From Singapore to Tallinn, governments, educators, and advocates from the tech industry argue that it has become crucial to hold at least a basic understanding of how the devices that play such a large role in modern life actually work.

10 Such knowledge, the advocates say, is important not only to individual students' future career prospects, but also for their countries' economic competitiveness and the technology industry's ability to find qualified workers. Exposing students to coding from an early age helps to **demystify** an area that can be intimidating. It also breaks down stereotypes of computer scientists as boring geeks, supporters argue. Plus, they say, programming is highly creative: studying it can help to develop problem-solving abilities, as well as equip students for a world transformed by technology.

[…]

Adapted from www.nytimes.com/2014/03/24/world/europe/adding-coding-to-the-curriculum.html. Accessed on August 22, 2018.

---

2. Read the fragment below and find out which initiative mentioned in the text in activity 1 it describes. Then exchange ideas about that project with a classmate. *Understanding details*

[…]
The _____ is an attempt to teach people the basics of computer programming in 60 minutes in a fun, simple way. It is part of a campaign that Code.org, a non-profit organization, launched in the U.S. with the goal of introducing coding into the U.S. curriculum and **raising awareness** around what coding is. The idea was to show that it's not just about the geek in the basement or the super-tech-savvy person but that it actually plays a role in everything we do and everybody should have access to it. And 20 million kids signed up to it.
[…]

Adapted from www.theguardian.com/technology/2014/mar/02/hour-of-code-get-with-program-try-coding. Accessed on August 22, 2018.

3. Now read the text carefully and decide if the sentences are true (T) or false (F). *Understanding details*

a. (   ) Computer scientists are often thought to be boring geeks.
b. (   ) According to the modern national curriculum in England, every child in the public school system should be exposed to computer programming from the age of five.
c. (   ) In Singapore, the government argues that it is not yet time for children to be learning the basics of computer programming.
d. (   ) Teaching students how to program means providing them with means to become more creative and better at problem-solving.

4. Read the extract below and answer the question: Does the verb form in italics focus on the result or on the duration of a situation that started in the past and continues up to the present?

> "From Singapore to Tallinn, governments, educators, and advocates from the tech industry argue that it *has become* crucial to hold at least a basic understanding of how the devices that play such a large role in modern life actually work."

_____

_____

5. Read a fragment from a text entitled "The hour of code: why we should get with the program… and try coding" and fill in the blanks with the verbs *build*, *get into*, and *work on* in the present perfect continuous.

> […]
> **Nicki Cooper**, *computing teacher at Northfleet School for Girls, Kent, and a Computing at School master teacher* […] I've found working in an all-girls school very different from a mixed school because here the girls are really free to express themselves. They're quite happy that they're into Minecraft or _____ computer games. That's what we _____ in lessons, and they _____ really _____ it. Whereas when I was in a mixed school, the girls took a back seat and it was the boys that would be shouting out and getting enthusiastic.
> They saw it as a boys' thing. […]
>
> Extracted from www.theguardian.com/technology/2014/mar/02/hour-of-code-get-with-program-try-coding. Accessed on August 22, 2018.

6. Choose between singular or plural verb forms to make subject-verb agreements and complete the quotes.
   a. "Computer science _____ (is not / are not) just for smart 'nerds' in hoodies coding in basements. Coding is extremely creative and is an integral part of almost every industry." (Reshma Saujani)
   b. "From building robots and video games to coding apps that solve a problem in your community, or 3D printing in fashion tech, it is important that we _____ (explores / explore) different ways to engage girls in STEAM and also ensure that _____ (there is / there are) many, and different, women role models that will inspire our girls to pursue STEAM careers." (Rana el Kaliouby)
   c. "Coding is like writing, and we live in a time of the new industrial revolution. What's happened is that maybe everybody _____ (knows / know) how to use computers, like they know how to read, but they _____ (doesn't know / don't know) how to write." (Susan Wojcicki)

7. Read the last quote in activity 6 again. The author uses an analogy to talk about people's ability to code. How does she do this? Do you agree with her views? Justify your answer.

_____

_____

_____

_____

_____

_____

_____

UNIT 3

Can We Eat with a Clear Conscience?

▶ IN THIS UNIT YOU WILL...

- reflect on making ethical food choices;
- talk about the impacts of food choices;
- learn how to use the second conditional for unreal and impossible situations;
- compare the uses of the zero, first, and second conditionals.

LEAD OFF

- ❯ What can you see in the picture? How is it linked to the question in the title of the unit?
- ❯ Which issues are involved in making food choices?
- ❯ Where does the food you eat come from? Do you care about its origin?

READING

›› BEFORE READING

Discussion and brainstorming

Read and discuss the comic strip below in pairs. Then list ideas relating to the topic of the text you are about to read.

_____

_____

Panel 1: "Sir, here's your food, but I can't help but notice your T-shirt."

Panel 2: T-shirt reads: "I think of my body as a temple"

Panel 3: "If you feel that way, how can you ingest fast food?"

Panel 4: "I'm non-practicing."

Extracted from www.gocomics.com/luckycow/2004/10/21. Accessed on August 17, 2018.

›› WHILE READING

Skim the text and check (✓) the correct alternative to complete the sentence.   *Skimming to identify the text genre*

The text is a...

a. ( ) cookbook recipe.   b. ( ) book description.   c. ( ) book excerpt.

The Omnivore's Dilemma
A NATURAL HISTORY of FOUR MEALS
MICHAEL POLLAN
Author of THE BOTANY OF DESIRE

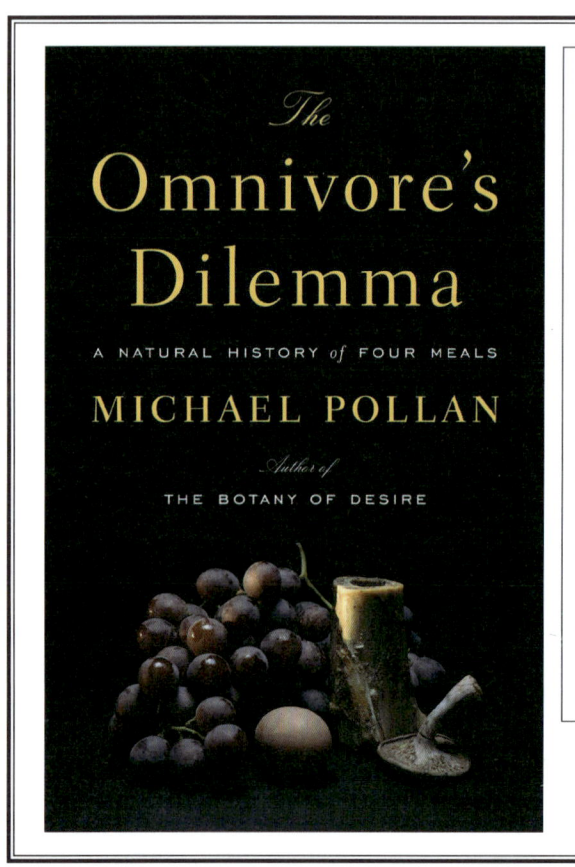

"Imagine if we had a food system that actually produced wholesome food. Imagine if it produced that food in a way that restored the land. Imagine if we could eat every meal knowing these few simple things: What it is we're eating. Where it came from. How it found its way to our table. And what it really cost. If that was the reality, then every meal would have the potential to be a perfect meal. We would not need to go hunting for our connection to our food and the web of life that produces it. We would no longer need any reminding that we eat by the grace of nature, not industry, and that what we're eating is never anything more or less than the body of the world. I don't want to have to forage every meal. Most people don't want to learn to garden or hunt. But we can change the way we make and get our food so that it becomes food again – something that feeds our bodies and our souls. Imagine it: Every meal would connect us to the joy of living and the **wonder** of nature. Every meal would be like **saying grace**." – Michael Pollan, The Omnivore's Dilemma: A Natural History of Four Meals.

Extracted from www.goodreads.com/work/quotes/3287769-the-omnivore-s-dilemma. Accessed on August 17, 2018.

AFTER READING

1. Read the text carefully. Check (✓) the statement that best summarizes the main idea of the book excerpt you have read. *Summarizing the main idea*

   a. ( ) The implications people's food choices have on the economy of the planet are shocking.
   b. ( ) How perfect our meals would be if we were really aware of where our food came from.
   c. ( ) The importance of gardening and hunting to restore the sacred value of eating and how we can contribute to that.

2. Underline the correct statements about the book cover and excerpt on page 28. *Understanding details*

   a. *The Botany of Desire* is the title of another book written by Michael Pollen.
   b. Many people are eager to learn the basics of gardening and hunting.
   c. Changing the way we get our food and how we make it is unlikely to happen.
   d. Knowing simple things like what we are eating and where the food came from would reestablish our connection to our food.
   e. Ideally, our daily meals should connect us to the joy of living and the wonder of nature.

EXPAND YOUR VOCABULARY

1. Refer to the text on page 28 to infer the meaning of the words from the box. Then match them with the definitions below.

> forage   hunt   omnivore
> restore   soul   wholesome

   a. _____ : likely to make you healthy
   b. _____ : to go around searching for food or other supplies
   c. _____ : the part of a person that is not physical, and that contains their character, thoughts, and feelings
   d. _____ : to chase animals and birds in order to kill or catch them
   e. _____ : to make something return to its former state or condition
   f. _____ : an animal that eats both meat and plants

   Extracted from www.ldoceonline.com. Accessed on August 18, 2018.

2. Use three words from activity 1 to complete the quotes below. Make any necessary adjustments.

   a. "Elsewhere the paper notes that vegetarians and vegans (including athletes) 'meet and exceed requirements' for protein. And, to render the whole we-should-worry-about-getting-enough-protein-and-therefore-eat-meat idea even more useless, other data suggests that excess animal protein intake is linked with osteoporosis, **kidney** disease, calcium stones in the urinary **tract**, and some cancers. Despite some persistent confusion, it is clear that vegetarians and vegans tend to have more optimal protein consumption than _____." – Jonathan Safran Foer, Eating Animals

   Extracted from www.goodreads.com/work/quotes/3149322-eating-animals. Accessed on August 18, 2018.

   b. "If you have a significant **layer** of fat around your **waist**, it means you have regularly consumed food in response to toxic hunger or have eaten recreationally. The body does not store large amounts of fat when fed a _____ natural diet and given only the amount of food demanded by true hunger." – Joel Fuhrman, Eat to Live: The Revolutionary Formula for Fast and Sustained Weight Loss

   Extracted from www.goodreads.com/work/quotes/389572-eat-to-live. Accessed on August 18, 2018.

   c. "Food should not only satisfy hunger, it should feed the _____, **nourish** the body, and **delight** the senses." – Karista Bennett

   Extracted from www.goodreads.com/quotes/search?commit=Search&page=3&q=food+to+feed+the+soul&utf8=%E2%9C%93. Accessed on August 18, 2018.

3. What should be people's primary concern when choosing their food?

   _____
   _____
   _____
   _____

Unit 3

29

VOCABULARY IN USE

1. Look at the book cover on page 28 again. Read the title of the book once more and complete the sentence.

   > The word _____ derives from the Latin **omnis** (which means **all**), and **vora** (which means **eat** or **devour**). Common examples of English words derived from Latin include the words **agriculture**, **digital**, **picture**, and **school**.

2. Now come up with other English words you already know to complete the chart. The words must be derived from the Latin ones listed in the first column.

Latin word	Meaning	English word
antiqua	old	
aqua	water	
divus	god	
domus	house	
finis	end, limit	
genus	birth, creation	

Latin word	Meaning	English word
lac	milk	
longa	long	
nominare	to name	
obscura	dark	
prima	first	
terra	land, earth	

3. The examples from the box below are also common words derived from Latin. Use them to complete the text.

   > progress   consecutive   items   percentage   organic

   Supermarket sales of organic food and drink continue to rise

   [...]

   Supermarket sales of organic food and drink in the UK have risen by 4% this year, new figures reveal, marking seven _____ years of growth.

   [...]

   Supermarket shoppers spent £1.5bn on _____ food and drink, including baby products, in the 52 weeks to the end of June, according to new independent data.

   That represents sales through "British retail outlets" – predominantly the big supermarkets but with a small _____ from chains such as Nisa and Costcutter. It does not include independent organic retailers or vegetable box schemes. The figures provide a half-year '_____ report' before publication of the sector's detailed Organic Market Report and full breakdown in February.

   Sales of fresh organic fruit and vegetables sales grew by 5.3% in the year to the end of June, while dairy – the largest overall market sector for organic – saw a sales increase of 3.5%.

   Other areas seeing strong growth are organic delicatessen _____ – including many chilled vegetarian and plant-based products – up 27.8% year on year, while sales of organic beer, wine and spirits were up by 8.7%.

   [...]

   Extracted from www.theguardian.com/environment/2018/sep/04/supermarket-sales-of-organic-food-and-drink-continue-to-rise. Accessed on December 4, 2018.

4. Why do you think people have been buying more organic food? Why is organic food considered better for you? Use at least three words derived from Latin in your answer.

   _____
   _____
   _____
   _____
   _____

LANGUAGE IN USE 1

Unit 3

SECOND CONDITIONAL

1. **The excerpt below was extracted from the text on page 28. Read it and underline the statement that best describes it.**

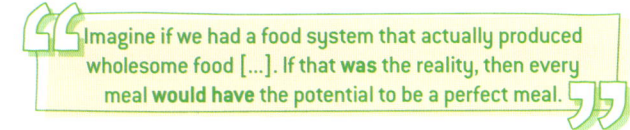

   > Imagine if we had a food system that actually produced wholesome food [...]. If that **was** the reality, then every meal **would have** the potential to be a perfect meal.

   a. The speaker is talking about an impossible situation in the past.
   b. The speaker is imagining what would happen in case a certain circumstance changed.
   c. The speaker is describing what happens every time a specific situation occurs.

2. **Choose the correct alternatives in parentheses to complete the sentences about the second conditional in English.**

   a. The second conditional is used to refer to _____ (hypothetical / definite) or unreal situations.
   b. We form the second conditional with *if* + subject + _____ (simple present / simple past) + *would / could / might* + base form of the main verb.
   c. It is possible to use *were* instead of _____ (is / was) in the second conditional.

3. **Use the second conditional to fill in the blanks in the comic strips below. Then work in pairs to explain the humor in both of them.**

   a. care about; buy (contraction)

   Extracted from www.gocomics.com/thatababy/2010/12/30. Accessed on August 19, 2018.

   b. cut out; start; not have (contraction)

   Extracted from https://licensing.andrewsmcmeel.com/features/bu?date=2018-01-21. Accessed on August 19, 2018.

4. **Complete the sentences below. If necessary, refer to activity 2 again.**

   a. If I were an advocate of animal rights, _____
   _____.

   b. Teenagers would be more worried about eating ethically if _____
   _____.

EXPAND YOUR READING

1. Skim the book cover, read the text title and subtitle, and answer: Is the author's position for or against fast food?

_____

No Accounting for Mouthfeel

Fast food is an inescapable part of the modern world, and the author thinks that's a very bad thing.

Related Links
- An Audio Interview With Eric Schlosser
- First Chapter: 'Fast Food Nation'

By ROB WALKER - January 21, 2001

[…]

Fast-food restaurants evolved from the drive-in eateries **spawned** by the post-World War II car culture of Southern California. The men who built the new industry were **rugged** individualists, but their insights all revolved around
5   **relentless** homogeneity – in the food they offered and in the way they acquired, produced and served it. […] Schlosser also calls on "the flavor industry" – labs where the taste of foods that are frozen and **otherwise** processed is **devised**. In what seems like an **outtake** from "Sleeper,"
10 scientists called "flavorists," wearing lab coats, **cobble** together chemicals to recreate the flavor of fresh cherries or grilled hamburgers, always keeping "mouthfeel" in mind. And then there's the hamburger itself, which has traveled a long road from being "a food for the poor" at the start of the
15 20th century to the down-home meal of choice for capitalist royalty at the start of the 21st. It was drive-ins and fast-food places that made hamburgers a national favorite, especially when the easy-to-eat burger was positioned as a great choice for kids. More recently, **cattle** raising and meatpacking
20 have been industrialized just like the potato business, flavor science, and fast-food outlets themselves. […] While the things Schlosser is concerned about (small farmers, mom-
25 and-pop store owners, low-skilled immigrant workers, child-focused marketing, the political **clout** of big business)
30 and the solutions he suggests (mostly better government regulation) will seem like predictable liberal **carping** to some,
35 the book manages to avoid **shrillness**. This is a fine piece of **muckraking**, alarming without being alarmist. At the very least, Schlosser makes it hard to go on eating
40 fast food in **blissful** ignorance. […] At one point, Schlosser quotes a scientist who specializes in food safety. This man is discussing the meat industry's **reluctance** to perform certain tests on its products, but he could be talking about almost any of the questions Schlosser raises about the fast-food
45 business – or, come to think of it, about the culture that **takes** that business **for granted**. "If you don't know about a problem," the man observes, "then you don't have to deal with it."

Rob Walker, a contributing writer for Money and Slate, lives in
50 New Orleans.

Extracted from https://archive.nytimes.com/www.nytimes.com/books/01/01/21/reviews/010121.21walkert.html. Accessed on August 20, 2018.

2. Read the text and underline the incorrect information in the sentences below. Then rewrite them with the correct information.

   a. Rob Walker is worried about issues related to small farmers, low-skilled immigrant workers, child-focused marketing, etc.

   _____
   _____

   b. Being classified as an excellent choice for parents made hamburgers a national favorite.

   _____
   _____

   c. "The Fast Food Nation" labs are, in Schlosser's opinion, places where the taste of processed and frozen foods is conceived.

   _____
   _____

3. Check (✓) the sentences that describe book reviews.

   a. (   ) They are always in informal language and written in the first person singular.
   b. (   ) They offer a critical assessment of the book.
   c. (   ) They may provide the reader with a concise summary of the content.
   d. (   ) They are written in chronological order and never include a personal judgment.
   e. (   ) They might suggest whether the reader would enjoy the book.

LANGUAGE IN USE 2

Unit 3

ZERO, FIRST, AND SECOND CONDITIONALS

1. Read these extracts from the texts on pages 28 and 32. Then use the suggestions from the box to complete the sentences and review what you have studied about the conditionals in English.

> I. If you feel that way, how can you ingest fast food?

> II. If that was the reality, then every meal would have the potential to be a perfect meal.

> III. 'If you don't know about a problem,' the man observes, 'then you don't have to deal with it.'

future	hypothetical	I	II	III
not	possible	result	second	
	when	will	zero	

a. The zero conditional used in extract _____ indicates that the _____ of the condition always happens or is always true. In this case, *if* can be replaced by _____ with no change in meaning.

b. The first conditional used in extract _____ indicates things that might happen in the future or results of imagined situations in the future. In the first conditional, the main clause may have any modal verb with _____ meaning, e.g., _____ , *can*, *may*, or the imperative.

c. While the _____ conditional describes what happens in general, the first conditional describes a particular situation.

d. The second conditional used in extract _____ indicates the _____ result of an unreal or _____ situation in the present or in the future.

e. While the first conditional describes things that will probably happen in the future, the _____ conditional describes things that are _____ likely to happen.

2. Use the correct conditional form to complete the quotes below. Then take some time to read them again and check (✓) the ones you agree with. Share your opinions with a classmate.

a. ( ) "If we _____ (give up) eating beef, we **would have** roughly 20 to 30 times more land for food than we have now." – James Lovelock, English scientist

Extracted from www.brainyquote.com/quotes/james_lovelock_314096. Accessed on August 20, 2018.

b. ( ) "If we _____ (pursue) organic farming as our healthy food style, we **can bring down** cost of treatment to a great extent." – Sulaiman Abdul Aziz Al Rajhi, Saudi Arabian businessman

Extracted from www.brainyquote.com/quotes/sulaiman_abdul_aziz_al_ra_732605. Accessed on August 20, 2018.

c. ( ) "If you truly _____ (get) in touch with a piece of carrot, you get in touch with the soil, the rain, the sunshine. You **get** in touch with Mother Earth and eating in such a way, you feel in touch with true life, your roots, and that is meditation. If we _____ (chew) every morsel of our food in that way, we **become** grateful and when you are grateful, you are happy." – Thich Nhat Hanh, Vietnamese clergyman

Extracted from www.brainyquote.com/quotes/thich_nhat_hanh_531558. Accessed on August 20, 2018.

d. ( ) "I'm an animal rights activist because I believe we _____ (have) a planet if we **continue** to behave toward other species the way we do." – James Cromwell, American actor

Extracted from www.brainyquote.com/quotes/james_cromwell_523948. Accessed on August 20, 2018.

e. ( ) "If everybody _____ (switch) to organic farming, we **couldn't support** the earth's current population - maybe half." – Nina Fedoroff, American scientist

Extracted from www.brainyquote.com/quotes/nina_fedoroff_512796. Accessed on August 20, 2018.

3. Answer the questions below. Then report your views to the class. If possible, use conditionals in your arguments.

a. Can you, as a consumer, be considered an accomplice in animal exploitation? Why (not)?

_____

_____

b. Have you heard of organic farming? If so, what is it?

_____

_____

c. What do you think would happen if people stopped eating beef?

_____

_____

d. Why do you think fast food is cheaper than fruits and vegetables in so many countries?

_____

_____

LISTENING COMPREHENSION

1. **In pairs, describe the photos below. Then match them with their corresponding captions.**

   a.

   b.

   ( ) At Granja Mantiqueira in Brazil eight million hens lay 5.4 million eggs a day. **Conveyor belts whisk** the eggs to a packaging facility. Demand for meat has tripled in the developing world in four decades, while egg consumption has increased **sevenfold**, driving a huge expansion of large-scale animal operations.

   ( ) On the Vulgamore farm near Scott City, Kansas, each combine can **harvest** up to 25 **acres** of wheat an hour – as well as provide real-time data on crop **yields**.

   Most of the food Americans eat is now produced on such large-scale, mechanized farms, which grow row after row of a single crop, allowing farmers to cover more ground with less labor.

   Extracted from www.nationalgeographic.com/foodfeatures/feeding-9-billion. Accessed on August 21, 2018.

2. **Listen to the first part of a talk on threats to the planet and complete the sentences accordingly.**

   06

   a. One of the biggest dangers to the planet is our need for _____.

   b. _____ contributes to global warming and accelerates the loss of biodiversity.

   c. If the spread of prosperity across the world continues, the amount of _____ will need to be doubled by _____.

   d. The debate over how to address the global food challenge has been polarized by those who favor _____ agriculture and proponents of local and _____ farms.

   e. As we try to meet the _____ for food worldwide, the _____ challenges posed by agriculture will become more urgent.

3. **Listen to the last part of the text and rephrase the speaker's conclusion using your own words. Then share your answer with your classmates.**

   07

   _____
   _____

>> EXPAND YOUR HORIZONS >>>>

Check (✓) the column that best describes your opinion about each statement. Then discuss your answers with your classmates and teacher, justifying your point of view.

	I agree.	I'm not sure.	I disagree.
a. As our food choices are almost endless nowadays, so are the methods of cultivating, transporting, preparing, and modifying food for our consumption.			
b. The food we choose to eat helps support unfair treatments of animals and the chaotic usage of natural resources that negatively affect ourselves and the environment in many different ways.			
c. A balance between producing more food and sustaining the planet is the answer to our present issues related to ethical eating in the face of an astonishing population growth, a worldwide financial crisis, and environmental chaos.			

UNIT 4
Extreme Weather Events Affecting the Planet

▶ IN THIS UNIT YOU WILL....

- talk about extreme weather conditions and environmental disasters;
- read and reflect about people who survived environmental disasters;
- learn how to refer to an action that happened before another with the past perfect tense;
- identify and use adverbs of intensity.

LEAD OFF

- What situations are represented in the picture?
- How are they related to the title of the unit?
- How important is it to understand the influence of human and natural factors on extreme weather events?

READING

►► BEFORE READING

Mention a natural disaster or an extreme weather condition that happened in the region where you live and explain its impact on your community. `Contextualizing`

_____

_____

_____

►► WHILE READING

Read the title of the text carefully. Does the author say that those people survived the disasters they faced? Justify your answer. `Locating key words`

_____

_____

4 People Who Faced Disaster – And How They Made It out Alive

Some disasters are simply not survivable. But most are, and research on human behavior suggests that the difference between life and death often comes down to the simple – yet surprisingly difficult – task of recognizing
5 **threats** before they **overwhelm** you, then working through them as discrete challenges. The people who survive disasters tend to be better prepared and more capable of making smart decisions under pressure. Not everyone is born with these traits, but almost anyone can learn them.
10 [...]

Rule 1:

It was early, 9:00 A.M., and **eerily** dark in Poway, Calif., as 75-**mph** winds drove **chaparral** *embers* through the air and **shook** the bones of Frank Vaplon's house. One ember
15 **lodged** in his woodpile and set it **ablaze**. Most of his neighbors had evacuated, but Vaplon had decided to stay and fight the wildfire that was closing in on his property.

Geared up in a mail-order *firefighter*'s outfit – helmet, **bunker coat**, respirator, the whole thing – Vaplon began
20 his *assault* by shooting a high-pressure stream of water at the flames, but it just blew back against him in a hot *mist*. "It was like **pissing into** the *wind*," Vaplon says. "So I turned around and started spraying down the house."

The Witch Creek fire was the fourth largest on record in
25 California. A reported 1,800 firefighters battled the *blaze* and several others nearby; more than 250,000 people in San Diego County were evacuated. Conventional wisdom says that when a wildfire is burning down your neighborhood, you shouldn't stick around. And, for most
30 homeowners, evacuation was certainly the smartest option. But Vaplon stayed and fought back against the fire. What did he know that everyone who followed the conventional **wisdom** didn't?

"The last thing I want from my story is for people to risk
35 their lives," Vaplon says. "But I'd thought about protecting my home, and I felt comfortable with my decision to stay." The day before the fire swept through his 2.5-acre spread, he woke up early to the distant smell of smoke. He immediately broke out 500 feet of fire **hose** and attached it
40 to a *standpipe* hooked up to a 10,000-gallon water tank. "I started watering down everything that I could," Vaplon says. "The roof, my lawn, everything."

[...]

"The brain is an engineering system," says John Leach, a
45 former Royal Air Force combat survival instructor who now works with the Norwegian military on survival training and research. "Like any engineering system, it has limits in terms of what it can process and how fast it can do so. We cope by taking in information about our environment,
50 and then building a model of that environment. We don't respond to our environment, but to the model of our environment." If there's no model, the brain tries to create one, but there's not enough time for that during an emergency. Operating on an inadequate mental model,
55 disaster victims often **fail** to take the actions needed to save their own lives.

Not Vaplon. As the firestorm approached, he stayed calm and **clearheaded**. He had done so much advance work that he had created a model for his brain to act on when
60 disaster came. [...]

Extracted from www.popularmechanics.com/adventure/outdoors/a4623/4331486.
Accessed on August 24, 2018.

Unit 4

» AFTER READING

1. Read the text carefully. Why was Vaplon able to survive the firestorm? `Understanding main ideas`

_____
_____

2. Check (✓) the correct alternative to complete the statements about the text. `Understanding details`

a. More than 250,000 people left San Diego County because of _____.
   ( ) Frank Vaplon   ( ) the Witch Creek fire

b. When Vaplon _____, he decided to start watering down the roof, the lawn, and everything he could.
   ( ) woke up to the smell of smoke
   ( ) got dressed in a firefighter's outfit

c. Vaplon challenged conventional wisdom when he _____.
   ( ) stayed and fought back against the fire
   ( ) did a lot of work in advance

EXPAND YOUR VOCABULARY

1. Look for the words and expressions listed below in the text and infer their meanings. Underline the one that does not belong in each group below. Then talk to a classmate about why the word is not part of the group.

a. helmet, hose, bunker coat
b. firestorm, wildfire, wisdom
c. property, house, chaparral
d. sweep through, water down, spray down

2. Write the words in italics in the text next to their corresponding definitions below.

a. _____: someone whose job is to stop fires burning

b. _____: a light cloud low over the ground that makes it difficult for you to see very far

c. _____: a piece of wood or coal that stays red and very hot after a fire has stopped burning

d. _____: an attempt to achieve something difficult, especially using physical force

e. _____: a big dangerous fire – used especially in news reports

f. _____: a pipe that provides water in a public place in the street

g. _____: moving air, especially when it moves strongly or quickly in a current

Extracted from www.ldoceonline.com. Accessed on August 24, 2018.

3. Choose words from activity 2 to complete the text. Make any necessary adjustments.

Brazil's worst month ever for forest fires blamed on human activity

Brazil has seen more forest fires in September than in any single month since records began, and authorities have warned that 2017 could surpass the worst year on record if action is not taken soon.

Experts say that the _____ are almost exclusively due to human activity, and they attribute the uptick to the expansion of agriculture and a reduction of oversight and surveillance. Lower than average rainfall in this year's dry season is also an exacerbating factor.
[…]
Burning is illegal and carries heavy fines, but fire is often used to clear land for pasture or crops and hunting or results from land conflicts.
[…]
In September, after a month-long battle, _____ gave up on a fire in Tocantins state park, believed to have been lit by local fishermen and carried by strong _____ during an intense dry period. An area three times the size of São Paulo was destroyed, according to local media.

Extracted from www.theguardian.com/world/2017/sep/28/brazil-forest-fires-deforestation-september-record-amazon. Accessed on August 24, 2018.

4. Do you agree that human activity is responsible for some disasters and extreme weather conditions we face around the world? Share your opinion with a classmate.

VOCABULARY IN USE

1. Pay attention to an extract from the text on page 36 and check (✔) the correct meaning for the phrasal verb in bold.

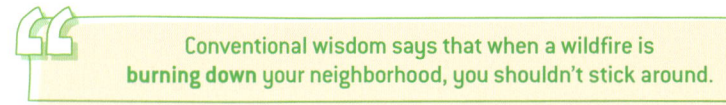

   > Conventional wisdom says that when a wildfire is **burning down** your neighborhood, you shouldn't stick around.

   a. ( ) to become weaker and produce less heat   **b.** ( ) to destroy by fire

2. Read some examples with other phrasal verbs related to weather conditions or environmental disasters. Match them with their corresponding meanings.

   a. The storm **had blown** itself **out**, leaving the sky pearly.

   b. By late fall, Mediterranean islands have **cooled off** and can have rainy days.

   c. Once the weather **warms up**, you can move the plants outdoors.

   d. I can't see where I'm going with the windows all **misted up** like this.

   ( ) becomes warm, or to make someone or something warm

   ( ) had ended

   ( ) became covered with very small drops of water

   ( ) returned to a normal temperature after being hot

   Adapted from www.ldoceonline.com. Accessed on August 26, 2018.

3. Circle the correct alternative to complete the explanation of the weather-related idiom pictured below.

   When someone says "it's raining cats and dogs", he/she means…

   a. it's raining a lot.

   b. it's raining pets.

   c. there are lots of cats and dogs walking around.

   d. cats and dogs are fighting.

   e. it's raining, but it's a very light rain.

4. The idioms in bold in the sentences have weather-related words. Infer their meaning and use them to fill in the blanks.

   > There is no need to make **a storm in a teacup**! It's just a small problem.
   >
   > Anna was **on cloud nine** after she got an A+ on her biology exam.
   >
   > Young man, you are going to the dentist's today **come rain or shine**, do you understand?
   >
   > We can't let the press **get wind of** the mayor's illness.
   >
   > Joshua is still a little **under the weather**, so he will stay home and rest.

   a. _____ : to hear or find out about something secret or private

   b. _____ : whatever happens or whatever the weather is like

   c. _____ : to be very happy about something

   d. _____ : slightly ill

   e. _____ : an unnecessary expression of strong feelings about something that is very unimportant

   Extracted from www.ldoceonline.com. Accessed on August 26, 2018.

5. Choose two idioms from activity 4 and contextualize them in a paragraph or dialogue. Then share your answer with your classmates.

   _____
   _____
   _____
   _____
   _____

LANGUAGE IN USE 1

Unit 4

PAST PERFECT

1. The excerpt below was extracted from the text on page 36. Read it, pay attention to the parts in bold, and underline the correct alternatives to complete the sentences about the past perfect tense.

> He **had done** so much advance work that he **had created** a model for his brain to act on when disaster came.

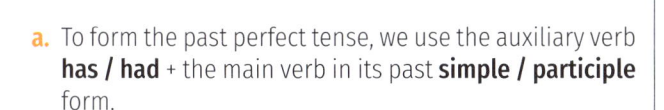

   a. To form the past perfect tense, we use the auxiliary verb **has / had** + the main verb in its past **simple / participle** form.

   b. The past perfect tense is used to refer to an action that occurred **before / after** another action in the **past / future**.

   c. Besides the verb tense, some words or expressions might also help identify which action happened first, such as **now / before**, *after*, and *previously*, for example.

2. Refer back to the text on page 36 and underline other past perfect occurrences.

3. In the extract "But I'd thought about protecting my home, and I felt comfortable with my decision to stay," what happened first: Vaplon's feeling comfortable with his decision or Vaplon's thinking about protecting his home?

_____

4. Below you will find two other stories about people who survived disasters. Use the past perfect tense of the verbs from the box to fill in the blanks.

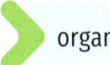

> organize   put   take shelter

[...]

Rule 2:
The tornado siren sounded at the Little Sioux Scout Ranch in western Iowa just before the power went out on June 11, 2008. Scout Leader Fred Ullrich, an IT manager at the University of Nebraska Medical Center, opened the door of the building where he and 65 Boy Scouts _____. [...]
Ullrich didn't know what he and his scouts were in for that day, but mental preparedness and responsibility are central to the Boy Scout philosophy. The night before the tornado, Ullrich _____ the boys through a first-aid drill. When emergency responders arrived after the tornado, what they saw was devastating – four scouts were dead or mortally wounded. Scores were suffering from broken pelvises, dislocated shoulders, lacerations and punctured lungs. Yet, amazingly, the rescue crew also saw that Ullrich and the uninjured scouts were putting their training to work. They _____ an on-the-spot triage center, helping to prepare the most seriously injured for their journey to the hospital. [...]

> lose   plan   suffer

Rule 3:
On Saturday, Nov. 18, 2007, Daryl Jané left his cottage on Bainbridge Island in Washington State to head for an overnight sky-watching event 190 miles southeast at Trout Lake. He _____ to be back the next day to watch a Seattle Seahawks game. Jané never made it to Trout Lake. Instead he became the prisoner of a tremendous late fall snowstorm. Jané was driving on a widely used – at least in good conditions – forest service road as the snow began to pile up. He became stuck 35 miles from his destination when the tires of his '93 Jeep Cherokee sank into deep snow. [...]
In the end, Jané was stuck for 14 days before a local snowmobile club found him. He _____ 10 pounds but _____ from neither frostbite nor hypothermia. [...]

Extracted from www.popularmechanics.com/adventure/outdoors/a4623/4331486.
Accessed on August 27, 2018.

5. Read and discuss the excerpt below in small groups. If possible, use the past perfect in your argumentation.

> **Why Save the Amazon?**
> For one, the Amazon is on the **frontlines** of the fight against global warming.
> Currently, the Amazon is a **carbon sink**, meaning it stores carbon dioxide and prevents it from entering the atmosphere and **fueling** climate change. Deforestation, on the other hand, releases that carbon into the air, making global warming worse. Because of this, deforestation accounts for about 10 to 15 percent of global greenhouse gas emissions. Losing the Amazon means more carbon emissions and a warmer world. No matter how far from the region you live, the Amazon plays an important role in all of our lives, and we all play a role in protecting the homes of thousands of people and some of the world's rarest wildlife.
> [...]

Extracted from www.greenpeace.org/usa/forests/amazon-rainforest.
Accessed on August 27, 2018.

EXPAND YOUR READING

1. **Read the text and check (✓) the alternative that best summarizes its main idea.**
   a. (　) As ocean waters are becoming warmer and more acidic, ocean circulation, chemistry, ecosystems, and marine life are affected.
   b. (　) Climate change and its impact on many sectors have become increasingly troublesome across the nation.

[...]

Introduction

Climate change is already affecting societies and the natural world. Climate change interacts with other environmental and societal factors in ways that can either moderate or intensify these impacts. The types and magnitudes of impacts vary across the nation and through time. Children, the elderly, the sick, and the poor are especially vulnerable. There
5 is **mounting** evidence that harm to the nation will increase substantially in the future unless global emissions of **heat-trapping gases** are greatly reduced.

Widespread Impacts

Because environmental, cultural, and socioeconomic systems are tightly coupled, climate change impacts can either be amplified or reduced by
10 cultural and socioeconomic decisions. In many arenas, it is clear that societal decisions have substantial influence on the vulnerability of valued resources to climate change. For example, rapid population growth and development in coastal areas tends to amplify climate change related impacts. Recognition of these **couplings**, together with recognition
15 of multiple **sources** of vulnerability, helps identify what information decision-makers need as they manage risks.

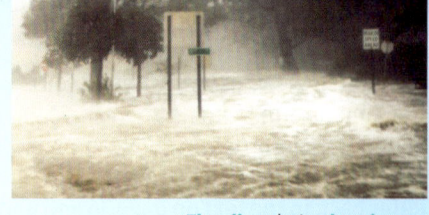

Flooding during **hurricanes**

Multiple System Failures During Extreme Events

Impacts are particularly severe when critical systems simultaneously fail. We have already seen multiple system failures during an extreme weather
20 event in the United States, as when Hurricane Katrina struck New Orleans. Infrastructure and evacuation failures and collapse of critical response services during a storm is one example of multiple system failures. Another example is a **loss** of electrical power during heat waves or wildfires, which can reduce food and water safety. Air conditioning has helped reduce illness
25 and death due to extreme heat, but if power is lost, everyone is vulnerable. By their nature, such events can exceed our capacity to respond. In succession, these events severely **deplete** resources needed to respond, from the individual to the national scale, but disproportionately affect the most vulnerable populations.
[...]

Katrina struck New Orleans

Cascading Effects Across Sectors

Agriculture, water, energy, transportation, and more are all affected by climate change. These sectors of our economy
30 do not exist in isolation and are linked in increasingly complex ways. For example, water supply and energy use are completely **intertwined**, since water is used to generate energy, and energy is required to pump, treat, and deliver water – which means that irrigation-dependent farmers and urban dwellers are linked as well.
[...]

Extracted from https://nca2014.globalchange.gov/highlights/report-findings/widespread-impacts. Accessed on August 27, 2018.

2. **Underline the alternative that best describes expository essays.**
   a. They are a mostly oral genre. They aim at convincing the reader to understand and accept the writer's point of view.
   b. They are a mostly written genre. They present facts, statistics, and definitions to inform the reader about a given topic.

LANGUAGE IN USE 2

Unit 4

ADVERBS OF DEGREE

1. Read these extracts from the text on page 40, pay attention to the words in bold, and answer: what's their function in the sentences? Then choose the best alternative to complete the sentences.

> "There is mounting evidence that harm to the nation will increase **substantially** in the future unless global emissions of heat-trapping gases are **greatly** reduced."

> "In succession, these events **severely** deplete resources needed to respond, [...]"

a. Adverbs of degree tell us about the _____ of an action, an adjective, or another adverb. These include *almost*, *enough*, *too*, _____, etc.

( ) manner / quickly ( ) intensity / very

b. Many adverbs of degree end in _____, for example: _____ and *intensely*.

( ) -ly / extremely ( ) -ing / intensifying

c. Adverbs of degree are usually positioned _____ the adjective, adverb, or _____ that they modify.

( ) after / pronoun ( ) before / verb

2. Read part of a text about the Mariana mining disaster effects and underline the adverb of degree. Then answer: what word does it modify?

_____

How Brazil's Worst Environmental Disaster Is Still Affecting Thousands of People

[...]
What could possibly be worse than one socio-environmental catastrophe?
Two of them.
On November 5, 2015, the Fundão dam, located in the sub-district of Bento Rodrigues, 35 km from the center of the Brazilian municipality of Mariana, Minas Gerais, ruptured. 60 million cubic meters of iron ore tailings were leaked from the Samarco-operated mining complex and traveled 55 km from the Gualaxo do Norte River and another 22 km from the Carmo River to the Doce River. In total, the mud traveled 663 km to find the sea.
It's been characterized by experts as the country's largest environmental disaster, altering the ecosystems along the Rio Doce basin tremendously in addition to killing 19 people and affecting more than 23 thousand families. Recently, the relationship between the yellow fever outbreak and this disaster have made their way into the mainstream media's narrative, just as biologist and environmentalist Augusto Ruschi predicted two years ago. [...]

Extracted from www.theinertia.com/environment/how-brazils-worst-environmental-disaster-is-still-affecting-thousands-of-people. Accessed on August 28, 2018.

3. Form *-ly* adverbs of degree to complete the chart below.

Adjectives	Adverbs of Degree
entire	_____
high	_____
huge	_____
moderate	_____
partial	_____
strong	_____
total	_____

4. In your notebook, summarize the text excerpt below using your own words. Insert two adverbs of degree from the previous activities.

Thailand cave: How the rescue operation unfolded

After a soccer practice on Saturday 23 June, 12 young players and their "Wild Boars" team coach entered the 10km (6 mile) Tham Luang cave complex in Chiang Rai province, northern Thailand.
When they failed to return home, a huge search operation was launched, with rescuers facing a race against time to find them as heavy rain battered the region and flooded parts of the cave.
After 10 days, they were found weak but alive. [...]

Extracted from https://news.sky.com/story/thailand-cave-rescue-how-the-boys-were-found-11424201. Accessed on August 28, 2018.

LISTENING COMPREHENSION

1. **Look at the magazine covers and answer: what do they have in common? Then work in small groups to discuss the issues shown on these covers.**

Extracted from http://content.time.com/time/covers/europe/0,16641,20051003,00.html. Accessed on August 28, 2018.

Extracted from www.nationalgeographic.com. Accessed on August 28, 2018.

Extracted from www.newsweek.com/archive/2014. Accessed on August 28, 2018.

2. **Listen to Alex Staniforth talk about his experience and infer what happened to him.**
   a. (   ) He fell 70ft into a **crevasse**.
   b. (   ) He was almost caught in an avalanche on Everest.
   c. (   ) He **rescued** someone from an underwater cave.

3. **Listen to the whole recording and order the sentences accordingly.**
   a. (   ) The earthquake struck.
   b. (   ) Alex realized he had escaped the worst of the avalanche.
   c. (   ) An avalanche killed 16 Sherpa guides on Mount Everest.
   d. (   ) Alex thought of his family and imagined the headlines announcing his death.
   e. (   ) Alex plans to return to Everest for a third attempt.
   f. (   ) After two days, they were helicoptered down.
   g. (   ) Twelve months later, Alex was ready to venture back.
   h. (   ) The avalanche hit Alex like an express train.

≫ EXPAND YOUR HORIZONS ≫≫≫

Check (✓) the column that best describes your opinion about each statement. Then discuss your answers with your classmates and teacher, justifying your point of view.

	I agree.	I'm not sure.	I disagree.
a. Disaster survivors are often more prepared and capable of making smart decisions when they are under pressure in future events.			
b. Although natural disasters are apparently caused by nature, they are usually at least partly caused or made worse by human decisions.			
c. Nations across the world must address issues related to global warming, climate change, and carbon emissions to reduce the risks of environmental disasters.			

REVIEW 2

Units 3 and 4

1. Read the title of the text carefully. Then list words or expressions relating to the theme you are going to read about. `Brainstorming`

_____

_____

_____

2. Work in pairs. Discuss some of the things you think the author of the text says you can do to help make our food and farming system better for the future. `Discussing and Predicting`

3. Now read the whole text and check your predictions.

What you can do – and ask others to do – to help make our food and farming system fit for the future

The Sustain Guide to Good Food

sustain

[...]

*Please consider adopting a Good Food at Work policy, **committing** your organisation to improve the food you buy and serve to staff, visitors, clients and the public, and to help communicate Good Food principles. If you do adopt a Good Food Policy, tell us. Share your story and inspire more organisations to get involved.*

[...]

Good food

What we mean by good food can be summed up by our seven principles:

1) Aiming to be waste-free

Reducing food waste (and packaging) saves the energy, effort, and natural resources used to produce and dispose of it, as well as money.

2) Eating better, and less meat and dairy

Consuming more vegetables and fruit, grains and pulses, and smaller amounts of animal products produced to high-welfare and environmental **standards** helps reduce health risks and greenhouse gases.

3) Buying local, seasonal, and environmentally friendly food

This benefits wildlife and the countryside, minimises the energy used in food production, transport, and storage, and helps protect the local economy.

4) Choosing Fairtrade-certified products

This scheme for food and drinks imported from poorer countries ensures a fair deal for disadvantaged producers.

5) Selecting fish only from sustainable sources

Future generations will be able to eat fish and seafood if we act now to protect our rivers and seas and the creatures living there.

6) Getting the balance right

We need to cut down on sugar, salt, and fat, and most of us want to avoid questionable ingredients and processes such as genetic modification (GM) and some additives.

7) Growing our own, and buying the rest from a wide range of outlets

Fresh out of the garden or **allotment** is **unbeatable**, and a vibrant mix of local markets, small shops and cafés, and other retailers provides choice, variety, and good **livelihoods**.

Extracted from www.sustainweb.org/sustainablefood/. Accessed on November 12, 2018.

4. Read the text and decide if the statements are true (T) or false (F).

a. (   ) The author defends that we should reduce the amount of meat that we eat.

b. (   ) You should give preference to imported food rather than local food.

c. (   ) If you buy imported food, you should give preference to smaller producers.

d. (   ) Even though we should eat less or avoid sugar, the same is not true for additives.

5. Read the text again and underline two first conditional sentences.

6. Now read these other sentences, paying close attention to the parts in bold, and match them with their use.

a. **If** we **reduce** packaging, we **will save** natural resources.

b. **If** we **want** to get a good eating balance, we **need** to reduce our consumption of sugar, salt, and fat.

c. We **would help** disadvantaged farmers **if** we **bought** more Fairtrade-certified products.

(   ) It describes a hypothetical situation and its hypothetical result.

(   ) It describes a general truth.

(   ) It describes a possible situation and its possible result.

43

7. Use the verbs in parentheses in the past perfect to complete the text.

Thai cave soccer players tell of how they tried to dig their way out

[…]
The press conference was a jovial affair. The boys, dressed in their matching Wild Boars soccer shirts, entered the packed hall dribbling soccer balls to loud cheers. They smiled, some widely, some more **shyly**, at the audience of hundreds who _____ (gather) to hear their account of the drama for the first time.
A video played at the beginning of the press conference showed the boys openly **weeping** as they thanked the medical
5 staff at the hospital who _____ (help) in their recovery over the past week.
[…]
Ekaphol, 25, said they _____ (decide) to make the trip to the Tham Luang cave complex on June 23 as a fun activity because none of them _____ (be) inside before.
They cycled there after soccer practice and planned to spend an hour in the caves but as they reached a junction on
10 the way out, they saw the water rising.
[…]
It was only after ten days, when many _____ almost _____ (lose) hope of finding them, that two British divers finally came across the boys sheltered on a shelf deep in the cave.
[…]
One of the first questions the boys had for the divers was how many days they had been there, since they had lost all track of the time. "Our brains were very slow," said Adul. "We _____ (forget) everything about mathematics."
15 They also revealed that the eventual decision about who should leave the cave first was not based on strength, but decided by the boys themselves. It was based on who lived furthest away from the cave and therefore would have the longest cycle back home.
[…]

Adapted from www.theguardian.com/news/2018/jul/18/thai-cave-rescue-footballers-and-coach-describe-ordeal. Accessed on August 29, 2018.

8. There are different types of adverbs in the following cartoon strip. Circle only the ones that indicate degree or intensity. Then work in pairs to discuss the writer's tone: is it serious or sarcastic? Justify your view.

The Boondocks by Aaron McGruder

Extracted from www.gocomics.com/boondocks/2006/01/18. Accessed on August 29, 2018.

UNIT 5
In the Limelight

IN THIS UNIT YOU WILL...
- talk about TV characters and shows;
- exchange ideas about binge-watching;
- learn how to talk about hypothetical situations in the past using the third conditional;
- learn how to express wishes and regrets.

LEAD OFF

- What does the idiom *in the limelight* mean? How does it connect to the picture?
- What are your favorite TV shows and characters of all time? Justify your answer.
- Do you agree that excessive watching of TV shows has become widespread across the world due to online streaming? Has it affected your daily life? If so, how?

READING

›› BEFORE READING

Read the title of the text below. In your opinion, who is its target audience? *Identifying the target audience*

›› WHILE READING

Read the whole text and answer: What is its main purpose? *Identifying the main purpose of a text*

What would have happened next if these TV characters hadn't died?

BY IAN SANDWELL 31 AUGUST 2018

We've already told you what your favorite TV characters are up to nowadays, but **spare** a thought for those characters killed off before their time.

So many storylines unfulfilled and promising futures **dashed** with one **tap** of the writer's keyboard, although if we're lucky, we'll get a **hint** of what they would have been *getting up to* if they hadn't been killed off.

Here are seven such occasions where we can fill in the 'what if?' question surrounding some major TV characters.

1. Poussey – Orange Is the New Black

Just in case you weren't devastated enough by Poussey's tragic death in Orange Is the New Black season four, writer Lauren Morelli revealed that if Poussey had survived, she would have *gone on* to get out of Litchfield and live a happy life.
[...]

2. Doyle – Angel

The sacrificial death of Angel's loveable psychic **sidekick** Doyle just nine episodes in wasn't originally planned, but it potentially wasn't going to be the end of Doyle – Joss Whedon wanted to bring the character back as a Big Bad in season three or four.
[...]

3. Professor Arturo – Sliders

In the season two episode "Post Traumatic Slide Syndrome" of cult sci-fi Sliders, Professor Arturo and his **double** have a battle. As the **vortex** opens, one Arturo *knocks* the other *down* and goes with the group to the next world.
[...]

4. Tara – Buffy the Vampire Slayer

There were actually two opportunities for Tara to come back in Buffy the Vampire **Slayer** after her cruel death in season six. [...] We don't know why it never happened, but maybe it's something to do with the choice not making sense in light of Buffy's traumatic return from the dead.

5. Tony Almeida – 24

We know that Tony Almeida eventually came back to life in 24 season seven and had turned **evil**, but before his "death" in season five, we were robbed of an exciting storyline for him – the writers had planned for him to go on a **revenge** mission after the death of his wife Michelle.
[...]

6. David Tennant – Doctor Who

When Steven Moffat took over as the Doctor Who **showrunner**, he almost persuaded David Tennant to *stick around* for one more season as the Doctor, before Tennant decided to leave and Matt Smith *took over* the iconic role for season five. The Tennant version of season five would have started off in similar fashion with the Doctor crashing into Amelia Pond's garden.
[...]

7. Carl – The Walking Dead

We're being a bit cheeky here as there's no guarantee that The Walking Dead would have followed the comic books with Carl's storylines. However, we do know that his shock death has robbed Carl of a host of storylines, including a romance with Lydia, the daughter of Whisperers leader Alpha, and a key role in the future of the Hilltop.
[...]

Adapted from www.digitalspy.com/tv/feature/a865204/dead-tv-characters-scrapped-storylines. Accessed on September 1, 2018..

>> AFTER READING

1. Which other TV characters would you add to the list on page 46? Work in pairs and justify your choices. *Discussing*

_____

_____

_____

2. Decide if the sentences are true (T) or false (F). *Understanding details*

a. ( ) According to Lauren Morelli, if Poussey hadn't died, she would have led a happy life.
b. ( ) In *The Walking Dead*, Lydia's death prevented her from having an affair with Carl.
c. ( ) Steven Moffat played the doctor in *Doctor Who*.
d. ( ) The writers of 24 had planned for Tony Almeida to seek revenge for Michelle's death.
e. ( ) Joss Whedon had decided to kill Doyle right at the beginning of season 3 or 4, but the character ended up dying in season 1.

3. What reasons might make a writer decide to kill off certain promising characters? Talk to your classmates.

EXPAND YOUR VOCABULARY

1. Scan the text to find the phrasal verbs in italics that match the definitions below. Write them in the base form.

a. _____ : to hit or push someone so that they fall to the ground
b. _____ : to stay in a place a little longer, waiting for something to happen
c. _____ : to take control of something
d. _____ : to continue doing something or being in a situation
e. _____ : to do something, especially something slightly bad

Extracted from www.ldoceonline.com. Accessed on September 3, 2018.

2. Read these extracts from the text on page 46 and check (✓) the word that best replaces the one in italics.

a. "We're being a bit cheeky here as there's no guarantee that The Walking Dead would have followed the comic books with Carl's *storylines*."
( ) climax   ( ) plot

b. "(...) Tennant to stick around for one more season as the Doctor, before Tennant decided to leave and Matt Smith took over the iconic *role* for season five."
( ) situation   ( ) part

c. "We know that Tony Almeida *eventually* came back to life in 24 season seven and had turned evil."
( ) finally   ( ) soon

d. "We're being a bit *cheeky* here as there's no guarantee that The Walking Dead would have followed the comic books with Carl's storylines."
( ) audacious   ( ) entertaining

3. Read the proverb below and answer the questions: Do you think it might apply to television programs as well? Can the shows you watch say anything about who you are or affect your behavior? Use some words from the previous activity in your answers. Then report your opinions to the class.

> You are what you eat.

_____

_____

_____

Unit 5

47

VOCABULARY IN USE

1. In "However, we do know that his shock death has robbed Carl of a host of storylines, including a romance with Lydia, the daughter of Whisperers leader Alpha, and a key role in the future of the Hilltop", what does the word *key* mean? Choose the correct alternative.

   a. ( ) a small specially shaped piece of metal that you put into a lock and turn in order to lock or unlock a door, start a car, etc.
   b. ( ) the buttons that you press on a computer keyboard to operate the computer
   c. ( ) very important or necessary
   d. ( ) the printed answers to a test or set of questions in a book

   Extracted from www.ldoceonline.com/dictionary/key. Accessed on September 4, 2018.

2. Read the dictionary entry below as well as the extracts from the text on page 46, paying special attention to the words in bold. Then check (✓) the meaning of each homonym in context.

   > **hom·o·nym** / noun [countable] *technical* a word that is spelled the same and sounds the same as another, but is different in meaning or origin. For example, the noun 'bear' and the verb 'bear' are homonyms.

   Extracted from www.ldoceonline.com/dictionary/homonym. Accessed on September 4, 2018.

   a. "So many storylines unfulfilled and promising futures dashed with one **tap** of the writer's keyboard, although if we're lucky, we'll get a hint of what they would have been getting up to if they hadn't been killed off."

   ( ) a piece of equipment for controlling the flow of water, gas etc. from a pipe or container
   ( ) an act of hitting something lightly, especially to get someone's attention

   b. "There were actually two opportunities for Tara to come back in Buffy the Vampire Slayer after her cruel death in **season** six."

   ( ) a series of films, plays, television programs, etc. that are shown during a particular period of time
   ( ) to add salt, pepper, etc. to food you are cooking

   Extracted from www.ldoceonline.com. Accessed on September 4, 2018.

3. Homonyms can be subdivided into homophones and homographs. Study the word clouds and match them with their corresponding categories.

   a. BYE FOUR BY BUY HERE HEAR HOUR NO FLOUR KNOW FLOWER FOR MEAT OUR SON WHERE SUN WEAR

   b. BAT WIND WOUND OBJECT BOW LEAD TEAR SECOND DESERT SUBJECT BASS FINE ROW

   ( ) **hom·o·graph** / noun [countable] *technical* a word that is spelled the same as another, but is different in meaning, origin, grammar, or pronunciation. For example, the noun 'record' is a homograph of the verb 'record'.

   Extracted from www.ldoceonline.com/dictionary/homograph. Accessed on September 4, 2018.

   ( ) **hom·o·phone** / noun [countable] *technical* a word that sounds the same as another but is different in spelling, meaning, or origin. For example, 'knew' and 'new' are homophones.

   Extracted from www.ldoceonline.com/dictionary/homophone. Accessed on September 4, 2018.

4. Use one homograph or homophone from the word clouds above to complete the cartoon. Then explain your choice to a classmate.

   Extracted from www.cartoonstock.com/directory/f/fining.asp. Accessed on September 4, 2018.

LANGUAGE IN USE 1

Unit 5

THIRD CONDITIONAL

1. Read the extracts from the text on page 46 and underline the correct alternatives to complete the sentences.

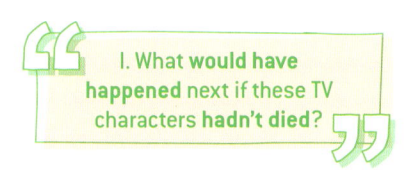

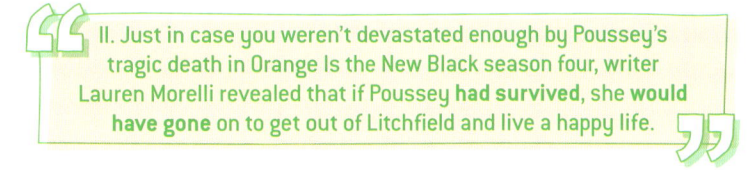

> I. What **would have happened** next if these TV characters **hadn't died**?

> II. Just in case you weren't devastated enough by Poussey's tragic death in Orange Is the New Black season four, writer Lauren Morelli revealed that if Poussey **had survived**, she **would have gone** on to get out of Litchfield and live a happy life.

About extract I, it is correct to say that…
- **a.** the TV characters died.
- **b.** the TV characters might not have died.

About extract II, it is correct to say that…
- **a.** it talks about a real possibility in the future.
- **b.** it talks about a hypothetical situation in the past.

We use the third conditional to refer to…
- **a.** an unlikely situation that probably won't be fulfilled, but we imagine its possible result.
- **b.** a situation that didn't happen and won't happen, but we imagine its hypothetical result.

2. Read the extracts again and fill in the blanks about the formation of the third conditional.

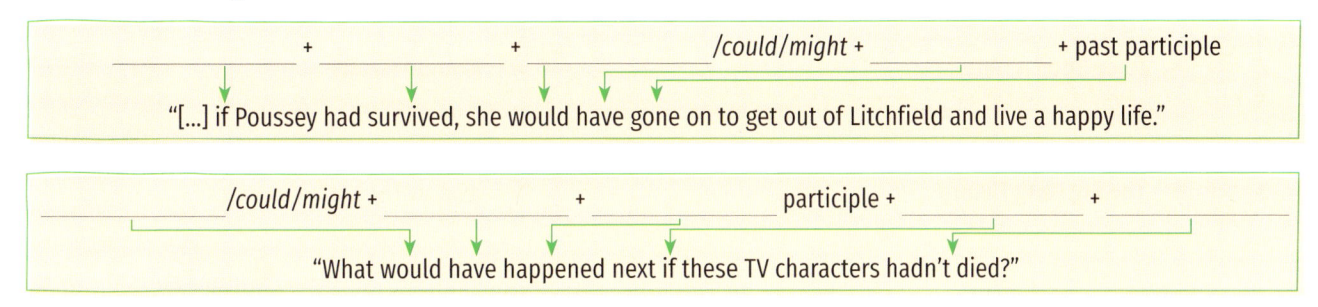

____ + ____ + ____ /could/might + ____ + past participle
"[…] if Poussey had survived, she would have gone on to get out of Litchfield and live a happy life."

____ /could/might + ____ + ____ participle + ____ + ____
"What would have happened next if these TV characters hadn't died?"

3. Use the verbs from the box to complete the extracts below. Remember to follow the rule for the third conditional.

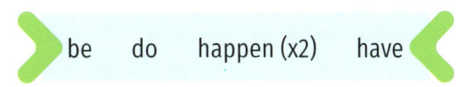

> be   do   happen (x2)   have

What if TV Had Never Been Invented?

Gloria   30-Aug-2018
"I _____ a lot better in school."

Aunt Sue   04-Sep-2018
"Grandma _____ so happy…"

Andrew   03-Sep-2018
"If the invention of the TV _____, globalization might not have been a reality."

Chris   05-Sep-2018
"If that _____, my life would have been miserable."

Dennis   04-Sep-2018
"Our lives _____ a smoother course."

4. Answer the questions below. Use the correct form of the third conditional in your answers.

- **a.** What TV show would you have watched until the end if it hadn't been canceled prematurely? Why?

  _____

- **b.** Which viewing habits might you have changed if you had been asked to?

  _____

49

EXPAND YOUR READING

1. Skim the text to find out its predominant genre. Then choose the correct alternative to complete the sentence.

The text is a/an _____ (advice letter / joke / list / song).

> **TV Shows You Wish You Were a Character On**
> […]
>
> Are you a huge fan of sci-fi? Do you want to believe that science can **transcend** what we know of the laws of physics? Perhaps joining the crew of *Battlestar Galactica* is your **jam**. Do you want to hang out with a bunch of crazy classmates in a Spanish study group that does anything but study? Hey, *Community's* probably your style. Or perhaps you want to **boldly** go where no one has gone before? *Star Trek: The Next Generation* has to be your choice. Whether you want to join the great big *Modern Family*, or you want to time travel with the **cast** of *Doctor Who*, there are plenty of awesome television worlds and TV shows you'd like to be part of.
>
> So vote up the television series you wish you were a character on and maybe the *Happy Endings* gang will invite you to sit with them, or you'll get a job in the Pawnee Parks Department. Even if the show is off the air, if you think it would be fun to have been a character on the series, vote it up!
>
> 1 ⬆⬇ **Friends**
> 221 135
> […]
>
> 2 ⬆⬇ **Once Upon a Time**
> 209 162
> […]
>
> 3 ⬆⬇ **The Big Bang Theory**
> 221 135
> […]
>
> 4 ⬆⬇ **How I Met Your Mother**
> 176 170
> […]
>
> 5 ⬆⬇ **Doctor Who**
> 155 165
> […]
>
> 6 ⬆⬇ **Sherlock**
> 70 59
> […]
>
> 7 ⬆⬇ **Modern Family**
> 137 168
> […]
>
> 8 ⬆⬇ **Avatar: The Last Airbender**
> 47 45
> […]
>
> 9 ⬆⬇ **When Calls the Heart**
> 47 49
> […]
>
> 10 ⬆⬇ **The Office**
> 120 156
> […]

Extracted from www.ranker.com/list/tv-shows-you-wish-you-were-on/ranker-tv. Accessed on September 3, 2018.

2. According to the text, which TV shows would you wish you were a character on if you...

a. were a sci-fi addict? _____

b. wanted to travel through time? _____

c. intended to visit unexplored places? _____

d. wanted to hang out with a group of mad classmates? _____

3. Check (✔) the items commonly found in lists.

a. ( ) standard language

b. ( ) complex questions

c. ( ) a set of items

d. ( ) a title for the list

e. ( ) organized information

f. ( ) the results of a research

4. Where do you often come across lists? Do you write lists yourself? What for? Exchange ideas with a partner.

_____

_____

LANGUAGE IN USE 2

Unit 5

WISH

1. **Read an extract from the text on page 50, paying attention to the verb structures in bold, and circle the correct alternatives to complete the sentences.**

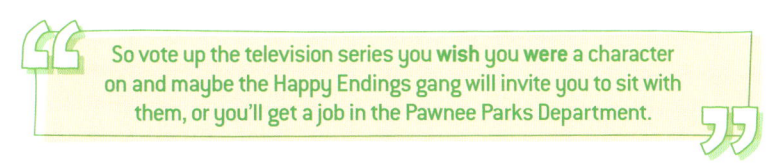

   > So vote up the television series you **wish** you **were** a character on and maybe the Happy Endings gang will invite you to sit with them, or you'll get a job in the Pawnee Parks Department.

   a. The readers who are invited to vote **are** / **aren't** TV characters.
   b. The structure in bold expresses a present wish that **is contrary to reality** / **might come true**.
   c. We should use the subjunctive form *did* / *were* instead of *was* when expressing wishes with the verb *be*.

2. **Now read a question from a question-and-answer website called Quora and underline the correct statements about it.**

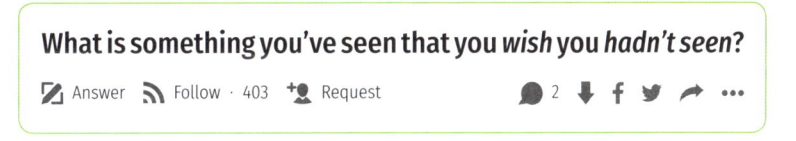

   > What is something you've seen that you *wish* you *hadn't seen*?
   > Answer · Follow · 403 · Request · 2

   Extracted from https://www.quora.com. Accessed on February 8, 2019.

   a. The author of the question assumes the reader has already seen something and disliked it.
   b. The question indicates that the reader might want to see that again.
   c. The verb structure in italics in the question expresses a regret about the past.

3. **Based on activities 1 and 2, complete the chart below with either *past perfect* or *simple past*.**

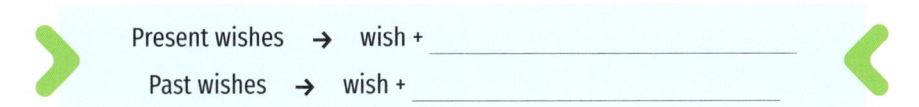

   Present wishes → wish + _____
   Past wishes → wish + _____

4. **Read the cartoon strip below and check (✓) the correct alternative to complete the sentence. Then discuss the strip content with a classmate. Try to use present and past wishes in your discussion.**

   Extracted from https://licensing.andrewsmcmeel.com/features/ch?date=1991-05-05. Accessed on September 5, 2018.

   In "When you're old, you'll **wish** you **had** more than memories of this tripe to look back on", the structure in bold…

   a. ( ) expresses a regret or a desire for a situation in the past to be different.
   b. ( ) indicates a wish for a situation in the present or future to be different.

5. **Work in pairs. Think of possible answers for the question posed in activity 2 and complete the sentence:**

   I wish I hadn't seen _____
   _____

LISTENING COMPREHENSION

1. **Look at the picture and infer what *binge-watching* means. Then underline the best definition for the expression.**
   a. to transfer or transmit (data) in such a way that it is processed in a steady and continuous stream
   b. to watch (multiple videos, episodes of a TV show, etc.) in one sitting or over a short period of time

   Extracted from www.dictionary.com. Accessed on September 5, 2018.

2. **Listen to the first part of a news program that talks about the results of a research on binge-watching TV shows and complete the transcript below.**

   Cancel your Netflix session: Binge watching TV makes it LESS enjoyable as you're more likely to forget plot details

   Binge watching television series like Game of Thrones could make it significantly less _____ than watching it on a weekly basis.

   New research found watching too much television in one go diminishes the _____ of the show with viewers getting 'significantly less' enjoyment than those who paced themselves.

   Research led by the University of Melbourne found how people watch television _____ affects how much enjoyment they get out of it.

   'Binge watching via video-on-demand services is now considered the new 'normal' way to consume television programs', _____, wrote in their paper in peer-reviewed journal First Monday.

   […]

   Researchers found that 'although binge watching leads to strong memory formation _____ following program viewing, these memories decay more _____ than memories formed after daily- or weekly-episode viewing schedules.'

   […]

   Extracted from www.dailymail.co.uk/sciencetech/article-4861672/Binge-watching-TV-makes-enjoyable-study-claims.html. Accessed on December 11, 2018.

3. **Listen to the second part of the video and match the columns accordingly.**
   a. A total of 51 students...
   b. Three groups of participants...
   c. None of the participants of this study...
   d. One of the tasks included...
   e. The results of the research showed that viewers...

   ( ) filling out a questionnaire with questions about the show.
   ( ) enjoyed the show more when they watched it only one hour a week.
   ( ) had watched the show before.
   ( ) watched *Cold War* for different periods of time.
   ( ) participated in the study.

4. **How much TV watching is too much? Are viewing habits different for older and younger generations? In what ways might binge-watching harm your health? Exchange ideas with your classmates.**

›› EXPAND YOUR HORIZONS ››››

Check (✓) the column that best describes your opinion about each statement. Then discuss your answers with your classmates and teacher, justifying your point of view.

	I agree.	I'm not sure.	I disagree.
a. Undoubtedly, everyone has dreamed of being a character in his/her favorite TV show.			
b. The old days when we needed to tune in live or buy expensive discs to watch our favorite shows and movies are gone. Streaming services are here to stay.			
c. Binge-watching has turned out to be a worldwide phenomenon, if not a disease.			

UNIT 6
Uncovering Blockchain and the Dark Web

▶ IN THIS UNIT YOU WILL...
- take part in discussions about bitcoins and blockchain;
- talk about the dark web;
- identify and use the determiners *some*, *any*, *no*, and *every*;
- learn how to use direct and indirect speech.

LEAD OFF

> Are you familiar with the situation represented in the picture? What does it refer to?
> What do you know about digital currencies? What about blockchain?
> Have you heard of the Internet's evil twin? Share what you know with your classmates.

» BEFORE READING — Identifying the source of the text

Scan the text you are about to read. What kind of publication was it extracted from?

» WHILE READING — Identifying the author's tone

Read the text and classify the author's tone as *regretful*, *nostalgic*, *objective*, or *ironic*. Justify your answer.

---

www.forbes.com/sites/jamiemoy/2018/02/22/forget-bitcoin-its-all-about-the-blockchain/#3028c50b5f6b

20,092 views | Feb 22, 2018, 06:33am

Forget Bitcoin, It's All About The Blockchain

Jamie Moy

[…]

Illustration of the blockchain network.
PHOTO COURTESY OF GERD ALTMANN VIA PIXABAY.

Bitcoin gets headlines. I see them too. I admit it **grabs** attention, but the substance is blockchain technology. That's why it's critical to get familiar with blockchain technology. To do so, start here:

Blockchain is a public distributed *ledger*. Throughout most of history, we've been living in a centralized world. We have governments, financial institutions, big tech companies, and credit bureaus as "**trusted**" third parties enabling us to transact and interact. These intermediaries control and have access to our money and data and are occasionally hacked. Blockchain technology allows for decentralization. It is essentially a **database** managed by a peer-to-peer *network* of computers. Blockchain facilitates the transfer and payment of digital money without the need for a trusted entity, such as a bank. The data it holds is public and **immutable**.

Blockchain is not bitcoin. Bitcoin is digital money, a virtual currency that was the first successful blockchain product. Blockchain is the technology that enables *cryptocurrency* like bitcoin. While they go hand-in-hand, there are other use cases for blockchain besides bitcoin. Blockchain can **ensure** that the terms of programmable autonomous contracts, known as smart contracts, are met. It can be used for online voting to address voter **fraud**. It can be used to secure identity and many other situations where transparency and security is lacking.
[…]

Blockchain is secure and safe. Security is a big topic and everyone should fully understand. Maybe you've heard about **hacks** of centralized **exchanges**. And you've probably heard about a person going "dumpster diving" to find an old hard drive because their private key was stored there. It's important to know that virtually all the **losses** were due to hacking of centralized exchanges, losing private key information and gaining control of private keys by bad actors, and not some security vulnerability in Bitcoin technology.
Blockchains, like Bitcoin and Ethereum, have not yet been hacked. They are considered to be very secure. It is very challenging, almost impossible, to change any *transaction* information once it is validated and becomes part of a block. Bitcoin is commonly referred to as digital gold. Referring to bitcoin as insecure or unsafe is like calling gold insecure or unsafe.

Blockchain allows for pseudonymity. The blockchain is public where transactions are recorded and visible to everyone, therefore it is not purely anonymous. But it does provide pseudonymity. For example, digital wallets are identified via the wallet's public address (aka public key). The public key is not connected to a person's other personal information such as name or address. This allows participants to transact privately and **reputably** with *data* remaining secure.

Blockchain technology has been referred to as the next revolution and although it's only in the early stages, it is here to stay.
[…]

Adapted from www.forbes.com/sites/jamiemoy/2018/02/22/forget-bitcoin-its-all-about-the-blockchain/#3028c50b5f6b. Accessed on September 8, 2018.

AFTER READING

1. What's the author's purpose? Use your own words to state it and justify your answer. *Stating the author's purpose*

   _____
   _____
   _____

2. Based on the information provided by the author, check (✓) the correct definition for *blockchain*. *Understanding the main idea*

   a. ( ) It's a crypto-currency allowing for anonymous transactions and using a decentralized architecture.

   b. ( ) It's a digitized, decentralized, and continuously growing public ledger that consists of records called blocks, which are linked and secured using cryptography.

3. Underline the true statements according to the text. *Understanding details*

   a. Blockchain allows digital information to be distributed, but not copied.

   b. Blockchain deals with cryptocurrency, contracts, or other data.

   c. Since blockchain's transactions are visible to everybody, one's personal information such as name and address is made public.

   d. Despite their popularity, bitcoins are proven to be unsafe.

EXPAND YOUR VOCABULARY

1. Read the text again, find the words in italics to fit each definition below, and use them to complete the infographic.

   a. _____ : a book in which a business, bank etc. records how much money it receives and spends

   b. _____ : a business deal or action, such as buying or selling something

   c. _____ : a set of computers that are connected to each other so that they can share information

   d. _____ : digital system or type of money

   e. _____ : information in a form that can be stored and used, especially on a computer

   Adapted from www.ldoceonline.com. Accessed on September 9, 2018.

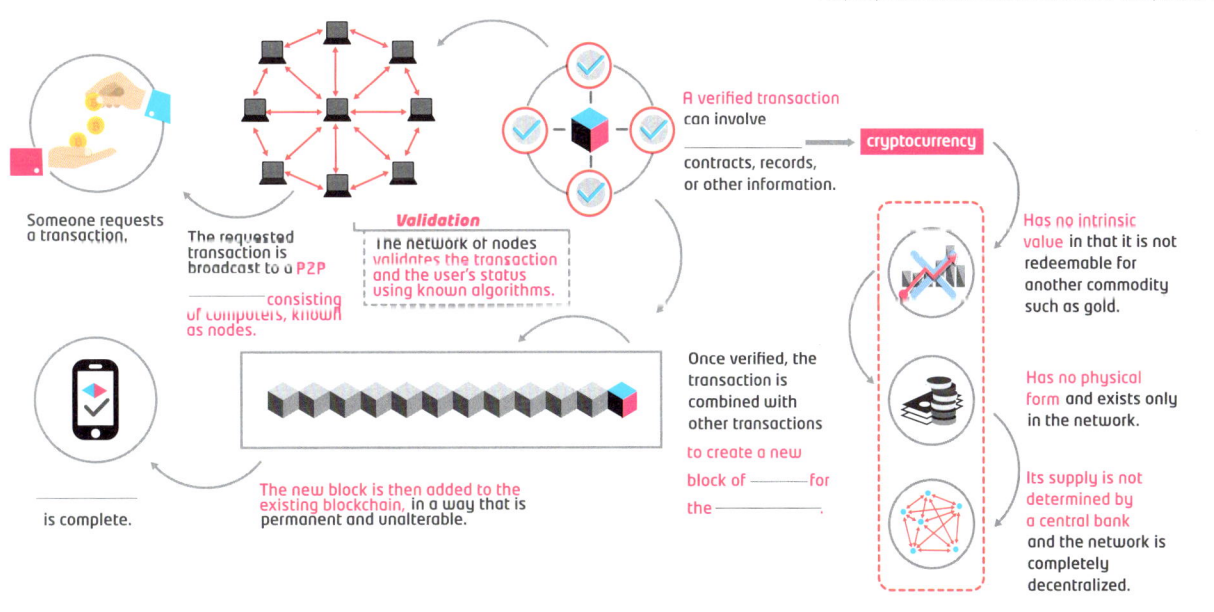

   Someone requests a transaction.

   The requested transaction is broadcast to a P2P _____ **consisting of computers, known as nodes.**

   Validation
   The network of nodes validates the transaction and the user's status using known algorithms.

   A verified transaction can involve → **cryptocurrency**
   contracts, records, or other information.

   Once verified, the transaction is combined with other transactions to create a new block of _____ for the _____.

   The new block is then added to the existing blockchain, in a way that is permanent and unalterable.

   _____ is complete.

   - Has no intrinsic value in that it is not redeemable for another commodity such as gold.
   - Has no physical form and exists only in the network.
   - Its supply is not determined by a central bank and the network is completely decentralized.

   Adapted from https://blockgeeks.com/guides/what-is-blockchain-technology. Accessed on September 9, 2018.

2. Read the last paragraph of the text again and answer: Do you agree that blockchain technology is revolutionary? Why or why not?

   _____
   _____

VOCABULARY IN USE

1. Read an extract from the text on page 54 and check the alternative that explains the expression in bold.

   > And you've probably heard about a person going **'dumpster diving'** to find an old hard drive because their private key was stored there.

   a. ( ) the sport of jumping from a plane and falling through the sky before opening a parachute

   b. ( ) the activity of looking through a large metal container for clothes, food, furniture, etc. that other people have thrown away

   Adapted from www.ldoceonline.com. Accessed on September 9, 2018.

2. Like the Internet or your bike, for example, you don't need to know everything about blockchain technology to use it. However, having some knowledge of this new technology language is useful. Use the terms related to blockchain technology listed below to complete their descriptions.

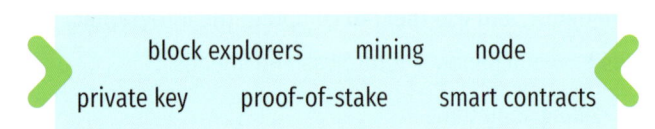

   > block explorers   mining   node
   > private key   proof-of-stake   smart contracts

   a. _____ are computer protocols that facilitate, verify, or enforce the negotiation or performance of a contract, or that obviate the need for a contractual clause. [...]

   b. [...] _____ can serve as blockchain analysis and provide information such as total network hash rate, coin supply, transaction growth, etc.

   c. _____ (PoS) is a method by which a cryptocurrency blockchain network aims to achieve distributed consensus. [...]

   d. _____ is the process of adding transaction records to Bitcoin's public ledger of past transactions or blockchain. [...]

   e. Any computer that connects to the blockchain network is called a _____. [...]

   f. [...] The _____ is a randomly generated number which allows users to transact over the blockchain. It is locally stored and kept secret. [...]

   Extracted from https://blockchainhub.net/blockchain-glossary. Accessed on September 10, 2018.

3. The phrasal verbs below also have to do with business, finance, or economy matters. Match them with their corresponding meanings.

   a. bail out   b. buy out   c. rake in
   d. shell out   e. go under   f. take over

   ( ) to spend a lot of money on something, often when you do not really want to

   ( ) to take control of a company by buying more than 50% of its shares

   ( ) to provide money to get a person or organization out of financial trouble

   ( ) to earn a lot of money without trying very hard

   ( ) to stop operating because of financial problems

   ( ) to buy someone's share of a business or property that you previously owned together, so that you have complete control

   Adapted from www.ldoceonline.com/dictionary. Accessed on September 10, 2018.

4. Choose two phrasal verbs from activity 3 to complete the text fragments that follow.

   a. Missed out on the bitcoin boom? Try these virtual currencies instead

   [...]

   Several alternative currencies have also seen significant movement in the past year, rising anywhere from 600 to 37,000 percent. But before you buy, do your research.

   The first thing to remember is that you can buy a fractional piece of almost any cryptocoin for just a few bucks – no need to _____ thousands of dollars for a full bitcoin, for example.

   [...]

   Extracted from www.euronews.com/2018/01/03/missed-bitcoin-boom-check-out-these-five-rising-cryptocurrencies-n834436. Accessed on September 10, 2018.

   b. Report: Nearly $2.5 Billion Paid Annually to Ethereum Miners, ETH Issuance Woes Continue

   [...]

   Despite **waning** prices and never-ending **scalability** debates, the Ethereum protocol continues to _____ massive **revenues** for network miners, with figures confirming $2.5 billion-a-year payouts.

   [...]

   Extracted from https://cryptoslate.com/report-nearly-2-5-billion-paid-annually-to-ethereum-miners-eth-issuance-woes-continue. Accessed on September 10, 2018.

5. Will blockchain technology have a huge impact on society? Exchange ideas with a classmate, justifying your point of view. Then report the main insights of your discussion to the rest of the class.

LANGUAGE IN USE 1

Unit 6

SOME, ANY, NO, EVERY

1. The excerpts below were extracted from the text on page 54. Read them and check (✓) the correct alternative to complete the sentence that follows.

> It's important to know that virtually all the losses were due to hacking of centralized exchanges, losing private key information and gaining control of private keys by bad actors, and not **some** security vulnerability in Bitcoin technology.

> It is very challenging, almost impossible, to change **any** transaction information once it is validated and becomes part of a block.

We use *some* and *any* to

a. ( ) talk about an indefinite quantity or number.

b. ( ) ask questions about number or quantity.

2. Pay attention to the words in bold in the quotes below. Then use the words from the box to complete the statements.

> There is **no** more reason to believe that Bitcoin will stand the test of time than that governments will protect the value of government-created money, although Bitcoin is newer, and we always look at babies with hope. (Paul Singer, American businessman)

Extracted from www.brainyquote.com/quotes/paul_singer_680170. Accessed on September 10, 2018.

> Assess Bitcoins? All you can do is examine the trading patterns, which do not provide a real analysis of **any** underlying economic value. The economics of investments are not solely based on supply and demand, and that is all that goes into Bitcoin prices. (Kurt Eichenwald, American editor)

Extracted from www.brainyquote.com/quotes/kurt_eichenwald_711317. Accessed on September 10, 2018.

> There is **some** risk that if the wrong regulatory regime gets adopted in the U.S., then the center of innovation could move to other countries. If blockchains are the next Internet, that would be a very unfortunate development for the U.S. (David O. Sacks, South African businessman)

Extracted from www.brainyquote.com/quotes/david_o_sacks_851308. Accessed on September 10, 2018.

> Bitcoin was created with security in mind. The Blockchain is Bitcoin's public ledger that records **every** transaction in the Bitcoin economy. (Perianne Boring, American businesswoman)

Extracted from www.brainyquote.com/quotes/perianne_boring_850612. Accessed on September 10, 2018.

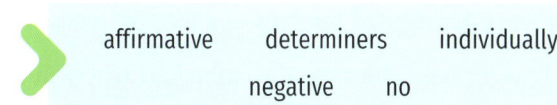

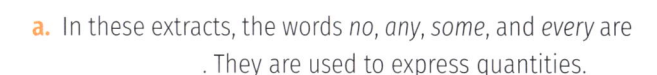

> affirmative   determiners   individually
> negative   no

a. In these extracts, the words *no*, *any*, *some*, and *every* are _____ . They are used to express quantities.

b. We use *some* in _____ sentences and in questions (often expecting a positive answer).

c. We use *any* in questions, _____ sentences, and to mean "it does not matter which or what".

d. We use *every* to refer _____ to all the members of a complete group and _____ to indicate *not any*. *Every* is always followed by a singular noun.

3. Choose the correct determiner in parentheses to complete the text below.

> _____ (Every / Some) things you need to know
>
> If you're getting started with Bitcoin, there are a few things you should know. Bitcoin lets you exchange money and transact in a different way than you normally do. As such, you should take time to inform yourself before using Bitcoin for _____ (any / no) serious transaction. Bitcoin should be treated with the same care as your regular wallet, or even more in _____ (any / some) cases!
> [...]

Extracted from https://bitcoin.org/en/you-need-to-know. Accessed on September 10, 2018.

4. Complete the meme with a determiner. Then exchange ideas with a classmate about what you understand from the text.

WHEN YOU'VE BOUGHT BITCOIN BUT YOU HAVEN'T TOLD _____ OF YOUR FRIENDS... IN 15 MINUTES

57

EXPAND YOUR READING

1. Have you ever heard of the deep and the dark webs? What are they? Exchange ideas with a classmate.
2. Read the text and underline the alternative that best describes its genre.

THE DARK WEB

MacKenzie Sigalos   Published 10:00 A.M. ET Sat, 14 April 2018
Updated 11:40 PM ET Sat, 14 April 2018

In 2015, the founder of a website called the Silk Road was sentenced to life in prison. The billion-dollar black market site was once the premiere online **bazaar** for drugs and other contraband, but it remained hidden from casual internet users for years because of something called the dark web.

Here's how that dark side of the Internet actually works.

Anatomy of the Internet

If you think of the web like an iceberg, you have the surface web up top. It's the Internet you see and use every day and consists of all the websites indexed by traditional search engines like Google. It's where you shop on Amazon and listen to music on Spotify.

What's submerged is the deep web – an anonymous online space only accessible with specific software. Then there's the dark web, which is the part of the deep web that hides your identity and location.

It's basically just "a series of encrypted networks that serve to **anonymize** peoples' use of the Internet," said Matthew Swensen, a Special Agent for the Department of Homeland Security with an expertise in cybercrimes.

[...]

Swensen said the most common dark web networks are Tor, I2P, and Freenet, but "Tor is, by far and away, the most popular."

Tor

Tor stands for "the onion routing project." It was developed by the U.S. Navy for the government in the mid-1990s. But it was open-sourced in 2004, and that's when it went public. Tor is now the dark web browser that the vast majority of people use to anonymously surf the Internet.

[...]

For some users – like journalists or **whistleblowers** – the dark web is about identity protection. It's where individuals can share anonymous tips with the press on secure drop sites. But more often than not, it's tied to the world of cybercrime. Special agents like Swensen are looking for the kinds of users who want this full cloak of anonymity in order to mask their illegal activity.

Putting a stop to this kind of crime has been described as a "never-ending game of whack-a-mole" for law enforcement. But even with the odds seemingly stacked against it, the anonymity of the dark web can sometimes play to the law's advantage. No ID and no location means you never really know who's communicating with you.

— CNBC's Ylan Mui and Karen James contributed to this report.

Adapted from www.cnbc.com/2018/04/13/the-dark-web-and-how-to-access-it.html. Accessed on September 10, 2018.

Information reports…

a) are texts written as requests for help. They are often written in the first person singular and present a problem or a specific situation. There are generally answers offering some advice and the use of should and the imperative are common.

b) provide readers with information on a chosen topic by presenting facts. They often give details about that topic and hardly ever contain personal views. These reports generally fall into three main categories: scientific, technological, and social studies.

3. Decide if the sentences are true (T) or false (F) according to the text.
   a. (   ) The dark web is part of the deep web.
   b. (   ) Being on the dark web makes it easier for someone to discover your true identity.
   c. (   ) Because of its virtually untraceable nature, the dark web is a center for criminal activity.
   d. (   ) Tor is a paid social media app that enables communication among peers on the Internet.

LANGUAGE IN USE 2

Unit 6

DIRECT AND INDIRECT SPEECH

1. Read these extracts from the text on page 58 and answer the questions.

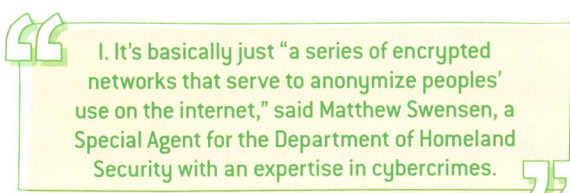

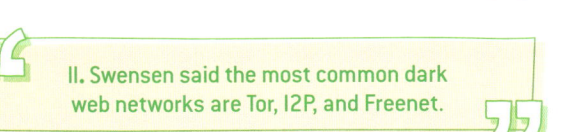

> I. It's basically just "a series of encrypted networks that serve to anonymize peoples' use on the internet," said Matthew Swensen, a Special Agent for the Department of Homeland Security with an expertise in cybercrimes.

> II. Swensen said the most common dark web networks are Tor, I2P, and Freenet.

a. Which extract contains Swensen's own words?
_____

b. Which extract reports what Swensen said?
_____

c. Which punctuation is used to indicate Swensen's exact words?
_____

d. Which verb is used to indicate Swensen's words?
_____

2. Based on the extracts and on your answers in activity 1, complete the statements with the words *direct* or *indirect*.

a. In _____ (or reported) speech, we report what the speaker says, but we don't use his/her exact words.

b. In _____ speech, we quote the speaker's exact words and use quotation marks.

3. Read the text carefully. Then look at the sentences extracted from it and complete the indirect speech sentences. Write two words in each blank.

> When a scam is targeted at a person it can be carried out via email, over the phone, via text, in person or without he or she knowing anything about it until something suspicious shows up on a statement or credit report.
> Married IT security consultant Tom Chantler […] discovered in May that contracts for top-end mobile phones had been taken out in his name.
> Tom says: "When I phoned the bank to ask if the account details matched one in my name, it became clear they were somebody else's. I am very careful with my personal information and always shred sensitive documents."
> […]
> He adds: "This can happen to anybody, even if they haven't done anything wrong."

Adapted from www.thisismoney.co.uk/money/bills/article-3287561/I-m-careful-phone-contracts-signed-cyber-attacks-sophisticated-look-protect-DARK-WEB.html. Accessed on April 5, 2019.

a. "I am very careful with my personal information."

Tom said that _____ very careful _____ personal information.

b. "This can happen to anybody, even if they haven't done anything wrong."

Tom explained _____ happen to anybody, even if they _____ anything wrong.

4. Work in pairs. Based on the previous activities, use the words or expressions from the box to complete the statements about direct and indirect speech.

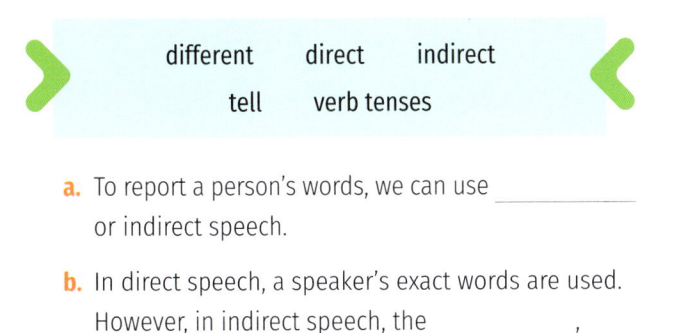

> different   direct   indirect
> tell   verb tenses

a. To report a person's words, we can use _____ or indirect speech.

b. In direct speech, a speaker's exact words are used. However, in indirect speech, the _____, pronouns, as well as place and time expressions may be _____ from those in the original sentence.

c. If we are reporting something that is a general truth, we keep the simple present in _____ speech.

d. Common reporting verbs are: *say*, _____, *ask, answer, warn, announce, add, argue,* and *urge,* among others.

LISTENING COMPREHENSION

1. You are going to listen to a text entitled *The Illicit World of Bitcoin and the Dark Web*. What comes to your mind when you read the title? How might bitcoins be related to the dark web? Exchange ideas in pairs.

2. Listen to the first part of the text and answer the questions.

   🎧 12

   a. Is Silk Road a digital currency or a dark market?
   _____

   b. Are dark markets inevitably illegal?
   _____

   c. Why do dark markets accept bitcoins as a method of payment?
   _____

   d. What kinds of products do most dark markets allow vendors to sell?
   _____

3. Listen to the second part of the text and decide if the sentences below are true (T) or false (F).

   🎧 13

   a. ( ) Created by Ross Ulbricht, Silk Road was a digital marketplace that connected vendors of illegal drugs with potential buyers.

   b. ( ) Customers buying drugs from vendors who listed on Silk Road would send their funds to Silk Road through bank deposits.

   c. ( ) Because Silk Road ran on Tor, it was an unprotected marketplace.

   d. ( ) The FBI arrested Ulbricht but many more dark markets have sprung up.

4. Listen to the last part of the text and order the sentences accordingly.

   🎧 14 [...]

   Dark Markets Under Attack

   ( ) In November 2014, Operation Onymous, an international law enforcement operation, **seized** over 400 dark web domains.

   ( ) Aside from the fact that they are breaking the law, one of the biggest concerns around dark markets is trustworthiness.

   ( ) Law enforcement is also getting better at targeting these dark markets and taking them down.

   ( ) Dark markets including CannabisRoad, Blue Sky, and Hydra have been taken down.

   ( ) Law enforcement says that it has found a way to target sites using Tor, although it has refused to reveal how.

   ( ) In several cases, dark markets have suddenly vanished with millions of dollars in escrow funds, leaving customers robbed of their funds.

   ( ) Dark markets continue to operate, and law enforcement continues to take them down in a continuous game of cat and mouse.

   Adapted from www.thebalance.com/what-is-a-dark-market-391289. Accessed on September 11, 2018.

›› EXPAND YOUR HORIZONS ››››

Check (✓) the column that best describes your opinion about each statement. Then discuss your answers with your classmates and teacher, justifying your point of view.

	I agree.	I'm not sure.	I disagree.
a. Bitcoin has turned out to be a lot more than just digital money because it tackles issues related to equality, access, and a more open framework for our society.			
b. Changing our passwords frequently and not using the same password on every site is enough for one to be protected against the dangers of the dark web.			
c. Although some products for sale on dark markets are legal, the offer of illicit goods such as drugs, stolen information, and weapons turns people who get involved with those dark websites into potential criminals.			

REVIEW 3

Units 5 and 6

1. Read the title of the following text. Who is its target audience? *Identifying the target audience*

_____

2. Now read the whole text and answer: What is its main purpose? *Identifying the main purpose of a text*

_____

Why binge-watching might actually be good for you

By Jim Medina, UC Santa Barbara
Tuesday, May 30, 2017

Joe Smith (not his real name) **cheated** on his wife. Up late one night alone, he watched half a season of "Game of Thrones" without her. Not cool, Joe.

Turns out Joe is not alone, though. In a recent Netflix survey, 46 percent of all respondents admitted to such infidelity. Worse, 81 percent admitted to being repeat offenders, and 45 percent never confess their betrayal at all.

[…]

Relationship issues aside, what benefits, if any, does binge-watching offer? Is it really just a waste of valuable time? According to UC Santa Barbara communication professor Robin Nabi, people are fascinated by a drama-filled series – from "Orange Is the New Black" to "Downtown Abbey" – and use them to escape daily stresses through what she described as "narrative transportation," in which they engage in a story world that seems "real."

"Typically, these shows are far more dramatic than our daily lives and the combination of the **plot**, the acting, and the music – all that combines to create this very strong emotional experience," said Nabi, whose research focuses on the interplay between emotion and the effects of mediated messages. "And emotional experiences keep our attention and we engage with them. We think about them. We talk about them. And then we look forward to having those emotions again."

[…]

Though research has been conducted on the value of media consumption, Nabi disagrees with critics who argue that TV watching is a waste of time. "They say you're ignoring your spouse, you're ignoring your work, and you're staying up too late, not getting enough sleep – and there's some truth to that," she said. "But another way of looking at this is there are times you just really need to do something for yourself to calm down."

For example, Nabi's media research with breast cancer survivors showed that people can watch TV to block out their concerns – from talking about illness, from engaging with others – and just be someplace where they're not dealing with that major stressor. "It can be very functional," she said, adding that people rely on TV for a range of psychological needs: **surveillance** (to be informed about what's happening in our environment), social connection, and diversion.

[…]

Adapted from www.universityofcalifornia.edu/news/binge-watching-healthy-diversion-or-waste-time. Accessed on September 12, 2018.

3. Underline the correct statements about the text. *Understanding details*

   a. In a recent survey, more than half of all respondents said that they cheated on their partners by watching TV series episodes without them.
   b. Nabi disagrees entirely with critics who say that TV watching is a waste of time.
   c. Nabi's media research showed that binge-watching can be beneficial for people who need to block out things that are worrying them.
   d. Binge-watchers are captivated by the drama in some TV series and tend to use them as a way out of the stress from their routine.

4. Work in pairs. Can you name other benefits to binge-watching?

_____

5. Refer to the text again and find a sentence that shows both direct and indirect speech.

_____
_____

61

6. Read these comic strips and complete the sentences about them. Pay attention to the parts in bold.

Grand Avenue – November 10, 2015

Extracted from https://assets.amuniversal.com/28fe05c063f00133182a005056a9545dw. Accessed on September 12, 2018.

If Grandma **hadn't told** Michael to always finish what he starts, _____

_____.

Grand Avenue – November 13, 2015

Extracted from https://assets.amuniversal.com/2cdb9b4063f00133182a005056a9545dw. Accessed on September 12, 2018.

Grandma **wishes** technology _____.

7. Check (✓) the correct alternative to complete the text.

> […]
> Google uses different methods to find new webpages. Among them are following links from known webpages to new ones, checking sitemaps, or receiving tips from one of our best web hosting providers about a new webpage.
>
> **Indexing content on the web**
>
> When a page is found, Google decides what it's about through indexing. This process includes studying and categorizing _____ the content, images, and video embedded on the webpage. The goal is to guess the intended topic so that a search for how to knit a llama sweater doesn't yield _____ webpages on how to make a pig fly.
>
> Google knows that it will stay the world's most popular search engine only by getting this stuff right, so it's sort of a big deal. After indexing, _____ webpage lands in the Google Index, which is a massive database stored across a huge computer network.
>
> […]

Adapted from www.cloudwards.net/the-deep-web/. Accessed on April 7, 2019.

a. ( ) all / every / any   **b.** ( ) every / any / all   **c.** ( ) all / any / every

UNIT 7
Digital Influencing

▶ IN THIS UNIT YOU WILL...
- talk about digital influencers;
- discuss issues related to influencer marketing;
- use the modal verbs *must* and *can* for assumptions;
- use the passive voice.

LEAD OFF

- What does the picture represent?
- Have you ever heard the expression *influencer marketing*? What do you think it means?
- In your opinion, what are some of the characteristics of an online influencer?

READING

BEFORE READING

Look at the picture that accompanies the text and read the two first paragraphs. What do you think it is about? Read the first paragraph and check your answer.

Predicting the topic of the text

WHILE READING

Read the whole text and check (✓) the best title for it.   *Selecting a good title*
a. ( ) The YouTube Phenomenon: a disruptive force
b. ( ) Under the Influence: The Power of Social Media Influencers

In the darkly comical Ingrid Goes West, a small-budget indie-flick that flew under the radar of many moviegoers last year, a young woman by the name of Ingrid becomes morbidly obsessed by Instagram-
5 famous blogger Taylor.
Ingrid becomes infatuated by Taylor's seemingly perfect life and starts mimicking her every move. Taylor posts a picture of her breakfast at her favorite bagel place, Ingrid stops by for lunch the same day. Taylor
10 quotes a passage from her favorite book, Ingrid orders it online right away.
While the events depicted in the film might be a little over-exaggerated for cinematic purposes, they are, in fact, closer to reality than you might think.
15 Promoting products via social media influencers can be categorized as a form of subconscious marketing. For ages, brands and advertisers have been seeking to shape consumers' thoughts, attitudes, and behavior, without us even being aware of it. [...]
20 **Why are social media influencers so influential?**
[...]
Credibility and social proof
[...]
According to French and Raven's (1960) framework
25 of power bases, one of the key elements to perceived power lies in expertise. A blogger that focuses on one particular subject, let's say cooking, will be perceived to have more authority when it comes to a particular brand of food (as opposed to a technology or sport blogger).
30 This authoritative position is further strengthened by a game of sheer numbers: a large number of followers, shares, and likes will provide viewers with a form of social proof. The notion that others value the opinion of an influencer, and adhere to their
35 judgments, assures viewers that doing so is okay. If the majority is doing something, they must be right.
Attractiveness
[...]
As humans are susceptible to attractiveness bias, we
40 subconsciously attribute attractive or charismatic people with many other qualities simply because they are good looking. Furthermore, this could lead to positive associations between the person and the brand as well. These opinions influence the
45 subconscious of the viewer, potentially priming them when faced with a product-related decision.
Relatability and the millennial crowd
But, what really sets social media influencers apart from other types of endorsers is their relatability.
50 Despite having a large popularity and internet following, influencers are still perceived as mostly normal, down-to-earth people.
[...]
More importantly, most influencers belong to the
55 younger age group of millennials, a demographic that is notoriously difficult to reach for marketers. They're a group that places strong value on forming their own identity, one of the most important parts of growing up. To do so, teens often look up to role models to
60 shape their own behavior. Having a role model that is relatable and easy to identify with makes it all the more likely that teens will copy their behavior.
[...]

Extracted from https://medium.com/crobox/under-the-influence-the-power-of-social-media-influencers-5192571083c3. Accessed on September 18, 2018.

» AFTER READING

1. Read the text again. Underline the correct endings to the phrase below.

Understanding main ideas

The author of the text states that…

a. consumers' thoughts, attitudes, and behavior have been modeled by brands and advertisers without our conscious acknowledgement.

b. when teens have a role model with whom they identify, it makes them more inclined to imitate that behavior.

c. the credibility of a peer depends only on expertise and attractiveness.

2. What makes social media influencers so attractive for brands? Read the fragments and write *1* for credibility and social proof, *2* for attractiveness, and *3* for relatability and the millennial crowd.

Understanding details

a. (   ) "[…] This is a strategy that marketers have already been using for ages—I'm sure you can think of numerous examples of advertisements featuring some handsome Hollywood actor recommending a certain luxury product. […]"

b. (   ) "[…] They post about their everyday life, stay connected with their followers, and are able to interact directly with them. Plus, they often share the same age group, demographics, interests, and behaviors of their target audience. […]"

c. (   ) "[…] Studies have shown that the credibility of a peer endorser depends on the factors of **trustworthiness**, expertise, attractiveness, and similarity. Taking the first two into account, we can note that the degree of influence a person possesses depends on his degree of perceived power. […]"

Extracted from https://medium.com/crobox/under-the-influence-the-power-of-social-media-influencers-5192571083c3. Accessed on September 18, 2018.

3. Work in small groups. Reread the questions in activity 2: What other reasons would you add to the ones listed?

_____

_____

EXPAND YOUR VOCABULARY

1. Scan the text on page 64 for the words or expressions from the box and infer their meanings. Then insert them in the text fragments that follow.

brand	expertise	followers
marketing	relatability	social proof

a. "[…] Social media influencers are people who have large audiences of _____ on their social media accounts, and they **leverage** this to influence or persuade this following to buy certain products or services. […]

Perhaps the most interesting aspect of this relatively new concept is that social media influencers do not necessarily have to be well-known celebrities or famous athletes. Instead, ordinary people have risen up the ranks of social media to **amass** hundreds, thousands, or even millions of followers due to their charisma, business **savvy**, and _____ on a given subject.. […]"

Adapted from www.forbes.com/sites/forbesagencycouncil/2018/08/21/are-social-media-influencers-worth-the-investment/#3dded9e8f452. Accessed on September 18, 2018.

b. "[…] One of the other important factors in influencer _____ is relatability. Even the most **sleek** and sophisticated social media personality will resonate better with their audience than a page-turning celeb. Micro-influencers and mid-range targets work well because they **max out** that _____ factor, offering a 'real-people' vibe. This shows your audience that, yes, this product is something that they can look fantastic in; it isn't just for elite 'fashion model' types. […]"

Extracted from https://jobs.sacbee.com/article/how-influencer-marketing-can-bolster-your-fashion-brand/7447. Accessed on September 18, 2018.

c. "[…] Whether you're familiar with social proof or not, chances are it has influenced decisions—both big and small—throughout your life.

_____ makes people pause to check out a social media post because it's **buzzing** with high engagement numbers. It gets them to take a chance on an unknown _____ because of the good things others are saying about it. […]"

Extracted from www.shopify.com/blog/social-proof. Accessed on September 18, 2018.

2. Some people say influencer marketing affects the way we feel toward a product or service. Do you believe that is true? How are you and your friends affected by influencer marketing? Exchange ideas with a partner.

VOCABULARY IN USE

1. **Reread these excerpts from the texts on pages 64 and 65, paying attention to the words in bold, and answer the questions.**

   > "In the darkly comical Ingrid Goes West, a small-budget indie-flick that flew under the radar of many moviegoers last year, a young woman by the name of Ingrid becomes morbidly **obsessed** by Instagram-famous blogger Taylor."

   > "Perhaps the most **interesting** aspect of this relatively new concept is that social media influencers do not necessarily have to be well-known celebrities or famous athletes."

   a. Which adjective in bold describes an emotion, how someone feels?

   _____

   b. Which adjective in bold describes a situation or what causes an emotion?

   _____

   Adjectives ending in -ed, such as bored, describe how someone feels, while adjectives ending in -ing, such as boring, describe a situation that leads to a feeling. Therefore, if something is boring, it causes someone to feel bored.

2. **Many adjectives end in -ed and -ing in English, and these are often based on verbs. Complete the chart below accordingly.**

Verbs	-ed adjectives	-ing adjectives
annoy		
challenge		
confuse		
disappoint		
entertain		
exhaust		
frighten		
inspire		
interest		
relax		
satisfy		
shock		
tire		
touch		
worry		

3. **Discuss the comic strip below in pairs. Then write sentences about it using at least two adjectives from each column in activity 2.**

   Comic strip – justgordon:
   - Panel 1: "Another Friday night alone. Another hot date with Netflix."
   - Panel 2: "Takeout imminent."
   - Panel 3: "I hope there's a clean-ish pair of underwear in there."
   - Panel 4: "THIS GUY'S INSTAGRAM ACCOUNT MAKES ME FEEL BETTER ABOUT MY LIFE." "HE'S AN UN-INFLUENCER!"

   Extracted from www.gocomics.com/thatababy/2018/11/09. Accessed on January 8, 2019.

   _____
   _____
   _____
   _____
   _____

4. **Work in pairs. List characteristics you think good digital influencers have. Then report your ideas to the class.**

   _____
   _____
   _____
   _____
   _____
   _____

LANGUAGE IN USE 1

Unit 7

MODAL VERBS FOR ASSUMPTION: *MUST* AND *CAN*

1. Read an excerpt from the text on page 64 and check (✔) the correct alternative to complete the sentence that follows.

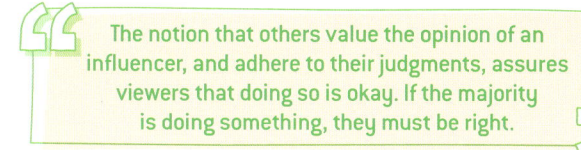

   > "The notion that others value the opinion of an influencer, and adhere to their judgments, assures viewers that doing so is okay. If the majority is doing something, they must be right."

   In "they <u>must</u> be right", the underlined modal verb indicates…
   a. ( ) an obligation.
   b. ( ) an assumption.

2. Now read the title of a text and check (✔) the correct alternative to complete the sentence that follows.

   ### 16 People on Social Media Who Can't Be Serious
   Katya Heckendorn

   [...]

   Extracted from https://diply.com/article/facepalm-social-media?config=101. Accessed on September 19, 2018.

   We can infer from the structure in italics that the author believes…
   a. ( ) those 16 people are probably satirizing or joking.
   b. ( ) those 16 people are obviously acting reasonably.

3. Use the words from the box to complete the paragraph below.

   | inferences | must | permissions |

   The modal verb _____ doesn't necessarily express obligations, as the modal verb *can* might convey other meanings besides abilities, _____, or requests, for example. Both verbs also express assumptions, _____, possibilities, or certainties.

4. Based on the text below, use the modal verbs *must* and *can* to come up with 2 assumptions about influencer marketing.

   ### 7 Predictions On The Future Of Influencer Marketing
   [...]

   1. **Status diversity.** Today, if you want to get in touch with an influencer and have them advocate for your brand, most companies start targeting people with 100,000 followers or more. They gravitate toward the biggest names in the industry, and understandably so; the more powerful an influencer is, the more valuable their advocacy will be. [...]

   2. **Influencer cliques and groups.** The nature of influencer marketing is interesting; if you're associated with an existing influencer, your reputation and authority will grow by proxy. It's a collective "rising tide" that affects all personal brands revolving around that influential center. [...]

   3. **Greater demand for authenticity.** The entire field of content marketing evolved from a consumer demand for authenticity. [...]

   4. **Bigger barriers to entry.** [...] Marketers everywhere are flocking to influencer marketing in droves, and accordingly, more individual personal brands are striving to become influencers in their own right. This is leading to a surge in content production and social media activity, which will make competition much fiercer if you want to earn your place as an expert in your field.

   5. **Transparency and regulatory crackdowns.** In April of 2017, the FTC sent out several letters and an official warning for influencers and brands to clearly disclose their relationships. [...]

   6. **Integrated functionality in platforms.** With platforms like Facebook, Twitter, LinkedIn, and Instagram noticing the importance (and potential) of influencer marketing, we may start to see platform-based innovations that make influencer marketing and outreach more convenient (or more profitable). [...]

   7. **Qualitative assessment tools.** Soon, it won't be enough to have a large quantity of followers on your account; marketers will also be looking to see how you engage with your followers, and what types of followers you have. [...]

   Adapted from www.forbes.com/sites/jaysondemers/2018/04/19/7-predictions-on-the-future-of-influencer-marketing/#b4742d6581df. Accessed on September 19, 2018.

   _____
   _____
   _____
   _____

5. From your point of view, can brands survive without influencer marketing? Share your opinions with a classmate. Use *must* and *can* for assumptions in your argumentation.

EXPAND YOUR READING

1. Skim the text to find out its genre.
  a. (　) a survey report   b. (　) a testimonial   c. (　) a guide   d. (　) an essay

How to make it as an Instagram influencer

From boosting your following to acing the lingo

The first influencer species evolved from the millennial. They were discovered around seven years ago on YouTube, where they spent their days vlogging about their pets and how many avocados they ate for lunch. They then briefly migrated to Twitter and Facebook, where they were bored and did nothing, before settling in their millions on the glossy plains of Instagram, where they now post selfies wearing athleisure and drinking turmeric lattes in an attempt to lure their primary source of sustenance: followers. Between followers, the influencer snacks on good lighting, symmetry and modishly shabby Shoreditch rooftops. The influencer's special treat is a juicy "paid-for-partnership".
[…]
So, who is part of this new breed? What do they want? How do they live? And, more importantly, what exactly is their game? Welcome to GQ's guide to influencers, where we put this strange creature under the microscope…

[…]
How to talk Influencer
[…]
Know your hashtags
[…]
Anatomy of a post
[…]
Three things you should never say as an influencer
[…]
How to buy friends and influence people
[…]
How to spot a bot buyer in three easy steps
[…]
Finally: know the law
Become an LAI: Law Abiding Influencer
[…]
1. Get your facts straight
"If promoting health products, it must be an authorized claim."
2. And the hashtag right
"Ads must be identifiable and therefore must be labelled with #Ad or Ad. #Sp or #Spon [sponsored] are unacceptable."
3. But don't be sneaky
"The word 'ad' must be one of the first words in the comment section. It cannot be lost under the 'view more' tab."
[…]

Adapted from www.gq-magazine.co.uk/article/how-to-be-an-instagram-influencer. Accessed on September 20, 2018.

2. What is the purpose of the text?

_____
_____

3. Underline the best definition for guides.
  a. They are short pieces that give brief instructions without detailing the steps to do something.
  b. They are testimonials of people who have done something and want to tell others how they did it.
  c. They are pieces of writing that provide information on a particular subject or explain how to do something.

Adapted from www.ldoceonline.com. Accessed on September 19, 2018.

LANGUAGE IN USE 2

Unit 7

PASSIVE VOICE II

1. Read the following extracts from the texts on pages 68 and 64, circle the verb forms, and write AV for active voice or PV for passive voice.

> Ads [...] must be labelled with #Ad or Ad. (   )

> Three things you should never say as an influencer. (   )

> Promoting products via social media influencers can be categorized as a form of subconscious marketing. (   )

> For ages, brands, and advertisers have been seeking to shape consumers' thoughts, attitudes, and behavior, without us even being aware of it. (   )

2. Now read a short fragment from a text entitled "Influencer Marketing Guide: How To Find And Verify Influencers For Your Next Campaign", paying attention to the part in bold. Then use the words from the box to complete the rules about the passive voice.

> When managed correctly, it [influencer marketing] can deliver wonders – A recent Collective Bias study proved that 60% of consumers **had been influenced** by a social media post or a blog review while shopping offline. It naturally has an enormous impact on purchasing online as well.

Adapted from https://wersm.com/influencer-marketing-guide-how-to-find-and-verify-influencers-for-your-next-campaign. Accessed on September 19, 2018.

| action | be | by | past participle | who |

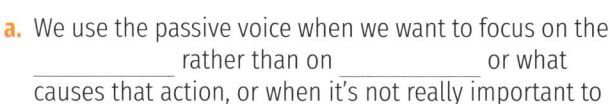

a. We use the passive voice when we want to focus on the _____ rather than on _____ or what causes that action, or when it's not really important to mention the doer of that action.

b. To form the passive voice, we use the auxiliary verb _____ and the main verb in the _____.

c. In the passive voice, to indicate who or what is responsible for the action, we use the particle _____ before the doer of that action.

3. Choose the appropriate verb form in parentheses to complete the first two paragraphs of this text.

Will fake social media followers derail the booming influencer marketing business?

August 22, 2018 by Christine Regan Davi, Northeastern University

Celebrities, social media stars, and other online personalities have taken a hit to their credibility in recent months, as millions of their followers _____ (have exposed / have been exposed) as fake or bought. This _____ (has created / has been created) a bigger problem for advertisers and consumers, who no longer can trust in high follower numbers as a measure of influence and credibility. Now, a machine-learning algorithm developed by Northeastern graduates is giving marketers a way to keep their advertising real—and rebuild consumer trust. Brands have always sought celebrity endorsements, but the mass adoption of social media _____ (has given / has been given) rise to a new kind of endorser: the influencer, an online personality with a large number of followers. [...]

Extracted from https://phys.org/news/2018-08-fake-social-media-derail-booming.html. Accessed on September 19, 2018.

4. Answer the question posed in the title of the text in activity 3. Use one passive structure in your answer. Then share your opinion with a partner.

_____
_____
_____
_____
_____
_____
_____
_____
_____

69

LISTENING COMPREHENSION

1. What makes someone an influencer? What types of online influencers have you heard of? Look at the picture and debate in small groups.

2. Listen to Dan Knowlton, from the agency KPS Digital Marketing, in Kent, England, and check (✓) the alternative that indicates what he's going to talk about.

   a. (   ) generating more leads and sales
   b. (   ) real influencers and fake influencers
   c. (   ) drone video businesses

3. Listen to the whole recording, read the sentences below, and underline the one that is incorrect.

   a. Dan Knowlton has been featured as an influencer.
   b. It's common to find lists of influencers on credible articles.
   c. There is always certified data to back up the identification of influencers and their naming on lists.
   d. When you see a list of influencers, question the methodology behind how the influencers were identified.

4. What was Dan's main purpose in recording the video?

5. Should we really question those lists or are they perfect? Is it important to be a critical consumer of information derived from all sources? Why (not)? Exchange ideas with a classmate and then report your views to the class.

» EXPAND YOUR HORIZONS »»»

Check (✓) the column that best describes your opinion about each statement. Then discuss your answers with your classmates and teacher, justifying your point of view.

	I agree.	I'm not sure.	I disagree.
a. Digital influencers make my world go round. I dedicate a good part of my time to consuming media content on digital platforms such as YouTube, Twitter, and Instagram.			
b. Influencer marketing is not going to disappear. It has evolved quickly and keeps up with changeable demands and rules of the existing and future social media platforms.			
c. A lot of people can be fooled by fake influencers and their messages; that's one of the reasons why it's important to be a critical information consumer.			

UNIT 8
The End of a Journey

IN THIS UNIT YOU WILL...

- take part in discussions about career preparation;
- exchange ideas about high school graduates' expectations;
- learn how to use the future continuous and the future perfect;
- review verb tenses.

LEAD OFF

- Which situation is represented in the picture?
- What are the causes and consequences of the so-called mismatch between education and occupation?
- Are you aware of your own skills and experiences? How ready are you to face the challenges that will come when high school ends?

READING

›› BEFORE READING — Discussion and Brainstorming

Work in pairs. Look at the picture that accompanies the text, read its caption, and share your opinions about it. Then list ideas to answer the question posed in the title of the text.

›› WHILE READING — Recognizing textual types

Read the whole text. Is it a technical, procedural, or expository writing? Justify your answer.

Too many graduates are mismatched to their jobs. What's going wrong?

Students often aren't aware of their own skills and experience, or what different jobs require. They need more meaningful careers advice.

Advice about the art of interview preparation and how to **craft** the perfect CV isn't enough to put every student on a **path** to a career they want. About one in three graduates
5 end up being "mismatched" to the jobs they find after leaving college, research by Universities UK suggests. These mismatched graduates face poorer prospects and lower earnings than their peers who embark on careers
10 that are a better fit for the knowledge and skills they have acquired through three or four years of study. It suggests that traditional careers advice isn't working.

Are students taking the wrong courses?
The problem isn't necessarily that too many students are taking the wrong course. There is little evidence that
15 graduates are studying the "wrong" subjects, according to the U.K. research, since most are on courses that offer subject knowledge and employability skills that are very much **in demand**.
Instead, students need better careers advice that will help
20 them define their skills and attributes – and understand how these match different career options. Students also need help finding out which skills they'll need to break into certain industries – particularly in sectors that aren't good at diversifying their recruitment, or when they have no family
25 or social network of contacts to call on for help and advice. Politicians complain of a skills **gap**, but graduates face an "experience gap" – with many employers preferring to recruit young people who have spent a couple of years in the workplace rather than raw recruitments from college.
30 Yet graduates have often picked up at university many of the soft skills that employers are looking for in more experienced recruits – they just don't know it yet.

"Students need better careers advice to help them define their skills and attributes – and understand how these match different career options." Photograph: Alamy

How can universities help?
To help graduates find the right jobs for them, lots of
35 universities are experimenting with new ways to make their career advice more accessible and meaningful.
[…]
At Norwich University of the Arts, we are gamifying career support. We've developed a career card game called
40 Profile, which provides students with a deck of cards in which half describe skills and attributes, and the other half describe workplace scenarios which require different tactics to resolve them.
Students are asked to match skills cards to the scenarios
45 – and think about how that applies to them and the best approach to overcome practical problems. It makes them aware of the skills they already have, and the ones they'll need in the workplace.
[…]
50 We should measure our success as universities by the extent to which we help students develop their talents and skills to a point where they are able to access industries and careers that will be fulfilling. Enabling students to play a **winning hand** after graduation is time
55 and effort well spent.

Adapted from www.theguardian.com/higher-education-network/2018/jan/25/too-many-graduates-are-mismatched-to-their-jobs-whats-going-wrong. Accessed on September 24, 2018.

Unit 8

>> AFTER READING

1. How is the text (introduction, body, and conclusion) organized? *Understanding text structure*
   a. ( ) story – examples – cause
   b. ( ) issue – reasoning – course of action
   c. ( ) dilemma – deductions – motivation

2. Refer back to the text and underline the topic sentences in each chunk. *Understanding main ideas*

3. Decide if the sentences are true (T) or false (F) according to the text. *Understanding details*
   a. ( ) The author thinks that universities shouldn't interfere with the students' choices because they need to be made by the students themselves.
   b. ( ) Graduates who are matched incorrectly to their careers have lower incomes than those who make a well-adjusted choice.
   c. ( ) Graduates are unaware of their skills and assume that employers are looking for more experienced recruits.
   d. ( ) Most employers tend to hire young people who have just left university instead of recruiting those that have spent a couple of years in the workplace.

EXPAND YOUR VOCABULARY

1. Match the words in bold with their meanings.
   a. "Too many graduates are **mismatched** to their jobs."
   b. "These mismatched graduates face poorer prospects and lower **earnings** than their peers [...]."
   c. "[...] with many employers preferring to recruit young people who have spent a couple of years in the workplace rather than **raw** recruitments from college."
   d. "[...] a point where they are able to access industries and careers that will be **fulfilling** [...]."
   e. "**Enabling** students to play a winning hand after graduation is time and effort well spent [...]."
   f. "At Norwich University of the Arts, we are **gamifying** career support."

   ( ) not experienced or not fully trained
   ( ) to combine things or people that do not work well together or are not suitable for each other
   ( ) making it possible for someone to do something, or for something to happen
   ( ) to design an activity such as learning, solving a problem, or being a customer so that it is like a game
   ( ) the money that you receive for the work that you do
   ( ) making you feel happy and satisfied because you are doing interesting, useful, or important things

   Adapted from www.ldoceonline.com/dictionary/mismatch. Accessed on September 24, 2018.

2. Besides the reasons mentioned in the text, what else might lead to the mismatch between graduates and their careers? Justify your views.

   _____
   _____
   _____
   _____

3. Work in pairs. How can you relate the word cloud below to the text on page 72? Discuss. Then share your opinions with your classmates.

   SKILLS SATISFACTION LIFE FUTURE
   KEY THINKING
   WORK DREAMS
   EXPECTATIONS MAKE IDENTIFY
   NEED CHALLENGE ATTITUDE CAREER
   JOB OPPORTUNITIES
   THINGS

   _____
   _____
   _____
   _____

VOCABULARY IN USE

1. **Pay attention to the subheading extracted from the text on page 72. Observe that the part in bold shows a collocation with the verb *take*. Check the correct meaning conveyed by that combination.**

   > Are students **taking** the wrong **courses**?

   a. ( ) to do something that involves risks

   b. ( ) to do a series of lessons in a particular subject

   c. ( ) to do something to deal with a problem

   Adapted from www.ldoceonline.com. Accessed on September 24, 2018.

2. **Choose the correct words in parentheses to complete the paragraph.**

   The verb _____ (be / take), as well as the verbs *have*, *make*, *do*, and *set*, for example, can often be confusing in English because they are delexical verbs. These are common verbs which have _____ (little / much) meaning of their own if used with particular nouns. In these collocations, most of the meaning is found in the _____ (noun / verb), not in the _____ (noun / verb) itself.

3. **Can you figure out new collocations with the verbs *take* and *have*? Complete the chart with the words from the box. Then use one collocation from each column to complete the texts. Make changes, if needed.**

   | a baby   a fight   a photograph   a risk |
   | an excuse   an experience   arguments |
   | care   charge   doubts   part   turns |

Take	Have

   a. **Survey reveals parental influence on students' career choices**

   The majority of students say their parents play a major role in their decision-making about careers and study, according to a report published last week. More than half (54%) of the students who _____ said that their parents tried to exert influence over their choice of course or career, while 69% said their parents had tried to influence their choice of university.

   [...]

   Extracted from https://targetjobs.co.uk/news/421008-survey-reveals-parental-influence-on-students-career-choices. Accessed on September 24, 2018.

   b. **Doubting your career choice**

   It is not uncommon to _____ about your career choice at some point in your studies. We give some insight into how to overcome career doubts.

   There can be a lot of excitement when starting a new qualification and taking your first class; however, after time it is not uncommon for feelings of doubt, restlessness, or uncertainty over your career choices to creep up.

   [...]

   Extracted from https://graduate.accaglobal.com/global/home/maximise-your-employability/doubting-your-career-choice.html. Accessed on September 25, 2018.

4. **Discuss the texts from activity 3 with a classmate. Try to use at least one collocation with *take* or *have* in your argumentation.**

LANGUAGE IN USE 1

Unit 8

FUTURE CONTINUOUS AND FUTURE PERFECT

1. Based on the fragment from the text on page 72, underline what you can infer about students' search for fulfilling careers.

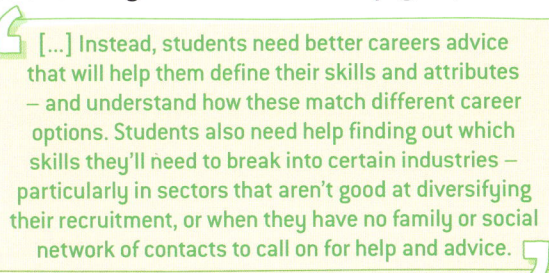

   > [...] Instead, students need better careers advice that will help them define their skills and attributes – and understand how these match different career options. Students also need help finding out which skills they'll need to break into certain industries – particularly in sectors that aren't good at diversifying their recruitment, or when they have no family or social network of contacts to call on for help and advice.

   a. Students will be able to define their abilities more effectively once they get better career advice.

   b. By the time students understand how their expertise matches distinct career alternatives, they will have already identified their skills and attributes.

   c. Students who don't have a short network of contacts won't need to search for help to enter some industries.

2. How do we form the future continuous and the future perfect in English? Underline their forms in the examples below and fill in the blanks accordingly.

Future continuous	Future perfect
Students will be defining their abilities more effectively once they get better career advice.	By the time students understand how their expertise matches distinct career alternatives, they will have found what it takes to get the right job.
will + _____ + main verb in the _____ form	will + _____ + main verb in the _____ form

3. Now reread the chart in activity 2 and complete the sentences about the usage of the future continuous and the future perfect tenses. Use the words from the box.

   > finished   progress   planned   time

   a. We use the future continuous to talk about something that will be in _____ at or around a time in the future and to talk about future actions that are already _____.

   b. We use the future perfect to talk about something that will be _____ or completed before a particular _____ in the future.

4. Read and complete the comic strips below. Use the verbs *drift* and *go* either in the future continuous or in the future perfect tense.

   Lucky Cow – June 22, 2005

   Extracted from https://licensing.andrewsmcmeel.com/features/luc?date=2005-06-22. Accessed on September 24, 2018.

   Grand Avenue for August 31, 2017

   Extracted from www.gocomics.com/grand-avenue/2017/08/31. Accessed on September 24, 2018.

5. Answer the questions with a classmate: What will you be doing one year after high school finishes? What goals will you have accomplished by then?

   _____
   _____
   _____
   _____
   _____
   _____
   _____
   _____

75

EXPAND YOUR READING

1. **Read the text and the genre descriptions that follow and write *A* if the description refers to advice letters, *E* if it refers to letters to the editor, or *O* if it refers to open letters.**

   a. (   ) They are sent to publications such as newspapers and magazines about issues of concern from their readers. They often rely on facts and opinions to try to persuade the reader.

   b. (   ) These are usually addressed to an individual, but intended for the general public, and often contain a protest or appeal.

   c. (   ) These letters are published in newspapers or magazines to offer advice to people who write to ask for help with a certain problem.

---

www.theguardian.com/education/2011/jul/17/graduate-jobs-advice-experts

"How do I deal with the post-university blues?"

It's normal to feel low just after graduation. For some, it's because the energy they needed is still flowing but now it has no **outlet**, so they feel anxious. For others, it's because they've realized how much effort they've expended, and they feel exhausted. Whatever the reason, here are three tips to help you feel more positive again:

1. Pay attention to the words you use. Graduation represents an ending, it's true – but it also represents new beginnings. It's more energizing to speak of new beginnings.
2. The key here lies in the word "beginnings" as opposed to "beginning". Instead of saying, "I need to start my career," break the task ahead into smaller steps and frame each step in a way that allows you to measure progress. So, for example, instead of expecting to "sort myself out", ask yourself to "prepare my CV", "find two **referees**", and "register with an employment agency". Put these goals in chronological order and focus on one at a time until you have **achieved** it.
3. In the long run you will almost certainly conclude that the most treasured aspect of your university experience wasn't your academic education or any career advice, but rather the friends you made. Make it a priority to stay in touch with those who **mattered** most to you during your university career.

Linda Blair, clinical psychologist

Adapted from www.theguardian.com/education/2011/jul/17/graduate-jobs-advice-experts. Accessed on February 5, 2019.

---

2. **Answer these questions about the advice letter in activity 1.**

   a. Why do some people feel anxious after graduating from college or university?

   b. Why does Linda Blair advise people to have "new beginnings" instead of "a new beginning"?

   c. What does Linda Blair say is the most valuable aspect of someone's university experience?

LANGUAGE IN USE 2

Unit 8

VERB TENSES REVIEW

1. Read a few extracts from the advice letter on page 76, paying attention to the verb forms in bold, and match them with their corresponding usage.

> a. [...] they **feel** anxious.

> b. [...] they**'ve realized** how much effort they**'ve expended** [...].

> c. [...] the most treasured aspect of your university experience **wasn't** your academic education or any career advice, but rather the friends you **made**.

> d. In the long run you **will** almost certainly **conclude** that the most treasured aspect of your university experience [...].

( ) Finished actions or states in the past
( ) Habits or generalizations in the present
( ) An action that happened at an indefinite time in the past
( ) A prediction based on an opinion

2. Scan the text below and provide the requested information.

Dear Graduate,

Congratulations, you have crossed the finish line. As you know, your route here was filled with tears of joy and sorrow, dreams shattered and fulfilled, moments that dispatched you to the arms of a beloved, remarkable beginnings, and ends sealed with generous promises.

Closing this chapter in your life offers a time of reflection on you. In fact, the day you were born, the world became more luminous. Chances are along the way you forgot this truth. At times it was overshadowed by fear or dismissed as insecurity, but I am here to remind you that it is still present. It is something that is uniquely yours, and can't be outsourced. In fact, there is no end to your luminosity. It is there amidst the lump in your throat and misty eyes. It is there in your sweaty palms and confused mind. It is there deep in your belly and lined in your heart. It is there.

[...]

Kristin

Extracted from www.huffpost.com/entry/an-open-letter-to-all-gra_b_9986202. Accessed on January 13, 2019.

a. An extract that indicates the action happened recently.

_____
_____

b. Three extracts that indicate a past action at a specific time.

_____
_____
_____

c. What is the difference in use between the verb tense from question *a* and the verb tense from question *b*?

_____
_____
_____

3. Read the text and choose the correct alternatives from the box to fill in the blanks.

> 's having / 'll have had
> had / 'll have   have worked / had worked
> is providing / provides

Letter to the editor: Congratulations, graduates.

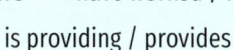

[...] So here you are, a high school graduate. [...] Whether you're going to Princeton or Penn, Rutgers or Rowan, higher education _____ unimaginable opportunities. Your parents _____ hard and saved long to give you this opportunity for a better life that they might never have had, but there really is no better life than a parent's selfless sacrifice for their child's future. For the next four years you'll be tested many times, but the most difficult test you _____ to take isn't one of essays or multiple choice but a test of will.
[...] As you listen to the commencement speaker's inspiring words, there are many serious things to consider, but for now, the only things to consider are who _____ the parties, whose parties you are going to, who'll be there and what kind of fun might develop. [...]
Savor your very special day.
George DeGeorge

Extracted from https://washingtontownshipsun.com/letter-to-the-editor-congratulations-graduates-ef1bfc0cfb0a. Accessed on September 25, 2018.

4. Based on the discussions throughout this unit and on the letter in activity 3, in your notebook, write a short message to your graduating high school classmates. Use mixed verb tenses in your writing.

LISTENING COMPREHENSION

1. Graduation speeches often aim at entertaining the audience. But what other functions might graduation speeches, whether delivered by students, school staff members, or even celebrities have?

   _____
   _____
   _____

2. Listen to the first part of the graduation speech given by Chase Dahl at the Weber High School graduation for the Class of 2015. Then complete the sentences.

   a. To ensure clear communication with the "_____ generation," Chase uses _____ and pop-culture references in his speech.

   b. **Ebola**, **ISIS**, _____, and facial acne are among the _____ that **plague** the world in Chase's opinion.

   c. Chase compares Weber High _____ to the changing _____ of Hogwarts.

3. Listen carefully, read the statements below, and decide if they are true (T) or false (F).

   a. (   ) In real life, we must count on being born great, or we'll never achieve greatness at all.

   b. (   ) Being recognized by the world is mandatory for one to reach greatness in his/her life.

   c. (   ) The legacies we must leave are the ones that are related to the kind of people we were.

4. Quotations are often used at graduation speeches to inspire the audience. Read the quote below, part of which was mentioned by Chase in his speech, and relate it to your reality as high school graduates. Share your opinion with a classmate.

   > It was the best of times, it was the worst of times, it was the age of wisdom, it was the age of foolishness, it was the epoch of belief, it was the epoch of incredulity, it was the season of light, it was the season of darkness, it was the spring of hope, it was the winter of despair. – Charles Dickens, *A Tale of Two Cities*

   Extracted from www.goodreads.com/quotes/341391-it-was-the-best-of-times-it-was-the-worst. Accessed on September 25, 2018.

>> EXPAND YOUR HORIZONS >>>

Check (✔) the column that best describes your opinion about each statement. Then discuss your answers with your classmates and teacher, justifying your point of view.

	I agree.	I'm not sure.	I disagree.
a. We don't need to be the wisest people in the world to be successful in finding a satisfying career. But we must know ourselves really well.			
b. Skills, communication and work styles, learning preferences, payment models, passions, and personal priorities altogether should be taken into account in the choice of a career.			
c. High school years are all about managing all kinds of conflicts, overcoming obstacles, and setting the goals we are to reach.			

REVIEW 4

Units 7 and 8

1. Work in pairs. Look at the picture, read its caption, and come up with an answer to the question raised. Then list ideas related to the content of the text. *Discussion and Brainstorming*

   _____
   _____

2. Read the whole text and check (✓) the best title for it. *Selecting a good title*
   a. (   ) It's time to address the elephant in the room: Influencers don't really influence anything or anyone!
   b. (   ) Brand Communities & Community Marketing: everything you need to know at once!

   [...]
   I think it's time we addressed the elephant in the room: Who really are these "influencers" and who do they "influence", if at all?
   The concept of an "influencer" is pretty clear. An individual who can reach many people through various communication channels and can therefore, potentially, influence them to like or dislike, to adopt or ban, to buy or skip buying, products and services.
   The more people the "influencer" can reach (read: the more "followers" they have), the better, stronger, and more of an "influence" he or she has. There is a whole marketing strategy called "influencer marketing" or "influencer outreach". There is even a concept called "micro influencer" to describe people with less following who are still considered "important" in their **niche**.

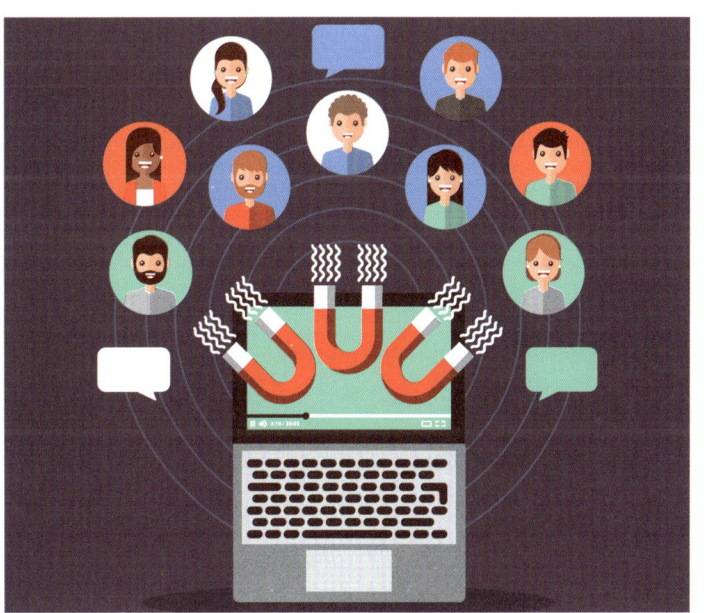

   Who are these people "influencing"?

   But let's consider a few of questions:
   1. What do numbers of followers mean in an age where buying likes and follows and YouTube video watches is easier than ever? [...]
   2. What does "coverage" even mean in a culture of multiple social media and new trends born daily? [...]
   3. Speaking of measuring and monitoring – how can you really tell that new business was generated by a particular collaboration with a specific influencer? [...]

   Let's face it, the concept of becoming an influencer is mostly appealing as a "job" to younger people who don't have many other options. When you look at the beauty segment, for instance, you can clearly see that the biggest YouTube channels with millions of followers, are usually ones that were built with hard work over years and years… and… the YouTubers are actually refusing "collabs" and sponsored content. Most of the time they pay for the products on their own, full price and they state so.
   But, since Instagram and Snapchat, more and more "web influencers" have popped up, especially in the lifestyle (beauty, fashion, travel) niche and in technology (consumer electronics) and they have been enjoying the **gullibility** of brands that think they can actually generate real business by working with them.

   Adapted from https://medium.com/21st-century-marketing/its-time-to-address-the-elephant-in-the-room-influencers-don-t-really-influence-anything-or-ee036b4abbb.
   Accessed on September 25, 2018.

3. Read the text and write its main idea using your own words. *Understanding main ideas*

   _____
   _____

4. Read the extract below. Does the modal verb in italics indicate an assumption or a possibility?

_____

> An individual who *can* reach many people through various communication channels and *can* therefore, potentially, influence them to like or dislike, to adopt or ban, to buy or to skip buying, products and services.

Now read these other examples. What do the modal verbs in italics indicate?

a. Harriet is an online influencer. She *must* know a lot about media contents.

b. Today is your prom. You *can't* be so calm!

_____

5. Scan the text below and find…

a. an action in progress in the present.

_____

b. three actions that happened at an indefinite time in the past.

_____
_____
_____

c. a prediction based on an opinion:

_____

Today's letters: Readers' sage advice for high school graduates

[…]

Be kind to others

— You are entering a world of challenges. Look at the big picture. Humanity has reached the limits to growth. Work with others to conserve what you value most. Natural ecosystems, which support all life on earth, must be protected. […] Nurture positive relationships with those you love.
Lyn Adamson, Toronto.

[…]

Never give up

[…]

— Progressive employers look for individuals who have experienced a significant setback and whether they have grown and learned from it. Failure, not success, is the best teacher. Find an intelligent way to include this as part of your qualifications and experience; don't hide it. And buy the best mattress you can't afford. You will spend more than one-third of your life on it.
Jim Sanders, Guelph, Ont.

[…]

Adapted from https://nationalpost.com/opinion/todays-letters-readers-sage-advice-for-highschool-graduates. Accessed on September 25, 2018.

6. Check (✓) the only extract from the text that is in the passive voice.

a. ( ) "And buy the best mattress you can't afford."

b. ( ) "Work with others to conserve what you value most."

c. ( ) "Natural ecosystems, […], must be protected."

d. ( ) "Failure, not success, is the best teacher."

7. Read the text and underline the verb form used to talk about something that will be in progress in the future. Then answer: Which verb tense is it?

_____

Overcoming Social Anxiety

So you've done it. You have survived several years of exam pressure and of dealing with stressful social situations, and you have graduated. And now "they" want you to stand up in front of a crowd and be the center of attention in a graduation ceremony? "Is there no end to the ways the world will torture me?", you may be thinking!
[…]
If you suffered from social anxiety at your high school graduation, chances are that you will be dreading your college graduation. However, remember what the ceremony is really about. It won't be like prom and its expectations of "performance" on the day. You have already done the work and you don't have to do anything except collect your symbolic reward – and standing up in front of everybody of course! The only response you will get from the audience is applause and congratulations.
[…]

Extracted from http://overcomingsocialanxiety.com/social-anxiety-college-graduation-tips. Accessed on September 25, 2018.

GRAMMAR OVERVIEW

Verb tenses

Tense	Use(s)	Example(s) – affirmative	Example(s) – negative	Example(s) – interrogative
Present perfect simple	To refer to actions that focus on length of time, achievements and results.	We **have eaten** all our meal at lunch.	They **haven't drunk** their milk during breakfast.	How long **have** you **had** this car?
Present perfect continuous	To refer to actions that started in the past and continue up to the present time; To refer to actions that started in the past and ended recently.	We **have been waiting** for you all day. It**'s been raining**. (the floor outside is wet)	Mary **hasn't been watching** TV for so long. I **haven't been eating** your cookies!	How **have** you **been coming** to work lately? How long **have** you **been living** here?
Past perfect	To indicate that an action was completed at some point in the past before something else happened.	The bus **had gone** before I reached the bus stop.	You **had not met** me when I was at school.	**Had** she **cooked** some food for the kids?
Future perfect	To refer to actions that will be completed before some other point in the future, or within a period of time.	Don't worry. By ten o'clock I **will have left** already.	We **will not have eaten** breakfast before we get to the game tomorrow morning.	**Will** you **have finished** your homework in an hour, so we can go to the movies?
Future continuous	To refer to an action that will occur in the future and continue for an expected length of time.	I **will be watching** the game with you.	When Mike gets home, I **won't be cooking** dinner.	What **will** you **be doing** next weekend?

Modal verbs

Modal verb	Use / meaning	Example(s) – affirmative	Example(s) – negative	Example(s) – interrogative
Wish	To refer to a situation that they want to be different; As an alternative to conditional sentences; As a formal alternative to refer to present and future wish situations; To criticize and talk about things we don't like and want to change.	I **wish** you **could** be here at the beach with me. I **wish** we **had met** before. I **wish to speak** to Ms. Smith, please. I **wish** I **were** there to help you with the project. I **wish** this rain **would** stop! I want to go out.	I **do not wish to** complain, but you are always late! I **do not wish to** do this, unless I'm forced to. I **wish** he **wasn't** so selfish.	**Do** you **wish** you **could** be someone else for a day? **Do** you **wish** you **had studied** more?
Will	To express assumptions with reference to present and future time; When followed by the perfect infinitive, it is used to express assumptions about past events.	They are calling out the numbers again. I **will be** next. I'm sure you **will have seen** me before.	I'm not repeating myself. You **won't** understand. Most of you **won't have seen** this yet.	
Should	To express assumptions with reference to present and future time; When followed by the perfect infinitive, it is used to express assumptions about past events.	I **should exercise** more often. I feel a little out of shape. We **should have worked** harder on the project.	You **shouldn't speak** to your teacher that way. Mike **should not have lied** about that.	The phone is ringing. **Should** that **be** for me? **Should** we **have studied** harder for the exams?
Ought to	When followed by the perfect infinitive, it is used to express assumptions about past events.	I **ought to have studied** harder for the test. Now, I'll have to take it again.	You **ought not to have told** her about the incident.	Questions with **ought to** are very formal. We use **should** instead.

81

GRAMMAR OVERVIEW

Homonyms

Category	Explanation	Examples
Homonyms	A word that is spelled the same and sounds the same as another, but is different in meaning or origin.	What's your e-mail **address**? This letter is **addressed** to Carl.
Homophones	A word that sounds the same as another, but is different in spelling, meaning, or origin.	Can I talk **to** you now? It's half past **two**. It's not **too** late to change your mind.
Homographs	A word that is spelled the same as another, but is different in meaning, origin, grammar, or pronunciation.	Don't forget to **wave** her goodbye. The **waves** are high today!

Extracted from www.ldoceonline.com/dictionary. Accessed on Dec. 29, 2018.

Conditional sentences

Conditional	Use	Form	Examples
Zero	To talk about things that are always true or always happen.	*If* + simple present → simple present	**If** babies **are** hungry, they cry.
First	To talk about real and possible situations.	*If* + simple present → *will* + infinitive	**If** you don't **leave** soon, you **will miss** the train.
Second	To talk about unreal or impossible situations.	*If* + simple past → *would* + infinitive	**If** I **won** the lottery, I **would travel** around the world!
Third	To talk about things that didn't happen.	*If* + past perfect → *would / could / might have* + main verb (past participle)	**If** they **had studied**, they **would have passed** the exams.

Some, any, no, every

Pronoun	Use	Examples
Someone Somebody Something Somewhere	Affirmative and interrogative sentences; When they mean invitation or when we expect an affirmative answer.	**Someone** is calling you outside. **Somebody** ate my sandwich. There is **something** missing in this room. Doesn't he live **somewhere** around here?
Anyone Anybody Anything Anywhere	Negative and interrogative sentences; Affirmative sentences meaning *every*.	I don't know **anyone** (**anybody**) in this room. He can do **anything** he wants to. They can be **anywhere** around town.
No one Nobody Nothing Nowhere	Affirmative sentences that have a negative meaning.	There is **no one** here to help us. She thinks that **nobody** likes her work. There is **nothing** here for you to see. This road will get us **nowhere**.
Everyone Everybody Everything Everywhere	Affirmative, interrogative, or negative sentences; When referring to a total number of people, things, or places.	Not **everyone** finished their work. **Everybody** loves chocolate! Is **everything** all right? **Everywhere** we go, people are so friendly!

Indirect / Reported speech

Verb tense in direct speech	Verb tense in indirect / reported speech	Example – direct speech	Example – indirect / reported speech
Simple present	Simple past	He said, "I always **drink** black coffee."	He said (that) he always **drank** black coffee.
Present continuous	Past continuous	"I'**m studying** for the math test," Mark said.	Mark said (that) he **was studying** for the math test.
Present perfect	Past perfect	She said to me, "I **have been** to the beach twice **this** year."	She told me (that) she **had been** to the beach twice **that** year.
Simple past	Past perfect	Sam said, "I **bought** a big new house."	Sam said (that) he **had bought** a big new house.
Will	Would	"We **will** do our homework," they said.	They said (that) they **would** do their homework.
Can / May	Could / Might	We explained, "It **can** be difficult to find a parking space **here**."	We explained that it **could** be difficult to find a parking space **there**.
Must	Had to	He said, "You **must** listen to me."	He told us (that) we **had to** listen to him.
Imperative	Infinitive	Lucy said, "**Be quiet**, please!"	Lucy told us **to be quiet**.

Compound adjectives

Form	Examples of compound adjectives	Examples in a sentence
Adjective + adjective	fat-free	I got a delicious **fat-free** yogurt.
Adjective + noun	last-minute	Joe was doing some **last-minute** revision.
adjective + verb –ing	long-lasting	I hope this is a **long-lasting** summer.
Adjective + verb (past participle)	absent-minded	She is such an **absent-minded** girl.
Noun + adjective	world-famous	Picasso is a **world-famous** painter.
Noun + verb + –ing	time-consuming	This is a **time-consuming** project.
Noun + verb (past participle)	sun-dried	I love **sun-dried** tomatoes.
Adverb + verb (past participle)	well-known	J. K. Rowling is a **well-known** writer.

Word categories

Category	Use / meaning	Examples
Expressions related to men and women	To say that you are related to that person; To say that a group of people do something together, at the same time; It is a traditional belief that is spread from one person to the other, over time.	We are **kissing cousins**. Let's all sing the song **as one man**. There are no werewolves. That's just **an old wives' tale**.
Types of technology	Scientific advanced technology; Scientific studies that involve transforming matter and developing gadgets on an atomic, or molecular scale.	This city has become the new **high technology** center of studies. They have been using **nanotechnology** in their field for some years.
Computer science abbreviations	Artificial Intelligence; Gigabytes.	**AI** is an area of computer science that develops intelligent machines. This cellphone has only 64 **GB** of storage.
English words derived from Latin	Postpone means *after*; Campus means *the land and buildings of a university or college*.	He has **postponed** the meeting again. Don't be scared. The college **campus** is very safe.
Idioms containing weather-related words	If someone has a face like thunder, they are very angry. Used to say that a problem is much bigger than is apparent.	She burst into the store with **a face like thunder**! Oh! This is just **the tip of the iceberg**. You know nothing.

GRAMMAR OVERVIEW

Category	Use / meaning	Examples
Adverbs of degree	To describe the intensity, degree, or extent of the verb, adjective, or adverb being modified; They can be mild, medium, strong, or absolute.	The pool was **extremely** cold today. This dress is **quite** expensive! The coffee is **somewhat** warm. She is swimming well **enough**. She can get into the pool.
-ed and –ing adjectives	-ed ending describes emotions; -ing ending describes what causes the emotion.	I'm **depressed** after watching that **depressing** movie. We are **thrilled** about our next vacation. It is a **thrilling** trip to Peru.

Passive voice

Verb tense	Form	Examples
Simple present	am / is / are + past participle	The library **is used** by the students.
Present continuous	am / is / are + being + past participle	The car **is being repaired**.
Simple past	was / were + past participle	The card **was sent** on time.
Modal verbs (present)	can / must / should / could / may / might + be + past participle	It **might be finished** by the end of the day.
Past continuous	was / were + being + past participle	The room **was being cleaned** yesterday.
Present perfect	has / have + been + past participle	The house **has been painted** since he left.
Past perfect	had + been + past participle	The chair **had been fixed** before you arrived.
Simple future	will + be + past participle	It **will be washed** tomorrow.
Imperative	let + object + be / get + past participle	**Let** the truth **be told**.
Modal verbs (past)	can / must / should / could / may / might + have been + past participle	This task **could have been done** this morning.

Subject-verb agreement

Use	Discourse markers	Examples
Use the verb form (singular or plural) that agrees with the subject closer to the verb.	or, nor	**The boys or the girls are** going to give the correct answer. Just wait. **The boy or the girls are** going to give the correct answer. Just wait. **The boys or the girl is** going to give the correct answer. Just wait. Neither **the boys nor the girl gets** the bus to school.
When group nouns are considered as a single unit, they take a singular verb. (AmE)	government, group, family, team, etc.	The **government decides** about the taxes we pay. The **group was** very happy with the results.
When some nouns end in -s, but are considered singular, they take a singular verb.	news, politics, mathematics, athletics, etc.	I think that **mathematics is** a very interesting subject. **Politics was** his favorite subject.
The indefinite pronouns take plural verbs.	both, few, many, several, others.	**Several are** often late. Just **a few are** here today.
Prepositional phrases between subject and verb don't change the conjugation.		The **bag** with toys **is** mine. The **cars** with a turbo **are** faster.

84

LANGUAGE REFERENCE

UNIT 1

PRESENT PERFECT CONTINUOUS

Usage Notes

The present perfect continuous is often used to refer to:

- actions that started in the past and continue up to the present time.

  I'm tired because I **haven't been sleeping** well at night.

- actions that started in the past and stopped recently.

  Why are you soaking wet? **Have** you **been walking** in the rain?

As not all verbs are compatible with continuous actions, they cannot be used in the present perfect continuous. A few examples are the verbs *be*, *arrive*, and *own*.

  I **have owned** a house at the beach since 2015.

NOT ~~I have been owning a house at the beach since 2015.~~

  They **have been** tired lately.

NOT ~~They have been being tired lately.~~

PRESENT PERFECT SIMPLE VS. PRESENT PERFECT CONTINUOUS

Usage Notes

- We use the present perfect continuous when we want to emphasize the length of time that an action has lasted or stress the fact that it is continuous. We use the present perfect simple when we want to focus more on achievements and results.

  I**'ve been studying** for this test for three days.

  (This focuses on the length of time.)

  I**'ve completed** my geography homework, but I **haven't started** my math assignment yet.

  (This focuses on the achievements and results.)

- We don't use the present perfect continuous when we are talking about amounts (*how much*) or quantities (*how many*). In these cases, we use the present perfect simple.

  The babies **have drunk** a lot of milk this afternoon.

NOT ~~The babies have been drinking a lot of milk this afternoon.~~

  I **have eaten** two donuts today.

NOT ~~I have been eating two doughnuts today.~~

- While the present perfect simple often focuses on the fact that the action is completed, the present perfect continuous focuses on the action itself.

  Sue**'s been watching** the TV series about vampires.

  (She hasn't finished watching the TV series.)

  Sue**'s watched** the TV series about vampires.

  (She's finished watching the TV series.)

- The present perfect continuous can also be used to emphasize that something is momentary.

  I**'ve been working** full-time this month.

  (I don't often do this.)

  They**'ve been coming** to school by bus recently.

  (They usually come by car.)

EXPRESSIONS RELATED TO MEN AND WOMEN

Expression	Meaning	Example
the poor man's something	used to say that something can be used for the same purpose as something else, and is much cheaper	Herring is **the poor man's salmon**.
as one	if a group of people do something as one, they do it together	The audience rose **as one** to applaud the singers.
it's every man for himself	used to say that people will not help each other	In journalism **it's every man for himself**.
father figure	an older man who you trust and respect	Ken was a **father figure** to all of us.
grandfather clause	a clause in a new rule stating that a person or business already doing the activity covered by the rule does not have to follow it	The new rule has a good chance of winning approval because it has a generous **grandfather clause**.
a man of his word	a man you can trust, who will do what he has promised to do	He had promised to help, and Sally knew that Dr. Neil was **a man of his word**.
man/woman of many parts	someone who is able to do many different things	He was a **man of many parts**: writer, literary critic, and historian.
old wives' tale	a belief based on old ideas that are now considered to be untrue	I think it's an **old wives' tale** that make-up ruins the skin.

Adapted from www.ldoceonline.com/dictionary. Accessed on October 16, 2018.

LANGUAGE REFERENCE

UNIT 2

SUBJECT–VERB AGREEMENT

Usage Notes

- When two or more singular subjects are joined by *or* or *nor*, use the verb form (singular or plural) that agrees with the subject closer to the verb.

  The teacher or the director is going to hand out the diplomas.

  The teachers or the director is going to hand out the diplomas.

  The teacher or the directors are going to hand out the diplomas.

- In American English, when group nouns such as *government, group, family, team,* etc. are considered as a single unit, they take a singular verb.

  My family makes the decisions over dinners.

  Their team wins all the games!

- Although some nouns such as *news, politics, mathematics, athletics,* etc. end in *s,* they are considered singular. So, they take a singular verb.

  Good news doesn't travel fast.

  Is mathematics your favorite school subject?

- The indefinite pronouns *both, few, many, several,* and *others* always take plural verbs.

  Many are joining us for Tom's party tonight.

  Both want to get married in December.

- When a prepositional phrase is placed between the subject and verb, it does not interfere in the agreement. To make the correct agreement, we address the subject and choose a verb that agrees with it.

  The woman at the counter **is** the cashier.

  The students with the best performance **are** going to be graded.

COMPOUND ADJECTIVES

Some compound adjectives in English:

adjective + adjective	fat-free
	dark-blue
adjective + noun	last-minute
	full-length
adjective + verb + -ing	long-lasting
	slow-moving
adjective + verb (past participle)	kind-hearted
	absent-minded
verb + adjective	smoke-free
	world-famous
noun + verb + -ing	mouth-watering
	time-consuming
noun + verb (past participle)	wind-powered
	sun-dried
adverb + verb (past participle)	brightly-lit
	well-known

Usage Notes

- For compound adjectives showing a number + a time period, the word referring to a time period takes the singular form.

  When will you take your **two-week** vacation?

  That was a **five-minute** delay.

COMPUTER SCIENCE ABBREVIATIONS

Abbreviation	Stands for
AI	Artificial Intelligence
ALGOL	Algorithmic Language
BASIC	Beginners All-purpose Symbolic Instruction Code
BIOS	Basic Input Output System
CASE	Computer Aided Software Engineering
CL	Command Language
CPU	Central Processing Unit
DDS	Digital Data Storage
DSN	Distributed Systems Network
EPG	Electronic Programming Guide
FM	Frequency Modulation
GB	Gigabytes
HTML	HyperText Markup Language
HTTP	HyperText Transport Protocol
ISDN	Integrated Services Digital Network
LAN	Local Area Network
MS-DOS	Microsoft Disk Operating System
NOS	Network Operating System
URL	Uniform Resource Locator
VoIP	Voice over Internet Protocol

Adapted from www.tutorialspoint.com/basics_of_computer_science/basics_of_computer_science_abbreviations.htm. Accessed on October 17, 2018.

UNIT 3

SECOND CONDITIONAL

Usage Notes

- The second conditional is used when we want to talk about the results of unreal or hypothetical situations or things we don't think will happen.

  If I **had** more time, I **would take up** gardening.

  We **would invite** Lenny and George for a drink if they **arrived** early.

- When the imaginary situation comes first in the sentence, we need to insert a comma between the clauses that indicate the situation and the result.

  If Lydia **didn't know** how to drive, it **would be** more difficult for her to keep her job.

- *Were* might be used instead of *was* to indicate the imaginary clause of a second conditional sentence. There is no change in meaning; however, *were* sounds more formal than *was*.

  If I **were** taller, I wouldn't sit in the front seats in the classroom.

- Although most conditional sentences use *if*, other words such as *when*, *in case*, *unless*, *if only*, *supposing*, etc. might be used as well.

  If only I had more money, I would be able to afford my son's college tuition.

  Unless students' parents signed the contract, they wouldn't be allowed to join us for the field trip.

ZERO, FIRST, AND SECOND CONDITIONALS

Usage Notes

- The zero conditional is used to talk about things that are always true or always happen. The simple present is used in both clauses.

  If you **heat** metals, they **expand**.

  If anyone **leans** against that wall, the alarm **goes off**.

- The first conditional is used to talk about real and possible situations. The structure is usually *if + simple present + will / can / may / might + infinitive*.

  I'**ll help** you with the housework if I **have** time.

  If Dennis **doesn't come**, we **may call** him.

- The second conditional is used to talk about unreal or impossible things. The structure is usually *if + simple past + would / could / might + infinitive*.

  If you **weren't** so sedentary, you **wouldn't feel** so tired every time you do some physical activity.

  Where **would** you **travel** to if you **won** the lottery?

ENGLISH WORDS DERIVED FROM LATIN

Latin Word	Definition	English Derivatives
amicabilis	kind (friendly)	amiable
annus	year	annual, annually, annuity
arma	arms (weapons)	arms, armed, armament, army
desidare	to want	desire, desirable, desirability
docere	teach	docent, doctrine, document, documentary
grata	pleasing	grateful, gratitude, gratuity
janua	door	January, janitor, janitress
libera	free	liberal, liberator, liberate
locus	place	locus, location, locate
magister	teacher	magistrate, magisterial, magistracy
morbus	disease	morbid, morbidity, morbific
mortuus	dead	mortuary, mortician, mortality
mutare	to change	mutation, commute, transmute
occupare	to occupy	occupy, occupation, occupational
patria	native country	patriotic, expatriate, patriotism
populus	people	populous, population, popular
post	after	postmortem, postnatal, postpone
temptare	to try	tempt, temptation, attempt
territa	frightened	terrified, terrific
trans	across	transport, transmit, transact
umbra	shade, ghost	umbrella, penumbra, umbra, umbrage
vitare	to avoid	inevitable, inevitably, inevitability
vulnerare	to wound	vulnerable, invulnerable, vulnerary

Extracted from www.enhancemyvocabulary.com/word-roots_latin_2.html. Accessed on October 19, 2018.

LANGUAGE REFERENCE

UNIT 4

PAST PERFECT

Usage Notes

- We use the past perfect when we want to refer to a past that is earlier than another past time in the narrative. Using the past perfect, we convey a sequence of the events.

    We **had seen** the weather forecast when you told us it was going to be a rainy weekend.

    (First we saw the forecast, then you told us it was going to be a rainy weekend.)

    When the ambulance arrived, the woman **had** already **died**.

    (First the woman died, then the ambulance arrived.)

- Don't use the past perfect tense if you aren't trying to convey some sequence of events. As the past perfect implies an action that occurred before another, when you don't say what that something else is (or if it's not inferred by context), the past perfect doesn't make sense.

- To distinguish the uses of the simple past and the past perfect, keep in mind that the past perfect is used to sequence events in the past and show which event happened first, whereas the simple past usually indicates a stronger connection between the time of the two events.

    When he **stepped** on the stage, everyone **applauded** wildly.

    (Everyone started applauding at the time he stepped on the stage.)

    The temperature **had fallen** when it **started** snowing.

    (It started snowing as soon as the temperature fell.)

ADVERBS OF DEGREE

Usage Notes

- To describe the intensity, degree, or extent of the verb, adjective, or adverb they are modifying, adverbs of degree can be mild, medium, strong, or absolute.

    She was **undoubtedly** the most beautiful girl at the party. (absolute degree)

    I'm **very** sorry for not being here for you guys when you needed me. (strong degree)

    The books you bought were **pretty** expensive. (medium degree)

    It'll take them **a little** longer to finish the task. (mild degree)

- Some adverbs of degree are easily identified because they end in -*ly*. However, many other adverbs of degree do not have the same ending. Some of them are: *enough, less, almost, even, just, most, quite, so, altogether, least, rather, somewhat, too, very*.

- When the word *enough* is used as an adverb of degree, it can only modify adverbs and adjectives and it is always positioned after the word it is describing.

    My students couldn't finish reading the text quickly **enough**.

    The movie was funny **enough**, but I wouldn't watch it twice.

IDIOMS CONTAINING WEATHER-RELATED WORDS

Idiom	Meaning
a face like thunder	if someone has a face like thunder, they look very angry
a ray of hope/light	something that provides a small amount of hope or happiness in a difficult situation
any port in a storm	used to say that you should take whatever help you can when you are in trouble, even if it has some disadvantages
ask for the moon	to ask for something that is difficult or impossible to obtain
keep/put something on ice	to do nothing about a plan or suggestion for a period of time
like greased lightning	extremely fast
shoot the bull/breeze	to have an informal conversation about unimportant things
the tip of the iceberg	a small sign of a problem that is much larger
under a cloud (of suspicion)	if someone is under a cloud, people have a bad opinion of them because they think they have done something wrong
windbag	someone who talks too much

*Extracted from www.ldoceonline.com/dictionary.
Accessed on October 19, 2018.*

UNIT 5

THIRD CONDITIONAL

Usage Notes

- The third conditional is used to describe something that didn't happen. The structure is usually *if + past perfect + would / could / might have + main verb in the past participle form*.

  If it **had rained**, I **wouldn't have traveled** to the beach.

  (But it rained.)

  They **would have had** better grades if they **had studied** harder.

  (But they didn't study harder.)

- Third conditionals may be used in mixed conditional sentences, which combine two different types of conditional patterns. The two most common mixed conditionals combine the third and the second conditionals.

- The mixed third / second conditional (a type 3 conditional in the *if-* clause — past perfect — followed by a type 2 conditional in the main clause — *would / could / might* + main verb in the base form) contrasts an imagined or real event in the past with its present result. This condition is used when we regret past action or inaction.

  If they**'d told** me they would be late, I **wouldn't** still **be** here waiting for them.

  If I **had followed** a balanced diet, I **would feel** healthier.

- The mixed second / third conditional (a type 2 conditional in the *if-* clause — If + past simple — followed by a type 3 conditional in the main clause — *would / could / might have* + main verb in the past participle form) describes ongoing circumstances in relation to a previous past event.

  If you **weren't** a good professional, I **wouldn't have hired** you for such an important position in my company.

  If you **didn't cover** up all his lies, he **would've realized** that he needed help much sooner than he did.

WISH

Usage Notes

- The use of *wish + simple past* or *wish + past perfect* is an alternative to conditional sentences.

  I **wish** you **could** spend Christmas with me this year.

  (If you could spend Christmas with me this year, that would be great.)

  We **wish** we **had studied** more before the test.

  (If only we had studied more before the test, our grades would've been better.)

- The structure *wish + infinitive* can also be used as a more formal alternative to *want* or *would like* when we refer to present and future wish situations.

  He **wishes to talk** to the admissions dean, but he hasn't scheduled an appointment.

  I **do not wish to sound** rude, but I'm running out of time here. Could you please go straight to the point?

- For present wishes with *wish* + simple past of verb *be*, *was* and *were* are interchangeable with first, second, and third person pronouns, singular and plural, although *were* sounds more formal than *was*.

  I **wish** I **weren't** here to witness the bankruptcy of our company.

  Chris **wishes** she **were** more hardworking.

- We often use *wish + would* to criticize and to talk about things that we don't like and want to change. It's not usually used to talk about ourselves, though.

  I **wish** my neighbors **would stop** making all that noise late at night.

  I **wish** you **wouldn't wake up** early so frequently!

HOMONYMS: HOMOPHONES AND HOMOGRAPHS

- Homophones are words that sound alike, whether they are spelled differently or not.

  pear (fruit) – pare (cut off) – pair (two of a kind)

  bear (carry) – bear (animal)

- Homographs are words that are spelled identically but may or may not share the same pronunciation.

  wind (an air current or to twist)

  fair (pleasing in appearance or a market)

- Homographs that are spelled the same but sound different are called heteronyms.

  tear (in the eye) – tear (rip)

  lead (to guide) – lead (metal)

LANGUAGE REFERENCE

UNIT 6

SOME, ANY, NO, EVERY – COMPOUNDS

Compounds

PEOPLE	somebody someone	anybody anyone	nobody no one	everybody everyone
THINGS	something	anything	nothing	everything
PLACES	somewhere	anywhere	nowhere	everywhere

Usages

Examples

Someone Somebody Something Somewhere	Affirmative sentences; Interrogative sentences when they show invitation or when we expect an affirmative answer.	Someone (Somebody) has to answer the phone. There's something under the mattress. Would you like to go somewhere special this Sunday?
Anyone Anybody Anything Anywhere	Negative and interrogative sentences; Affirmative sentences meaning *every*.	I don't know anyone (anybody) in this picture. I didn't do anything interesting last night. Does she intend to travel anywhere in July? You can buy anything you want on the Internet.
No one Nobody Nothing Nowhere	Affirmative sentences which have a negative meaning.	No one (Nobody) told me to keep quiet. I could do nothing to prevent her from falling. There's nowhere like home.
Everyone Everybody Everything Everywhere	Affirmative, negative, or interrogative sentences.	Everyone (Everybody) can be assigned for the role. He told us everything he remembered about the accident. I've looked everywhere but my socks are still missing.

INDIRECT / REPORTED SPEECH

Observe the changes in verb tenses.

Direct speech	Indirect / reported speech
Simple present He said, "I **want** to get home before noon."	Simple past He said (that) he **wanted** to get home before noon.
Present continuous She said, "**I'm doing** the laundry."	Past continuous She said (that) she **was doing** the laundry.
Present perfect They said, "We **haven't worked** together before."	Past perfect They said (that) they **hadn't worked** together before.
Simple past You said, "I **didn't forget** to do the homework."	Past perfect You said (that) you **hadn't forgotten** to do the homework.
Will We said, "We **will** arrive late."	Would We said (that) we **would** arrive late.
Can / May I said, "I **can't** control his attitude." He said, "I **may** need some help."	Could / Might I said (that) I **couldn't** control his attitude. He said (that) he **might** need some help.
Must She said, "I **must** check the attendance every class."	Had to She said (that) she **had to** check the attendance every class.
Imperative They said to us, "**Slow down**."	Infinitive They told us **to slow down**.

Observe the changes in time and place expressions.

Direct speech	Indirect / reported speech
a week / a month / a year ago	a week / a month / a year before
last week / month / year	the week / month / year before
next	the following
now	then / at that time
today	that day
tomorrow	the next day / the following day
tonight	that night
yesterday	the day before / the previous day
here	there

Usage Notes

- Note that *could, might, would,* and *should* don't show any changes.

  He said, "I **could** contact a lawyer." (Direct speech)

  He said (that) he **could** contact a lawyer. (Indirect / reported speech)

  She said, "It **might** take a little time." (Direct speech)

  She said (that) it **might** take a little time. (Indirect / reported speech)

- To change a *yes/no* question from direct to indirect speech, we use if + the affirmative form and make all the necessary changes in verbs, time, and place expressions.

  Louis asked her sister, "**Will you invite** Joan to the party?"

  Louis asked her sister **if she would invite** Joan to the party.

- To change a *wh-* question from direct to indirect speech, we repeat *the question word* + the affirmative form and make all the necessary changes in verbs, time, and place expressions.

  The teacher asked, "Where **are you** going?"

  The teacher asked where **we were** going.

- The demonstrative pronouns *this* and *these* are often changed to *that* and *those* in indirect speech.

  Lucca said, "I can't work with **this** old computer."

  Lucca said (that) he couldn't work with **that** old computer.

TYPES OF TECHNOLOGY

Collocation	Meaning
assistive technology	technology which helps people who have a disability
biotechnology	the use of living things such as cells, bacteria, etc. to make drugs, destroy waste matter, etc.
high technology	the use of the most modern machines and methods in industry, business, etc.
information technology	the study or use of electronic processes for gathering and storing information and making it available using computers
nanotechnology	a science which involves developing and making extremely small but very powerful machines
niche technology	technological products that are designed for a particular small area of a market

Extracted from www.ldoceonline.com/dictionary. Accessed on October 22, 2018.

UNIT 7
EXPRESSING ASSUMPTIONS

Besides *must* and *can,* there are other modal verbs that might be used to express assumptions.

- *Will* and *should* are used when we want to express assumptions with reference to present and future time. Note that assumptions with *will* are more probable.

  There's someone at the door. That**'ll** be the mailman.

  I have never gone skiing, but it **shouldn't** be too difficult.

- *Will*, *should*, and *ought to* followed by the perfect infinitive can be used to express assumptions about past events.

  Most of the students **will have seen** me around before.

  Mark **should have arrived** home by now.

PASSIVE VOICE
Formation chart

Passive forms are composed by an appropriate form of the verb *be* followed by the past participle form of the main verb.

Verb tense	Passive voice
Simple present	am / is / are + past participle
Present continuous	am / is / are + being + past participle
Simple past	was / were + past participle
Modal verbs (present)	can / must / should / could / may / might + be + past participle
Past continuous	was / were + being + past participle
Present perfect	has / have + been + past participle
Past perfect	had + been + past participle
Simple future	will + be + past participle
Modal verbs (past)	can / must / should / could / may / might + have been + past participle

Usage Notes

- When we have a whole sentence as the object of the active voice, there are two possibilities to make the passive voice.

  They say (that) she is British. (active)

  It is said that she is British. (passive)

  She is said to be British*. (passive)

- With verbs of opinion like *say, think, expect, know, believe, understand, consider, find,* etc., there are also two possible options to make the passive.

  They thought (that) I was stupid. (active)

  It was thought (that) I was stupid. (passive)

  I was thought to be stupid*. (passive)

- When we want to change an imperative form into the passive voice, we use the structure: *let* + object + *be/get* + past participle.

  Play the best music. (active)

  Let the best music be played. (passive)

LANGUAGE REFERENCE

Don't change the subject. (active)
Let the subject not be changed. (passive)

* Most frequent option.

OTHER -ED AND -ING ADJECTIVES

-ed adjectives	Meanings	-ing adjectives	Meanings
alarmed	worried or frightened	alarming	making you feel worried or frightened
charmed	have / lead a charmed life	charming	very pleasing or attractive
convinced	feeling certain that something is true	convincing	making you believe that something is true or right
depressed	very unhappy	depressing	making you feel very sad
disturbed	worried or upset	disturbing	worrying or upsetting
embarrassed	feeling uncomfortable or nervous and worrying about what people think of you	embarrassing	making you feel ashamed, nervous, or uncomfortable
fascinated	extremely interested by something or someone	fascinating	extremely interesting
surprised	having a feeling of surprise	surprising	unusual or unexpected
thrilled	very excited, happy, and pleased	thrilling	interesting and exciting
troubled	worried or anxious	troubling	worrying

Extracted from www.ldoceonline.com/dictionary. Accessed on October 22, 2018.

UNIT 8

FUTURE PERFECT AND FUTURE CONTINUOUS

Usage Notes

- We can also use the future continuous to talk about what we assume is happening at the moment.

  The students' behavior seems very suspicious to me. They**'ll be doing** something wrong, for sure!

  Give Gabriel a call. He**'ll be having** dinner already.

- We usually use the future perfect with *by* or *in*. *By* indicates *not later than a specific time* and *in* indicates *within a period of time*.

  I think technology **will have taken** control of school curricula by the year 2030.

  Will you **have finished** your work in one hour, so we can talk?

FIGURES OF SPEECH

Term	Definition
alliteration	the commencement of two or more words of a word group with the same letter, as in "apt alliteration's artful aid"
anaphora	the use of a word as a regular grammatical substitute for a preceding word or group of words, as in the use of *it* and *do* in "I know it and he does too."
antithesis	the placing of a sentence or one of its parts against another to which it is opposed to form a balanced contrast of ideas, as in "Give me liberty or give me death."
euphemism	the substitution of a mild, indirect, or vague expression for one thought to be offensive, harsh, or blunt. […] "To pass away" is a euphemism for "to die"
hyperbole	an extravagant statement or figure of speech not intended to be taken literally, as in "to wait an eternity"
irony	the use of words to convey a meaning that is the opposite of its literal meaning: the irony of her reply, "How nice!" when I said I had to work all weekend
metaphor	a figure of speech in which a term or phrase is applied to something to which it is not literally applicable in order to suggest a resemblance, as in "A mighty fortress is our God."
metonymy	a figure of speech that consists of the use of the name of one object or concept for that of another to which it is related, or of which it is a part, as "scepter" for "sovereignty," or "the bottle" for "strong drink," or "count heads (or noses)" for "count people"
onomatopoeia	the use of words that sound like the thing that they are describing, for example "hiss" or "boom"
simile	a figure of speech in which two unlike things are explicitly compared, as in "She is like a rose."

Based on www.ldoceonline.com and www.dictionary.com. Accessed on October 23, 2018.

READING STRATEGIES

Ao longo da coleção, estamos sinalizando algumas estratégias de leitura voltadas à melhora na compreensão de textos.. O principal objetivo dessas estratégias é fazer com que você, aluno, torne-se um aprendiz mais eficaz e alcance resultados positivos nos exames e vestibulares a serem realizados ao final do Ensino Médio.

A seguir você encontrará uma breve explicação sobre as estratégias mais comumente abordadas antes e durante a leitura dos textos.

Activating or using previous knowledge – Esta estratégia consiste em acionar, quando preciso, o conhecimento que você tem guardado em sua mente. Quando falamos em conhecimento prévio na leitura, estamos nos referindo às informações que você precisa ter para ler um texto sem muita dificuldade para compreendê-lo.

Brainstorming – O termo foi criado a partir da junção das palavras *brain* (cérebro) e *storm* (tempestade), portanto, significa "tempestade cerebral" ou "tempestade de ideias". A estratégia propõe que você e seus colegas de sala explorem sua capacidade criativa, na medida em que trocam ideias a respeito do assunto que será abordado no texto.

Bridging – O termo vem da palavra *bridge*, que significa "ponte". A estratégia consiste, então, em "fazer uma ponte", isto é, em estabelecer uma relação entre o seu conhecimento prévio sobre o assunto que será explorado no texto e o texto propriamente.

Finding organizational patterns or understanding text structure – A estrutura de um texto diz respeito à forma como as informações estão nele organizadas. Artigos, por exemplo, contam com uma introdução, um desenvolvimento e uma conclusão; as informações nas biografias são, em geral, organizadas em sequência cronológica; as receitas, na maioria das vezes, são divididas em duas partes – ingredientes e modo de preparo. Assim, estar atento aos padrões de organização de um texto ajuda-o a identificar seu gênero e, consequentemente, sua função social.

Predicting – A palavra *predict* significa "prever". Ao lermos o título de um texto ou observarmos as imagens que o acompanham, por exemplo, podemos prever ou deduzir seu conteúdo. Quanto mais conhecimento geral você tiver, mais facilmente vai prever o assunto de um texto. Em algumas atividades, você é convidado especificamente a prever o tema e o gênero do texto (*predicting the theme and the genre*).

Recognizing or identifying – Reconhecer significa identificar algo que se conhece. Portanto, reconhecer ou identificar o tipo textual (*textual type*), a voz, ou seja, quem está falando no texto (*voice in a text*), a perspectiva do autor (*the author's perspective*), a fonte do texto (*the source of the text*), o público ao qual o texto se destina (*the target audience*), o propósito principal do texto (*the main purpose*) etc. ajuda-o a antecipar o que está por vir no texto a ser lido.

Skimming – Consiste em observar o texto rapidamente para detectar o assunto geral ou o seu propósito geral (*skimming to identify the main purpose*), por exemplo. Nesse momento, não há nenhuma preocupação em se atentar aos detalhes. É importante que você observe o *layout* do texto, seu título e sub-títulos, cognatos, primeiras e últimas linhas de cada parágrafo, bem como as imagens, gráficos e tabelas que o acompanham.

Scanning – É uma técnica de leitura que consiste em correr rapidamente os olhos pelo texto até localizar a informação específica desejada. O *scanning* é prática rotineira na vida das pessoas. Alguns exemplos típicos pode. Alguns exemplos típicos são o uso do dicionário para obter informação sobre o significado de palavras ou a utilização do índice de um livro para encontrar um artigo ou capítulo de interesse.

Há, também, estratégias que são trabalhadas após a leitura dos textos. Observe:

Making inferences or inferring – A estratégia de inferência tem como objetivo fazê-lo capturar aquilo que não está dito no texto de forma explícita. Essas adivinhações podem ter como base as pistas dadas pelo próprio texto ou o seu próprio conhecimento. Trata-se de uma estratégia de leitura extremamente importante, pois um texto só terá sentido se você puder estabelecer relações entre as partes, ou seja, entre as palavras, frases, parágrafos etc.

Selecting a good title – Muitas vezes o título de um texto resume sua ideia central. Para selecionar o título mais apropriado para o texto que você acabou de ler, leia-o novamente e anote os pontos que mais chamaram sua atenção. O mesmo se aplica para quando você tiver que afirmar ou declarar a ideia ou o propósito principal do texto lido (*stating the main idea or the main purpose of the text*).

Understanding details – Para entender os detalhes de um texto é preciso fazer uma leitura lenta e concentrar-se durante essa leitura, isto é, ficar longe de qualquer coisa que possa distraí-lo. Recorrer a um dicionário para consultar as palavras e expressões desconhecidas e anotar seu significado, bem como fazer paráfrases durante a leitura, são algumas das ações que contribuem para a compreensão detalhada do texto. Podem contribuir, também, para as atividades que pedem que você resuma o texto lido (*summarizing*).

Understanding main ideas – Para realizar atividades que têm esta estratégia sinalizada, não é necessário fazer uma leitura tão detalhada, nem mesmo procurar todas as palavras desconhecidas em um dicionário. Basta fazer uma leitura geral do texto com atenção e compreender sua mensagem principal.

IRREGULAR VERBS

Base form	Past form	Past participle	Translation
awake	awoke	awoken	acordar
be	was, were	been	ser, estar
become	became	become	tornar-se
begin	began	begun	começar
bend	bent	bent	dobrar
bet	bet	bet	apostar
bite	bit	bitten	morder
blow	blew	blown	soprar
break	broke	broken	quebrar
bring	brought	brought	trazer
build	built	built	construir
burn	burnt/burned	burnt/burned	queimar
buy	bought	bought	comprar
catch	caught	caught	pegar
choose	chose	chosen	escolher
come	came	come	vir
cut	cut	cut	cortar
do	did	done	fazer
draw	drew	drawn	desenhar
dream	dreamed/dreamt	dreamed/dreamt	sonhar
drink	drank	drunk	beber
drive	drove	driven	dirigir
eat	ate	eaten	comer
fall	fell	fallen	cair
feed	fed	fed	alimentar
feel	felt	felt	sentir
fight	fought	fought	lutar
find	found	found	achar
fly	flew	flown	voar
forget	forgot	forgotten	esquecer
forgive	forgave	forgiven	perdoar
get	got	got/gotten	conseguir
get up	got up	got up/gotten up	levantar-se
give	gave	given	dar
go	went	gone	ir
grow	grew	grown	crescer
hang out	hung out	hung out	passar tempo
have	had	had	ter
hear	heard	heard	ouvir
hide	hid	hidden	esconder
hit	hit	hit	atingir
hold	held	held	segurar
hurt	hurt	hurt	machucar
keep	kept	kept	manter

Base form	Past form	Past participle	Translation
know	knew	known	saber, conhecer
lean	leant/leaned	leant/leaned	inclinar-se
learn	learnt/learned	learnt/learned	aprender
leave	left	left	deixar, sair
lend	lent	lent	emprestar
let	let	let	deixar
lose	lost	lost	perder
make	made	made	fazer
mean	meant	meant	significar
meet	met	met	encontrar, conhecer
overcome	overcame	overcome	superar
pay	paid	paid	pagar
put	put	put	colocar
read	read	read	ler
ride	rode	ridden	andar de
ring	rang	rung	tocar
rise	rose	risen	subir, aumentar
run	ran	run	correr
say	said	said	dizer
see	saw	seen	ver
sell	sold	sold	vender
send	sent	sent	enviar
set	set	set	estabelecer
show	showed	shown	mostrar
sing	sang	sung	cantar
sit	sat	sat	sentar
sleep	slept	slept	dormir
speak	spoke	spoken	falar
spell	spelled/spelt	spelled/spelt	soletrar
spend	spent	spent	gastar, passar tempo
split	split	split	dividir
stand up	stood up	stood up	ficar de pé
steal	stole	stolen	roubar
swim	swam	swum	nadar
take	took	taken	pegar, tomar
teach	taught	taught	ensinar
tell	told	told	contar
think	thought	thought	pensar
throw	threw	thrown	jogar
understand	understood	understood	entender
wake up	woke up	woken up	acordar
wear	wore	worn	vestir
win	won	won	ganhar
write	wrote	written	escrever

COMMON MISTAKES

Speakers of Portuguese are more likely to make certain mistakes in English because of interference from Portuguese. Let's take a look at some common mistakes:

TOPIC	COMMON MISTAKE	RIGHT FORM	SOME EXPLANATION
BEEN VS. *BEING*	I have ~~being~~ abroad twice in my life. My car is ~~been~~ washed.	I **have been** abroad twice in my life. My car **is being washed**.	With both the present perfect simple and the present perfect continuous, the verb that comes after *have / has* is in the past participle (i.e., *been*), not in the present participle (i.e., *being*). The words *been* and *being* differ in use, spelling, and pronunciation.
COUMPOUND SUBJECT: USING *I*	Jenny and ~~me~~ are from South Africa.	Jenny and **I** are from South Africa.	*I* is a subject pronoun so it comes before the verb.
AGE AS AN ADJECTIVE BEFORE A NOUN	Two-year~~s~~-old children are still learning to speak.	**Two-year-old** children are still learning to speak.	When we place someone's age before the noun, we are using it as an adjective, and adjectives don't have a plural form in English, so we can't use any of the words that are part of the compound adjective in the plural form.
WOULD IN SECOND CONDITIONAL SENTENCES	If I ~~would have~~ more money, I would travel all over the world.	If I **had** more money, I would travel all over the world.	In second conditional sentences, the *if* clause is in the simple past, and *would* can only be used in the result clause.
THE FORMATION OF PAST PERFECT	When my parents got home, I had already ~~did~~ my homework.	When my parents got home, I had already **done** my homework.	Making mistakes with past participles is common. In the past perfect tense, we always use the past participle as the conjugation of the main verb.
ADVERBS OF DEGREE AND GRADABLE / UNGRADABLE ADJECTIVES	This house is ~~very~~ enormous!	This house is **enormous**! OR This house is **very big**!	Gradable adjectives are those that you can use an adverb of degree with, such as *big* and *good*. With ungradable adverbs we can use only a few adverbs: *absolutely, really, completely, totally, utterly*.
FORMATION OF SENTENCES WITH *WISH*	I wish ~~that~~ I ~~have~~ a brother.	I wish **I had** a brother.	When expressing wishes in the present, we use a past verb; when expressing a past wish, the main verb is in the past perfect.

TOPIC	COMMON MISTAKE	RIGHT FORM	SOME EXPLANATION
USING THE DETERMINER *EVERY*	Every ~~people~~ in my school must wear a uniform, students, teachers, and even the principal.	**Every member** of my school must wear a uniform, students, teachers, and even the principal.	We use the determiner *every* with a singular noun, even though it refers to more than one of the nouns.
TIME EXPRESSIONS IN INDIRECT / REPORTED SPEECH	He said (that) he ~~will~~ buy a car ~~today~~.	He said (that) he **would** buy a car **that day**.	Although the use of *will* and *today* in the first example can be accepted when the sentence is reported on the same day, the same is not true when the sentence is reported some time after it was first said.
TOLD VS. *SAID*	She said ~~me~~ that her name was Emma.	**She said that** her name was Emma. OR **She told me that** her name was Emma.	The verb *tell* usually requires an object, we *tell someone something*; the verb *said* can only have an object if we add the preposition *to* after the verb: we *say something to someone*.
MODAL VERBS FOR ASSUMPTION	You ~~mustn't~~ be serious!	You **can't** be serious!	When we are making an assumption and we are sure of something, we use the modal verb *must*; however, the negative assumption uses a different modal verb, *can't*. *Mustn't*, or *must not*, is not possible when referring to assumptions.
FUTURE PERFECT AND FUTURE CONTINUOUS	At 10:25 my plane will ~~have~~ landing.	At 10:25 my plane **will be landing**. OR At 10:25 my plane **will have landed**.	Portuguese speakers sometimes make mistakes in verb conjugation when there is more than one verb in a structure. Beware! Continuous tenses always have the main verb in the *–ing* form, while perfect tenses have the main verb in the past participle.
PRESENT SIMPLE VS. PRESENT PERFECT	I ~~live~~ in this town since my childhood.	I **have lived** in this town since my childhood.	In English, we can't use the present simple if we are also talking about the past. If you want to say *"Eu moro nesta cidade desde minha infância."* you need to use the present perfect, as the activity started ten years ago (past) and is still true now (present).

FALSE FRIENDS

False friends are similar-sounding words with different meanings. When we look at the word *actually*, for example, we immediately associate it with the Portuguese word "*atualmente*", because of its similarity. However, *actually* means "*na realidade*" as in "It **actually** costs three thousand dollars, not three hundred." Let's take a look at some other examples.

English	Portuguese translation	Example	Don't get confused with...	Which in English is...
alias	pseudônimo, nome falso	He used to work under an **alias**.	aliás	by the way
anthem	hino	Are you able to sing the American national **anthem**?	antena	antenna
appoint	nomear	Tom Leary was **appointed** to a new position.	apontar	point
assist	ajudar	Who is going to **assist** the new judge?	assistir	watch
college	faculdade	I can't believe you are not excited about going to **college**!	colégio	school
comprehensive	abrangente, amplo	It was a very **comprehensive** report.	compreensível	understandable
convict	condenado(a)	The **convict** had to be handcuffed.	convicto(a)	certain
costume	fantasia	How much is the vampire **costume**?	costume	habit
data	dados	We have gathered a lot of **data** on the subject.	data	date
exit	saída	Where is the **exit** door?	êxito	success
fabric	tecido	Silk is a very expensive **fabric**.	fábrica	factory
hazard	risco	This medicine presents no **hazard** to your health.	azar	bad luck
inhabited	habitado(a)	It is an **inhabited** island.	inabitado(a)	uninhabited
journal	revista especializada, diário	Tom is the editor of a very important medical **journal**.	jornal	newspaper
lecture	palestra	The **lecture** had a very young audience.	leitura	reading
legend	lenda	Have you heard of the **legend** of Billy Jack?	legenda	subtitle
library	biblioteca	Is there a **library** around here where I can take out some comics?	livraria	bookstore
novel	romance	*My Brilliant Friend* is a **novel** written by Elena Ferrante, a mysterious Italian writer.	novela	soap opera
notice	notar, observar	Have you **noticed** the new furniture in the Study Hall?	notícia	news
parents	pais	My **parents** got married in the early nineties.	parentes	relatives
physician	médico	He is a respected **physician** who is looking after the president's health.	físico	physicist
prejudice	preconceito	We must always fight against all kinds of **prejudice**.	prejuízo	harm
pretend	fingir	Stop **pretending**! I know you are not telling the truth.	pretender	intend
realize	perceber	Have you **realized** how far we are from our goal?	realizar	accomplish
resume	recomeçar	After a long break they **resumed** the session.	resumir	summarize
sensible	sensato(a)	Choosing to cross the river in such a small boat is not a **sensible** option.	sensível	sensitive
support	apoiar	The homeless shelter is **supported** by a group of volunteers.	suportar	bear

98

GLOSSARY

Unit 1

craved – ansiar (infinitivo: *crave*)

empowerment – empoderamento

enhancers – potenciadores

figures – estimativas

fortnight – período de 14 dias

hence – logo, por isso

Kohl-lined eyes – olhos delineados

K-pop bands – bandas de música pop coreana

leadership – liderança

outstanding – excepcional

overlap – sobrepõe

pride – orgulho

range – variedade

ratio – proporção

rear – traseira

reiterating – repetindo, reiterando (infinitivo: *reiterate*)

roles – papéis

skincare – cuidados com a pele

skull – crânio

speed up – acelerar

targeted – direcionado(a)

tingling – formigamento

wresting – obtido à força

Unit 2

approaches – abordagens

bootcamps – campo de treino de recrutas

buzz language – linguagem do momento

coincide – coincidir

conspicuously – visivelmente

decree – decreto

despite – apesar de

disproportionately – desproporcionalmente

disrupted – perturbado(a)

fire up – entusiasmar

geeks – nerds

interface – interface fronteira

mastery – domínio

offspring – prole

pattern – padrão

pursuing – buscar (infinitivo: *pursue*)

STEM – sigla em inglês para *science, technology, engineering, and mathematics*

tech-savvy – inteligência tecnológica

Review 1

acquainted – familiarizado

awareness – consciência

demystify – desmistificar

entice – convencer

persuaded – persuadiu (infinitivo: *persuade*)

raising – aumentando (infinitivo: *raise*)

shatter – estilhaçar-se

stuck to – preso a

undergraduates – não-graduados(as)

Unit 3

acres – medida para terrenos

as a whole – como um todo

available – disponível

behavior – comportamento

blissful – feliz

carping – resmungo

cattle – gado

clout – golpe

cobble – remendar

conveyor belts – esteiras rolantes

delight – agradar

devised – criado(a) (infinitivo: *devise*)

harvest – colheita

herds – rebanhos

kidney – rim

layer – camada

leap – salto

GLOSSARY

morsel – bocado
muckraking – sensacionalismo
nourish – nutrir
nurture – educar
offsetting – compensação
otherwise – de outra forma
outcome – resultado
outtake – corte
regardless of – independente de
relentless – implacável
reluctance – relutância
rugged – bruto(a)
saying grace – orando (infinitivo: *say grace*)
sevenfold – sete vezes
shrillness – estridor
spawned – gerado(a) (infinitivo: *spawn*)
standpoints – posições
sticking with – aderindo a (infinitivo: *stick with*)
takes […] for granted – tem como certo (infinitivo: *take […] for granted*)
tract – trato (intestinal)
waist – cintura
weight – peso
whisk – bater
wonder – maravilha
yields – produções

Unit 4

ablaze – ao fogo
attics – sotãos
bunker coat – casaco de bombeiro
chaparral – tipo de vegetação chamada chaparral
clearheaded – lúcido(a)
couplings – acoplamentos
crevasse – fenda
deplete – esgotam
drizzle – garoa
eerily – sinistramente
embroidered – bordado
fail – falhar
failures – falhas
floodings – alagamentos
frontlines – linhas de frente
fueling – alimentando (infinitivo: *fuel*)
geared up – preparado(a)
hazardous – perigoso
heat-trapping gases – gases retentores de calor
hose – mangueira
hurricanes – furacões
intertwined – entrelaçado(a)
lightweight – leve (em peso)
lodged – alojou-se (infinitivo: *lodge*)
loose-fitting – folgado(a)
loss – perda
mounting – organizando (infinitivo: *mount*)
mph – abreviação para *miles per hour*, milhas por hora
overwhelm – sobrecarregar
pissing into – urinando em (infinitivo: *piss into*)
rags – trapos
replenished – reabastecido (infinitivo: *replenish*)
rescued – resgatou (infinitivo: *rescue*)
scramble – engatinhar
shook – sacudiu (infinitivo: *shake*)
sources – fontes
spinning – rodando
thaw – descongelamento
threats – ameaças
tremendously – tremendamente
widespread – generalizado(a)
wisdom – sabedoria
yelling – gritando (infinitivo: *yell*)

Review 2

aiming – objetivando (infinitivo: *aim*)
allotment – lote
committing – comprometendo (infinitivo: *commit*)

livelihoods – subsistências
range – extensão
shyly – timidamente
standards – padrões
unbeatable – invencível
weeping – chorando (infinitivo: *weep*)

Unit 5

abducts – sequestra (infinitivo: *abduct*)
airbender – controlador de ar
boldly – corajosamente
cast – elenco
concoct – fabricar
dashed – arruinado(a) (infinitivo: *dash*)
doomed – condenado(a) (infinitivo: *doom*)
double – dupla
hint – dica, ideia
jam – favorito (gíria)
kidnapping – sequestrando (infinitivo: *kidnap*)
mayhem – desordem
measly – miserável
misunderstood – mal-compreendido(a)
preying – predando (infinitivo: *predar*)
revenge – vingança
sequel – sequência
showrunner – produtor do programa
sidekick – aliado(a)
slayer – assassino(a)
spare – reservar
starvation – fome
tap – batida
transcend – ultrapassar
vortex – vórtice
wasteland – terreno baldio

Unit 6

aided – ajudava (infinitivo: *aid*)
anonymize – ocultar
assets – bens
bazaar – bazar

censorship – censura
credentials – credenciais
database – base de dados
downtime – tempo de inatividade
ensure – assegurar
exchanges – trocas
fraud – fraude
grabs – chama (infinitivo: *grab*)
grants – garante (infinitvo: *grant*)
hacks – alterações
harvested – colhido(a) (infinitivo: *harvest*)
immutable – imutável
litany – ladainha
losses – perdas
pseudonymity – estado de identidade disfarçada
redress - retificação
reputably – respeitavelmente
revenues – receitas
scalability – escalabilidade
scammers – fraudador
scoured – corroeu (infinitivo: *scour*)
seized – confiscou (infinitivo: *seize*)
trusted – confiável
volatility – volubilidade
waning – decrescente
whistleblowers – informantes

Review 3

cheated – traiu (infinitivo: *cheat*)
plot – narrativa
surveillance – vigilância

Unit 7

abiding – durável
albeit – embora
amass – aglomerar
assessment – avaliação
athleisure – roupas de ginástica para outras ocasiões
bagel – rosca (alimento)
bias – inclinação, propensão

GLOSSARY

buzzing – zunindo (infinitivo: *buzz*)
claim – afirmação
crackdowns – medidas enérgicas
creepy – assustador
derail – descarrilhar
disclose – revelar
droves – bandos
endorsers – endossadores
fiercer – mais feroz
framework – estrutura
increase – aumento
indie-flick – filme independente (gíria)
infatuated – obcecado(a)
leverage – influenciar
lingo – jargão
lure – atrair
max out – estourar
measure – medida
mimicking – fazendo mímica, copiando (infinitivo: *mimick*)
modishly – de acordo com o padrão da moda
morbidly – morbidamente
notoriously – infamemente
nutshell – casca de noz
proxy – procuração
rising tide – maré crescente
savvy – habilidade
shabby – esfarrapado
sheer – total
sleek – elegante
smutty – manchado(a)
sneaky – ordinário
theft – roubo
trustworthiness - confiança
turmeric – cúrcuma (tempero)
ubiquitous – onipresente
wannabes – que querem ser (gíria)
whether – se

Unit 8

achieved – alcançou (infinitivo: *achieve*)
billboard – outdoor de propaganda
biohackers – pessoa que mistura biologia com ética hacker
blues – tristeza
counseling – orientação
craft – produzir
depletion – esgotamento
earnings – ganhos
ebola – doença por vírus, ebola
enabling – possibilitando (infinitivo: *enable*)
gap – brecha
in demand – desejado(a)
ISIS – Sigla para Estado Islâmica do Iraque e da Síria
mattered – importou, deu importância (infinitivo: *importar*)
mismatched – mal combinado
outlets – saídas
path – caminho
plague – praga
raw – cru
referees – referências
sift – peneirar
stunning – deslumbrante
triggering – provocando (infinitivo: *trigger*)
whooping – gritando (infinitivo: *whoop*)
winning hand – mão vitoriosa (termo usado em poker)

Review 4

niche – nicho
gullibility – ingenuidade
sage – sábio

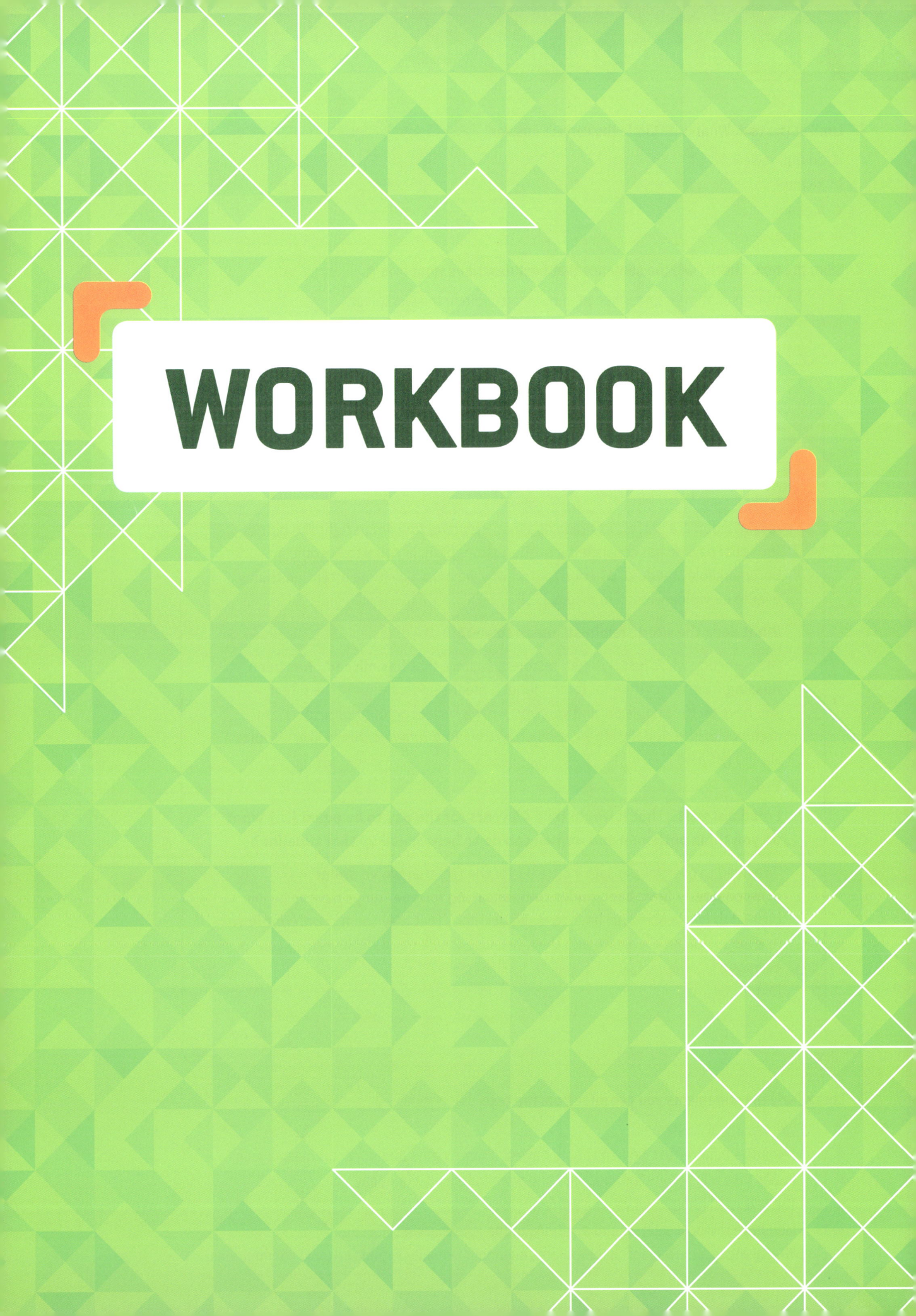

WORKBOOK

Unit 1   **Gender Equality Is for Everybody**

1. **Look at the text. What is it? Circle the correct answer.** *Identifying the genre*
   a. an film review
   b. a story
   c. a poem
   d. an interview

2. **Skim the text. Check (✓) the sentence that best describes what is in it.** *Skimming*
   a. (   ) A conversation with Joss Whedon about men's role in the workplace.
   b. (   ) A discussion where Joss Whedon shows advantages and disadvantages of working with women.
   c. (   ) A conversation with Joss Whedon about men and women having equal roles in the workplace.

A Talk with Joss Whedon on Women's *Equality* in the Workplace

[…]

Joss Whedon is a perfect example of a man *stepping forward* to fight the battle for *equal pay*. He has consistently pushed strong female **roles** to become an unremarkable standard. Whedon told us why we must pay more attention than ever to elevating women in media. […]

What does the word "feminist" mean to you?

"It's someone who's just trying to restore a *balance* that **has missed / has been missing** from our culture for far too long. It means understanding the effect you have on the people around you, and what a certain amount of respect can *accomplish* in your daily life — as much as the more *tangible* things like, 'People should get paid.'"

[…]

I read a statistic that it would take 44 years for the pay to be equal […] What do you think both men and women can do to help speed up that timeline?

"We need to overcompensate a little bit for the fact that **we've under compensated / have been under compensating** forever. Things have to be pushed to be even. People have to make decisions that may seem *counterintuitive* to a businessman every now and then, because they'll pay as little as they can to everyone.

[…]

<sub>Adapted from https://businesscollective.com/an-interview-with-joss-whedon-on-womens-equality-in-the-workplace/index.html.
Accessed on September 17, 2018.</sub>

---

3. **Check (✓) the statements you can infer from the text.** *Inferring*
   a. (   ) Women are all underpaid.
   b. (   ) Feminists believe that women should have the same rights and opportunities as men.
   c. (   ) It may take a long time for both men and women to have equal pay.
   d. (   ) The text is all about men valuing women.
   e. (   ) Men have the best salaries and positions in the jobs market.
   f. (   ) #HeForShe is a movement that promotes economic equality within the local communities.

Unit 1

4. Read the text again. Think of the rules about present perfect simple and present perfect continuous and underline the correct alternative to complete the sentences in the interview on page 104. Then write the form of each of these verb tenses.

_____

_____

5. Reread these sentences from the interview on page 104 and circle the correct alternative.
   a. The sentence "It's someone who's just trying to restore a balance that has been missing from our culture for far too long" focuses on the **completion** / **duration** of an action.
   b. The sentence "We need to overcompensate a little bit for the fact that we have been under compensating forever" focuses on the **completion** / **duration** of an action.

6. Look at the words in italics in the interview on page 104. Use them to complete the dictionary entries below.

_____ (noun): a state in which opposite forces or influences exist in equal or the correct amounts, in a way that is good

_____ (adjective): clear enough to be easily seen or noticed

_____ (phrasal verb): to come and offer help, information, etc.

_____ (adjective): not based on a feeling

_____ (noun): the principle that men and women should have the same salary if they do the same work

_____ (noun): a situation in which people have the same rights, advantages, etc.

_____ (verb): to succeed in doing something, especially after trying very hard

Adapted from www.ldoceonline.com. Accessed on September 18, 2018.

7. Read the testimonials below. What are the people talking about? Check (✓) the correct alternative.
   a. "In my job both men and women are treated the same way. Women are respected and can also take leading posts. In fact, my boss is a woman, and she is one of the best managers in our factory." - Dylan, 28
   ( ) unequal pay   ( ) balance of power   ( ) equal pay
   b. "I have been working at my current job for about six years. Last month I found out my male colleague, who has been working with me for less than a year, gets around 15% more than me and does the same job. It is so unfair!" - Sonia, 33
   ( ) unequal pay   ( ) equal pay   ( ) balance of power
   c. "I work for a clothing store. Sometimes I feel that my boss comments on our appearance way too much. Just last week he told me to stand by the front door because I was pretty and I would attract lots of customers. I have more qualities than just being pretty! I'm a good salesperson!" - Vivian, 24
   ( ) unequal pay   ( ) sexual harassment   ( ) women's empowerment

105

8. Complete the sentences with the verbs in brackets in the present perfect continuous.

a. My mom _____ (read) a lot of articles about feminist movements lately.
b. You have a lot of good ideas. _____ you _____ (study) about the subject recently?
c. We _____ (wait) here for over an hour.
d. Women _____ (fight) for gender equality for a very long time.
e. I _____ (do) research for a new article on equal pay.
f. Mark _____ (work) for us for a year now.

9. Read the quotes about gender equality. Complete the sentences with the verbs from the box to form present perfect simple or present perfect continuous sentences.

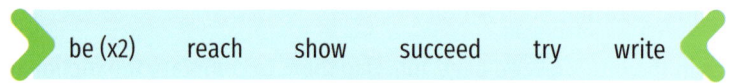

> be (x2)   reach   show   succeed   try   write

a. Women's value _____ under-recognized for far too long. (Sidney Sheldon)

b. The failure of women to _____ positions of leadership has been due in large part to social and professional discrimination. In the past, few women _____, and even fewer _____. (Rosalyn Sussman Yalow)

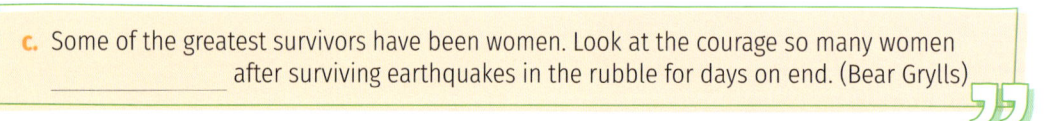

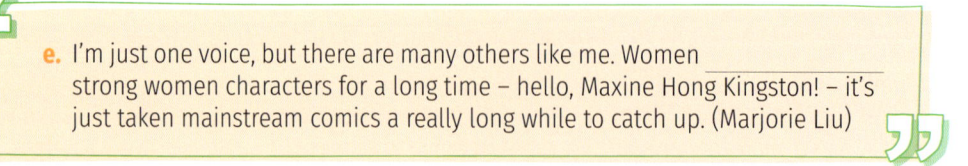

c. Some of the greatest survivors have been women. Look at the courage so many women _____ after surviving earthquakes in the rubble for days on end. (Bear Grylls)

d. Women's progress _____ a collective effort. (Gloria Steinem)

e. I'm just one voice, but there are many others like me. Women _____ strong women characters for a long time – hello, Maxine Hong Kingston! – it's just taken mainstream comics a really long while to catch up. (Marjorie Liu)

Extracted from www.brainyquote.com. Accessed on September 18, 2018.

10. Refer back to the quotes in activity 9. Identify and write two time expressions that focused on the duration of the action.

11. Answer the questions with your own information.

  a. How long have you been living in this town/city? What do you like most about it?
  ___
  ___
  ___

  b. How long have you been studying English? In your opinion, is it important to learn a foreign language? Justify your answer.
  ___
  ___
  ___

  c. Do women in your family work outside of the home? If so, how long have they had a job? Did your great-grandmother have a job or was she a housewife?
  ___
  ___
  ___

  d. How long have women in your country been allowed to vote?
  ___
  ___
  ___

AN EYE ON VESTIBULAR

VESTIBULAR UNICAMP 2016 – Provas Q e Z
1ª Fase – Questões 36 e 37

Advice for new students from those who know (old students)

"The first day of college I was a ball of nerves. I remember walking into my first class and running to the first seat I found, thinking everyone would be staring at me. But nobody seemed to notice and then it hit me: The fact that nobody knew me meant nobody would judge, which, upon reflection, was what I was scared of the most. I told myself to let go. All throughout the year, I forced myself into situations that were uncomfortable for me — for example, auditioning for a dance piece. Believe it or not, that performance was a highlight of my freshman year. My advice: challenge yourself to try something new, something you couldn't have done in high school."

– Ria Jagasia, Vanderbilt University, '18.

(Adaptado de www.nytimes.com/2015/08/02/education/edlife/advice-for-new-students-from-those-who-know-old-students.html?ref=edlife.)

No primeiro dia de faculdade, Ria ficou muito nervosa
  a. por não conhecer ninguém.
  b. por achar que seria julgada pelos colegas.
  c. porque ninguém olhou para ela.
  d. porque não sabia dançar.

Para lidar com a situação, a estratégia adotada foi deixar de se preocupar e
  a. fazer coisas que nunca fez antes.
  b. fazer novos amigos.
  c. fazer um curso de dança como ouvinte.
  d. abandonar o curso.

Unit 2 — **Technology in the School Curriculum**

1. Read the article and answer: What's the main purpose of the text? *Understanding the purpose of a text*

---

10 signs a career in coding and software development might be right for you

[…]
To help present the skills needed for computer programming in a different light, here are 10 signs coding could be right for you; signs that aren't always accounted for in academic tests.

1. You're a problem-solving pro
Lots of people will simply tolerate problems without looking for a proactive way to solve them, particularly if tolerating the problem is easier. If you don't take this approach, but actually enjoy the challenge of solving problems of all kinds, then that's a great sign that you could be **suited to** software development. If, in your desire to solve problems, you also take into account realistic **constraints** – such as timeframes and budgets – then this could be a real **asset** in your search for a career.

2. You have a passion for strategy games
Yes, it can be true that gaming is good for you, particularly where strategy games are concerned. These help **hone** your ability to make decisions based on a number of relevant factors, taking into account both short and long-term consequences. As well as computer games, those who enjoy offline games like chess, bridge or risk, could also have an underlying aptitude for programming. […]

3. _____
While the evidence for the correlation between music and maths is still in debate, it seems commonplace for those with musical talent to have mathematical abilities too. […]

4. You have a talent for winning arguments
No, we're not talking about **full-blown** shouting matches. But if your logical approach to arguing your points in a structured way means that you frequently win over your opponents, this could be a sign that you have the systematic thinking needed for software development.

5. _____
You can get the same sense of satisfaction from making something in the virtual world as you can in the physical world. Indeed, in the digital world, you aren't constrained by practicalities like materials and space, so imagination is your only limit. Having a natural curiosity for how things work, and how to make them work better, is a good indication of a nascent software developer.

6. You're a people person
Contrary to the stereotype of the IT team **hidden away** from the rest of the company, working as a developer can actually involve a great deal of interaction with others across the business. This means that an enjoyment of communicating and an ability to explain things in a way that is easily understood by others are both really important.

7. You'd like to know more about the theory of computer science
While you may not have digested the full history of computer science, an interest in the theory behind software engineering is an important aspect of a coder's skillset. You don't want to spend your time re-inventing the wheel, so being interested in what others have discovered, and being prepared to build on those foundations, will fast-track your potential **achievements**.

8. _____
Coding itself is a very collaborative process; continuously reviewing and redefining code with others helps you to shake out bugs, makes your work more likely to meet users' needs and is one of the best ways to learn. Developers therefore need to enjoy working together and should be prepared to study, critique, and improve one another's work.

9. You are intrinsically motivated
Putting some amateur psychology to use, it seems to be true that the best developers are intrinsically motivated. This means they take their reward and motivation from the process of finding a solution to a problem, or creating something innovative in itself. In other words, developers often do what they do for the love of doing it, rather than just being paid to do it.

10. _____
This is fairly obvious, but it is worth re-iterating that if you want to work in software engineering, you need to have an appreciation for the amazing possibilities that technology brings to the world. Being interested in how you can **harness** the potential of technology, for whichever company you want to work in, will definitely stand you in good **stead**, and is a sure sign you are on the right career track for success in coding.

Adapted from www.theguardian.com/careers/ten-signs-career-coding-software-development-right-for-you. Accessed on December 5, 2018.

---

2. Complete the text with the headings from the box. *Understanding details*

> You're a team player
> You have a musical mind
> You love technology
> You love making things

Unit 2

3. Match some words from the article with their meanings.

a. problem-solving ( ) abilities to do something well, talents
b. systematic ( ) when you find ways of doing things, or answers to problems
c. skills ( ) someone who you think is not very skilled at something
d. bugs ( ) faults in the system of instructions that operates a computer
e. critique ( ) to say how good or bad a book, play, painting, or set of ideas is
f. amateur ( ) organized carefully and done thoroughly

Adapted from www.ldoceonline.com. Accessed on December 5, 2018.

4. Read this summary from the text on page 108 and underline the correct alternative.

> The article "10 signs a career in coding and software development might be right for you" **present / presents** ten characteristics people may have that could help them to pursue a career in coding. **Most / Few** skills are simple personality traits that many people have. If you **like / likes** technology, music, making things, and solving problems, for instance, it **mean / means** that you could start thinking about working with coding in the future. A surprising factor that is presented in the text **is / are** the ability to interact with others from your team.

5. Which of the characteristics presented in the text in activity 1 do you think you have? Would you like to pursue a career in coding? Justify your answer.

_____
_____
_____
_____
_____
_____
_____

6. Circle the correct option to complete the sentences.

a. I believe that _____ (each / all) skills presented in the text may be important for someone who wants to learn to code.
b. When I read the article, I noticed that I have more than _____ (half of / all of) the skills needed.
c. I believe that we can learn to do things if we practice _____ (every / each) day.
d. If you think you have _____ (all of / none of) the skills presented in the article, don't worry. You can learn new skills.

7. Complete the extracts with the words from the box. There are two extra words.

> algorithm   variable   iteration   sandbox

a. "Is Facebook's advertising _____ sexist? That's what Tobias Dengel, CEO of WillowTree is claiming after a job advertisement was rejected because of the use of the term 'equal pay' in a job announcement run on November 5, 2018. [...]"

Extracted from www.forbes.com. Accessed on December 5, 2018.

b. "Fortnite is getting a major new _____ mode, separate from battle royale."

Extracted from www.eurogamer.net. Accessed on December 5, 2018.

109

8. Read an excerpt from another article about coding. Then identify and circle the compound adjectives you find.

https://www.theguardian.com/technology/2016/sep/11/make-computer-coding-childs-play-programming-apps

HOW TO MAKE COMPUTER CODING CHILD'S PLAY

With *programming* lessons now part of the school day, can parents help their *offspring* get top grades? Fear not – toys, gadgets, and *apps* are all available to make *coding* a fun part of growing up. [...]

Nowadays there's a renewed wave of interest in the topic, thanks partly to programming being part of England's national curriculum starting at five-year-old children. [...] There are inevitably apps for that, but also some inventive hardware. For children wanting to get in some extracurricular practice, these *gadgets*, programs, and books could be just the thing.

Gadgets

Kano

Billed as "an easy-to-build computer", Kano arrives in its constituent parts, which children put together as the first step in their journey towards programming. [...]

Fisher-Price Code-a-pillar

Aimed at pre-school children, this certainly looks the part as a Fisher-Price toy: a characterful plastic caterpillar with bold, bright colours. It's one of the most accessible introductions to computational thinking in the guise of fun play. [...]

Osmo coding kit

Osmo is an iPad *accessory*, that functions as a stand-up base for your tablet, and a mirror that clips on to its top, enabling the camera to "see" what's in front of the device.

[...]

LittleBits Arduino coding kit

With this kit children can build their own Etch-a-Sketch toy or a version of arcade game Pong. It uses the Arduino computer, an alternative to the Raspberry Pi, and is aimed at children aged 14 and older to hack together their own inventions, including *hardware* and software.

[...]

PROGRAMMING READS

A selection of old-fashioned printed books that could fire up children's interest in coding.

Hello Ruby: Adventures in Coding [...]
Coding for Beginners: Using Scratch [...]
Computer Coding for Kids [...]

Adapted from www.theguardian.com/technology/2016/sep/11/make-computer-coding-childs-play-programming-apps. Accessed on September 21, 2018.

9. The words in italics in the excerpt are related to education and technology. Read and complete the definitions below.

a. _____ are small, useful, and cleverly-designed machines or tools.

b. _____ is the activity of writing programs for computers, or something written by a programmer.

c. _____ are some pieces of software for a particular use or job.

d. _____ is the activity of writing computer programs.

e. An _____ is something such as a piece of equipment or a decoration that is not necessary, but that makes a machine more useful or more attractive.

f. _____ is computer machinery and equipment, as opposed to the programs that make computers work.

Adapted from www.ldoceonline.com. Accessed on September 24, 2018.

10. Now choose three of the compound adjectives from activity 8 and write sentences that are true for you.

_____
_____
_____

110

Unit 2

11. Complete the sentences with the correct compound adjective from the box.

> well-known   state-of-the-art   two-year-old
> time-saving   20-page   fastest-growing

a. Let's buy it. It's a _____ gadget. We can spend more time on other things then.

b. Do you know what the _____ programming language is? I need to have these figures for my coding class.

c. The municipality is building a new _____ hospital, where only the latest devices are going to be used.

d. Mark Zuckerberg is one of the most _____ programmers in the world.

e. Mike has just submitted a _____ project. He will only get his grade on it next week, as it will take his teacher some time to read it all.

f. This is Simba. He's my _____ dog.

AN EYE ON VESTIBULAR

VESTIBULAR FUVEST 2018 – Prova V

1ª Fase – Questões 89 e 90

Algorithms are everywhere. They play the stockmarket, decide whether you can have a mortgage, and may one day drive your car for you. They search the Internet when commanded, stick carefully chosen advertisements into the sites you visit, and decide what prices to show you in online shops. (…) But what exactly are algorithms, and what makes them so powerful?

An algorithm is, essentially, a brainless way of doing clever things. It is a set of precise steps that need no great mental effort to follow but which, if obeyed exactly and mechanically, will lead to some desirable outcome. Long division and column addition are examples that everyone is familiar with—if you follow the procedure, you are guaranteed to get the right answer. So is the strategy, rediscovered thousands of times every year by schoolchildren bored with learning mathematical algorithms, for playing a perfect game of tic-tac-toe. The brainlessness is key: each step should be as simple and as free from ambiguity as possible. Cooking recipes and driving directions are algorithms of a sort. But instructions like "stew the meat until tender" or "it's a few miles down the road" are too vague to follow without at least some interpretation.
(…)

The Economist, August 30, 2017.

No texto, um exemplo associado ao fato de algoritmos estarem por toda parte é

a. o cartão de crédito.
b. o livre mercado.
c. a dieta.
d. o jogo de xadrez.
e. o comércio eletrônico.

Segundo o texto, a execução de um algoritmo consiste em um processo que

a. prevê a memorização de tabelas e fórmulas.
b. envolve mecanismos de seleção e detecção de erros.
c. se apoia em um número infinito de etapas.
d. é incompatível com análises subjetivas e imprecisas.
e. alterna níveis altos e baixos de esforço intelectual.

Unit 3 — Can We Eat with a Clear Conscience?

1. **Read the title of the blog post. What can you infer from it? Check (✓) all the possible answers.** *Inferring*
   a. ( ) All unhealthy food is expensive.
   b. ( ) Some healthy foods are cheap.
   c. ( ) Healthy food is not cheap.
   d. ( ) Unhealthy food is cheaper than healthy food.

2. **Read the whole text. What is the author's purpose?** *Identifying the purpose of the text*

---

www.huffingtonpost.com/deane-waldman/what-if-healthy-food-were_b_323831.html

THE BLOG

What if healthy food were cheaper?
By Deane Waldman

Choose!

Everyone knows that obesity is a major health problem in the USA. One estimate suggests that 30% of *health care* costs (actually the cost of sickness care) can be attributed to the consequences of obesity.

Obesity clearly reduces productivity. Thus, from the national commercial standpoint, obesity produces a *double whammy*: it both reduces *revenue* and at the same time increases costs.

While there are some endocrine conditions and genetic disorders that predispose to obesity, the vast majority of obesity is culturally driven and over-eating is under conscious control.

If we ate properly, most obese people would not be obese. Unfortunately, unhealthy foods are generally cheaper and much more available. Worst of all, people are programmed to think they taste better.

The production and distribution of unhealthy foods is very big business and highly *profitable*. Big food, like big pharma, is politically active and quite effective at defending their profitable position.

Consider obesity from the **standpoints** of three different people: provider, taxpayer, and President. The health care provider doesn't care about your weight other than the medical complications. It is part of their moral code to provide services to sick people **regardless of** all other factors.

Both healthy-sized people and super-sized people pay the same amount into the healthcare system. Yet the super-sized take more out because they require more health care services. The healthy-eating taxpayer feels this is unfair.

Finally, imagine yourself the CEO of Corporation USA, also known as the President of the USA. Your primary goal is to protect and **nurture** the nation **as a whole**. In contrast to either the provider or the taxpayer, you have power. You can encourage passage of laws, rules, and regulations. You have influence over the tax code.

You cannot legislate morality or **behavior** in the national best interest or even behavior in the individual's best interest. Intellectually, people know they should eat "healthy" but the bad stuff tastes sooooo good and besides, it's cheaper.

So, Mr. CEO of Corporation U.S.A., what can you do? You can change *incentives*. You know that incentives affect behavior and behavior determines **outcome**. If the people ate more healthy foods, they would be less obese. Health care would cost less, and productivity would increase (the reverse of the double whammy above).

Finally, Mr. CEO, you know that carrots work better than sticks. It is always better to offer a positive incentive to encourage the behavior you want than to punish the behavior you do not want.

If you want to reduce obesity, instead of punishing super-sized persons, *subsidize* healthy foods. Make them cheaper and more **available**. What if apples and vegetables were easier to come by than coke, French fries, and cheetos?

Imagine diverting 10% of what we spend now on obesity-care – say $60 billion – to subsidize healthy foods. How much less might we spend later on obesity-care – $100 billion, $300 billion? Then add the gains in productivity. Sounds to me like a win-win scenario.

Adapted from www.huffingtonpost.com/deane-waldman/what-if-healthy-food-were_b_323831.html. Accessed on September 23, 2018.

3. Read the blog post on page 112 again. Underline two problems that can be attributed to obesity. `Understanding details`

4. Scan the text. Circle the healthy food and cross out the unhealthy food you find. `Scanning`

5. Scan the text on page 112 to find the words in italics that match the definitions below. Then complete the paragraph that follows with one of the words.

  a. _____ : things that encourage you to work harder, start a new activity, etc.
  b. _____ : producing a profit or a useful result
  c. _____ : money that a business or organization receives over a period of time, especially from selling goods or services
  d. _____ : two bad things that happen together or one after the other
  e. _____ : if a government or organization does it, it pays part of the cost
  f. _____ : the services that are provided for looking after people's health, or the activity of doing this

  Adapted from www.ldoceonline.com. Accessed on September 26, 2018.

> "Can thoughtful legislation help tackle the challenge of food recovery? Italy is optimistic that it will, hoping to reduce its 5.6 million tons in annual food waste by 20 percent through a law that rewards positive behaviors in the marketplace. The measure includes _____ for donating food, in addition to removing restrictions that have stood in the way of such benevolent actions. […]"

Extracted from http://blog.ifco.com/how-incentives-could-reduce-food-waste. Accessed on November 26, 2018.

6. Match the columns to form second conditional sentences.

  a. If we had a better diet, …   ( ) people would eat in restaurants that offer healthy food.
  b. We would buy those pears…   ( ) if he went to a nutritionist.
  c. If the government invested more in health care, …   ( ) if they were cheaper.
  d. If there weren't so many fast-food franchises, …   ( ) the people in that country would be healthier.
  e. Daniel wouldn't have stomachaches so often…   ( ) obesity wouldn't be a problem for us.

7. Look at some sentences extracted from the text on page 112. Then complete the sentences that follow with your own ideas using the second conditional form.

  a. "What if healthy food were cheaper?"
     If healthy food were cheaper, _____
     _____.

  b. What if "10% of what we spend now on obesity-care – say $60 billion – were diverted to subsidize healthy foods"?
     If _____
     _____.

  c. "What if apples and vegetables were easier to come by than coke, French fries, and cheetos?"
     If _____
     _____.

  d. What if "super-sized people paid a different amount to the healthcare system"?
     If _____
     _____.

8. Read the two first paragraphs of an article about changing your eating habits and underline a first and a second conditional sentence.

Changing Your Habits for Better Health

Are you thinking about being more active? Have you been trying to cut back on less healthy foods? Are you starting to eat better and move more but having a hard time **sticking with** these changes?

Old habits die hard. Changing your habits is a process that involves several stages. Sometimes it takes a while before changes become new habits. And you may face roadblocks along the way.

Adopting new, healthier habits may protect you from serious health problems like obesity and diabetes. New habits, like healthy eating and regular physical activity, may also help you manage your **weight** and have more energy. After a while, if you stick with these changes, they will probably become part of your daily routine. [...]

Contemplation: Are you thinking of making changes?

Making the **leap** from thinking about change to taking action can be hard and may take time. Asking yourself about the pros (benefits) and cons (things that get in the way) of changing your habits may be helpful. How would life be better if you made some changes?

Think about how the benefits of healthy eating or regular physical activity might relate to your overall health. [...]
You may learn more about the benefits of changing your eating and physical activity habits from a health care professional. This knowledge may help you take action.
Look at the list of pros and cons below. Find the items you believe are true for you. Think about factors that are important to you.

If you eat more healthily, you...	
Pros	**Cons**
• will have more energy • will improve your health • will lower your risk of health problems • will maintain a healthy weight • will feel proud of yourself • will set an example for friends and family	• will probably spend more money and time on food • will probably need to cook more often at home • will probably need to eat less of foods you love • will probably need to buy different foods • will probably need to convince your family that you all have to eat healthier foods

Adapted from www.niddk.nih.gov/health-information/diet-nutrition/changing-habits-better-health. Accessed on September 26, 2018.

9. Read the pros and cons list in the chart in activity 8. Think of two more pros and cons for the list in the text in activity 8. Then complete the chart below with them.

If I eat more healthily...	
Pros:	**Cons:**
a. _____	c. _____
b. _____	d. _____

10. Read again a question from the text and write your own answer for it. Use the second conditional in your answer.

"How would life be better if you made some changes?"

_____

_____

Unit 3

11. Complete the zero and first conditional sentences with the verbs in parentheses.

   a. If you don't eat any vegetables, you _____ (develop) nutrient deficiencies.
   b. People usually have constipation if they _____ (not drink) water every day.
   c. If you eat bananas before going to the gym tomorrow, you _____ (probably avoid) having muscle cramps.
   d. If Ana _____ (never drink) water, she will end up having some severe symptoms, such as increased blood sugar.
   e. You _____ (get) more vitamin A into your body if you eat carrots.
   f. What _____ (happen) if someone eats too much sugar?

12. Complete the conditional sentences with your own ideas using the correct conditional form.

   a. If someone eats too much chocolate, _____
   _____.

   b. If you stop having breakfast, _____
   _____.

   c. If you stopped eating at fast-food restaurants, _____
   _____.

   d. If you don't eat dessert every day, _____
   _____.

   e. If you could grow your own vegetables, _____
   _____.

AN EYE ON ENEM

ENEM 2014 – 2º dia Caderno Cinza
Questão 91

Disponível em: http://1.bp.blogspot.com. Acesso em: 30 jul. 2012.

Implementar políticas adequadas de alimentação e nutrição é uma meta prioritária em vários países do mundo. A partir da campanha *If you can't read it, why eat it?*, os leitores são alertados para o perigo de

a. acessarem informações equivocadas sobre a formulação química de alimentos empacotados.
b. consumirem alimentos industrializados sem o interesse em conhecer a sua composição.
c. desenvolverem problemas de saúde pela falta de conhecimento a respeito do teor dos alimentos.
d. incentivarem crianças a ingerirem grande quantidade de alimentos processados e com conservantes.
e. ignorarem o aumento constante da obesidade causada pela má alimentação na fase de desenvolvimento da criança.

Unit 4 — Extreme Weather Events Affecting the Planet

1. Look at the title, headings, and pictograms in the text in activity 2. What is it about? List some ideas of what you expect to find in the text. *Predicting and taking notes*

   _____

   _____

2. Read some safety guidelines from "Winter Storm Safety," by redcross.org. Underline the words related to the weather. Then infer their meaning by context or look them up on a dictionary, if necessary. *Scanning*

Winter Storm Safety

Learn how to stay safe during a blizzard and how to prevent or **thaw** frozen pipes.

About

Each year, hundreds of Americans are injured or killed by exposure to cold, vehicle accidents on wintry roads, and fires caused by the improper use of heaters. Learn what to do to keep your loved ones safe during blizzards and other winter storms!

Take immediate precautions if you hear these words on the news:

Winter Storm WARNING: Life-threatening, severe winter conditions have begun or will begin within 24 hours.

Blizzard WARNING: Sustained winds or frequent gusts of 35 miles per hour or greater, plus considerable falling or blowing snow reducing visibility to less than a quarter mile, expected to prevail for three hours or longer. […]

Staying Safe During a Winter Storm or Blizzard

- Stay indoors and wear warm clothes. Layers of **loose-fitting**, **lightweight**, warm clothing will keep you warmer than a bulky sweater. If you feel too warm, remove layers to avoid sweating; if you feel chilled, add layers. […]
- Bring your companion animals inside before the storm begins.
- Move other animals to sheltered areas with a supply of non-frozen water. Most animal deaths in winter storms are caused by dehydration.
- Eat regularly. Food provides the body with energy for producing its own heat.
- Keep the body **replenished** with fluids to prevent dehydration. […]
- Conserve fuel. Winter storms can last for several days, placing great demand on electric, gas, and other fuel distribution systems (fuel oil, propane, etc.). Lower the thermostat to 65° F (18° C) during the day and to 55° F (13° C) at night. Close off unused rooms, and stuff towels or **rags** in cracks under the doors. Cover the windows at night.
- Check on relatives, neighbors, and friends, particularly if they are elderly or if they live alone.

Driving in Winter Conditions

- Check your vehicle emergency supplies kit and replenish it if necessary. […]
- Let someone know your destination, your route, and when you expect to arrive. If your vehicle gets stuck along the way, help can be sent along your predetermined route.
- Before leaving, listen to weather reports for your area and the areas you will be passing through, or call the state highway patrol for the latest road conditions.
- Be on the lookout for sleet, freezing rain, freezing **drizzle**, and dense fog, which can make driving very **hazardous**. […]

If You Become Stranded

- Stay in the vehicle and wait for help. Do not leave the vehicle to search for assistance unless help is visible within 100 yards (91 meters). You can quickly become disoriented and confused in blowing snow. […]
- Run the engine occasionally to keep warm. Turn on the engine for about 10 minutes each hour (or five minutes every half hour). Running the engine for only short periods reduces the risk of carbon monoxide poisoning and conserves fuel. Use the heater while the engine is running. Keep the exhaust pipe clear of snow, and slightly open a downwind window for ventilation.
- Do light exercises to keep up circulation. Clap your hands and move your arms and legs occasionally. Try not to stay in one position for too long. […]

Extracted from www.redcross.org/get-help/how-to-prepare-for-emergencies/types-of-emergencies/winter-storm.html. Accessed on September 27, 2018.

3. Now that you have read the text, were your predictions in activity 1 correct? Write a comparison between your predictions and what is in the text.

_____
_____
_____
_____

4. Complete the statements below using the idioms containing weather-related words from the box.

> be on cloud nine
> a storm in a teacup
> to be under the weather
> it's raining cats and dogs
> take a rain check
> come rain or shine

- **a.** Oh, no! Look outside, _____ .
- **b.** Susan has _____ since she heard how well she did on her final papers.
- **c.** I couldn't understand why he was so angry. His protest was nothing but _____ .
- **d.** I'm feeling a little _____ today, so I won't be able to come to your party.
- **e.** Put on your sweater and let's go. The concert is happening _____ .
- **f.** I can't meet you guys today. Sorry, I'll _____ .

5. Now use the words from the box to complete these other idioms containing weather-related words. Read the definitions to help you.

> break   storm   cloud   pours   rainy

- **a.** *every* _____ *has a silver lining:* used to say that there is something good even in a situation that seems very sad or difficult
- **b.** *it never rains but it* _____ : used to say that as soon as one thing goes wrong, a lot of other things go wrong as well
- **c.** _____ *the ice:* to make people feel more friendly and willing to talk to each other
- **d.** *save something for a* _____ *day:* to save something, especially money, for a time when you will need it
- **e.** *the calm before the* _____ : a calm, peaceful situation that will not continue because a big argument, problem, etc. is coming

Adapted from www.ldoceonline.com. Accessed on September 28, 2018.

6. Read the extracts from page 116. Underline the adverbs of intensity that best convey the ideas of the words in bold.

- **a.** "If you feel **too** (nearly / extremely) warm, remove layers to avoid sweating."
- **b.** "Be on the lookout for sleet, freezing rain, freezing drizzle, and dense fog, which can make driving **very** (extremely / moderately) hazardous."
- **c.** "Run the engine **as much as needed** (a lot / enough) to keep warm."
- **d.** "Running the engine for **a short** (a lot / a little) while reduces the risk of carbon monoxide poisoning and conserves fuel."
- **e.** "Keep the exhaust pipe clear of snow, and **slightly** (a little / totally) open a downwind window for ventilation."

7. Read part of a Katrina survivor's tale. Then complete the blanks with a verb from the box in the past perfect.

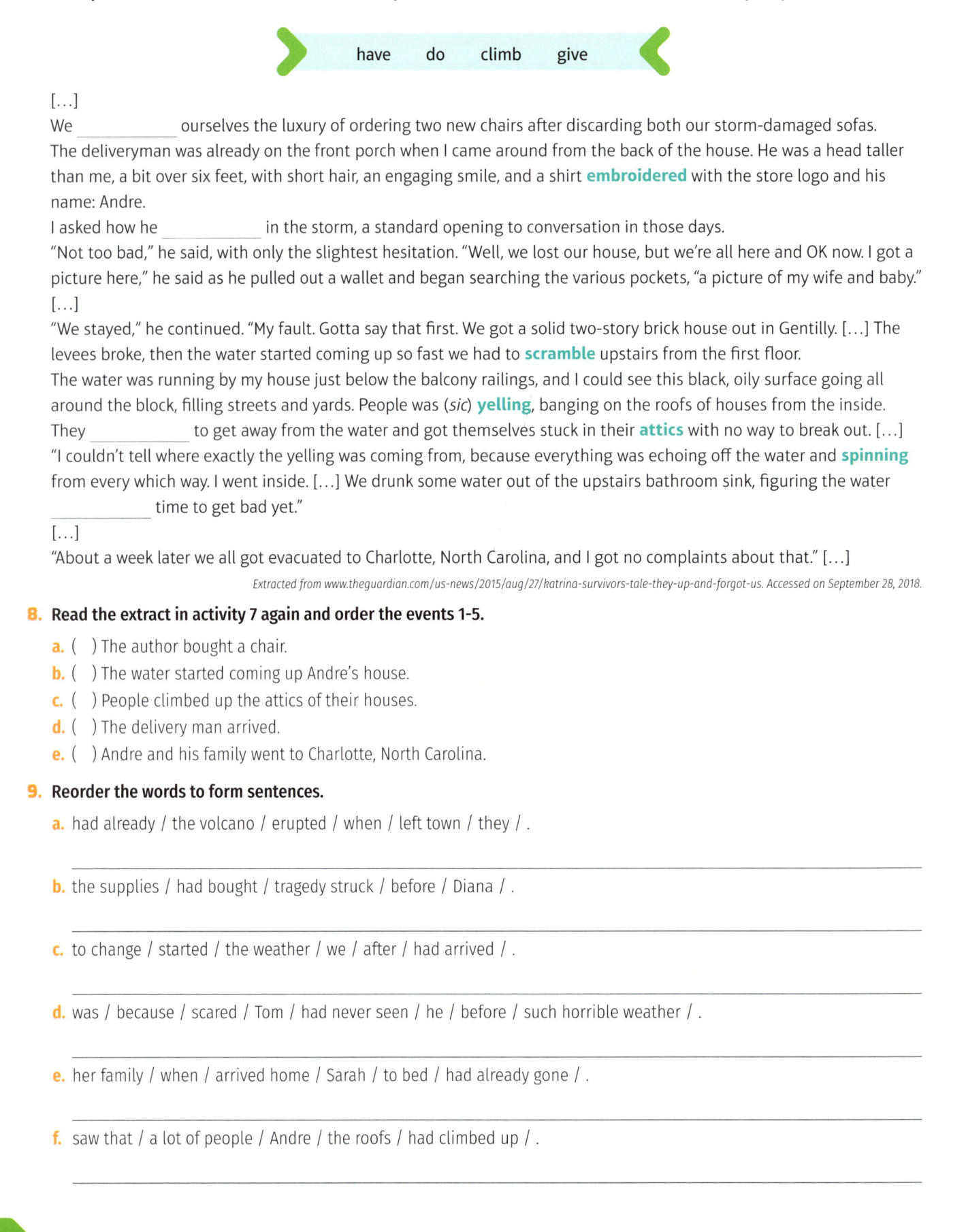

> have   do   climb   give

[…]
We _____ ourselves the luxury of ordering two new chairs after discarding both our storm-damaged sofas. The deliveryman was already on the front porch when I came around from the back of the house. He was a head taller than me, a bit over six feet, with short hair, an engaging smile, and a shirt **embroidered** with the store logo and his name: Andre.
I asked how he _____ in the storm, a standard opening to conversation in those days.
"Not too bad," he said, with only the slightest hesitation. "Well, we lost our house, but we're all here and OK now. I got a picture here," he said as he pulled out a wallet and began searching the various pockets, "a picture of my wife and baby."
[…]
"We stayed," he continued. "My fault. Gotta say that first. We got a solid two-story brick house out in Gentilly. […] The levees broke, then the water started coming up so fast we had to **scramble** upstairs from the first floor.
The water was running by my house just below the balcony railings, and I could see this black, oily surface going all around the block, filling streets and yards. People was (sic) **yelling**, banging on the roofs of houses from the inside. They _____ to get away from the water and got themselves stuck in their **attics** with no way to break out. […]
"I couldn't tell where exactly the yelling was coming from, because everything was echoing off the water and **spinning** from every which way. I went inside. […] We drunk some water out of the upstairs bathroom sink, figuring the water _____ time to get bad yet."
[…]
"About a week later we all got evacuated to Charlotte, North Carolina, and I got no complaints about that." […]

Extracted from www.theguardian.com/us-news/2015/aug/27/katrina-survivors-tale-they-up-and-forgot-us. Accessed on September 28, 2018.

8. Read the extract in activity 7 again and order the events 1-5.
   a. (   ) The author bought a chair.
   b. (   ) The water started coming up Andre's house.
   c. (   ) People climbed up the attics of their houses.
   d. (   ) The delivery man arrived.
   e. (   ) Andre and his family went to Charlotte, North Carolina.

9. Reorder the words to form sentences.
   a. had already / the volcano / erupted / when / left town / they / .
   _____

   b. the supplies / had bought / tragedy struck / before / Diana / .
   _____

   c. to change / started / the weather / we / after / had arrived / .
   _____

   d. was / because / scared / Tom / had never seen / he / before / such horrible weather / .
   _____

   e. her family / when / arrived home / Sarah / to bed / had already gone / .
   _____

   f. saw that / a lot of people / Andre / the roofs / had climbed up / .
   _____

Unit 4

10. Complete the sentences below with the verbs in parentheses in the simple past or past perfect.

a. Alan didn't want to watch the news with us because he _____ (read) about the hurricane in the morning.
b. Lizzy hadn't seen a snowstorm before, so she _____ (get) very interested in the pictures.
c. By the time Terry arrived, we _____ (finish) the research on natural disasters.
d. We _____ (not say) anything until she had finished talking.
e. I _____ (help) people who _____ (be) through natural disasters before, so I knew I could help them, too.
f. After Cindy _____ (move out), I found her notes.

11. Read the paragraph below. Then write two things Collin had done before the school bus arrived.

> I woke up at 6:30. Then I put on my school uniform and went to the kitchen. I ate my breakfast, cereal with fruit and milk. Then I brushed my teeth and heard the school bus stopping in front of my house.

Before the bus arrived, Colin _____.

AN EYE ON VESTIBULAR

VESTIBULAR PUC-RJ – 2015
1º dia – Questão 12

Tsunami Science:
advances since the 2004 Indian ocean tragedy

The Indian Ocean tsunami was one of the worst natural disasters in history. Enormous waves struck countries in South Asia and East Africa with the little to no warning, killing 243,000 people. The destruction played out on television screens around the world, fed by shaky home videos. The outpouring of aid in response to the devastation in Indonesia, Sri Lanka, Thailand and elsewhere was unprecedented.

The disaster raised awareness of tsunamis and prompted nations to pump money into research and warning systems. Today (Dec. 26), on the 10th anniversary of the deadly tsunami, greatly expanded networks of seismic monitors and ocean buoys are on alert for the next killer wave in the Indian Ocean, the Pacific, and the Caribbean. (...)

By Becky Oskin, Senior Writer. Adapted from htttp://www.livescience.com/49262-indian-ocean-tsunami-anniversary.html. December 26, 2014.

In the sentence "The disaster raised awareness of tsunamis and prompted nations to pump money into research and warning systems", the word *prompted* means

a. motivated.
b. persuaded.
c. suggested.
d. restricted.
e. impeded.

Unit 5 — In the Limelight

1. **Skim the text and check (✓) the correct alternative to complete the sentence.** *Skimming and identifying the genre*

   The text is from…
   - **a.** (   ) a TV guide.
   - **b.** (   ) a comic strip.
   - **c.** (   ) an interview.
   - **d.** (   ) a blog.
   - **e.** (   ) an advertisement campaign.

   ## Two post-apocalyptic movie endings that were changed by audience opinions

   Companies selling products aren't the only businesses using paid surveys to increase sales. There are other industries that collect opinions in different ways and use them to drastically change projects and outcomes.

   The movie industry is well-known for using test audiences to alter your favorite movies. In fact, oftentimes a crowd's reaction to a rough cut can change the way a movie ends, which is essentially the most important part of many cinematic adventures.

   For better or worse, studio executives weren't happy with the way audiences reacted to the original endings of these movies, so viewers got something drastically different than what was first intended. Read on if you don't mind spoilers.

   ### 'I Am Legend'

   This 2007 post-apocalyptic film starred Will Smith as Doctor Robert "Legend" Neville. He's perhaps the only survivor of a plague that has turned the citizens of New York City – and maybe the world – into vampires, and he's frantically working to **concoct** a cure using his natural immunity and vampire test subjects he **abducts**.

   The movie is an adaptation based on a novella by Richard Matheson of the same name. However, the two end quite differently because the original was disliked by test audiences. The original cut of the movie and the book end with Neville realizing that he is the monster **preying** on the **misunderstood** vampires. The vampires reveal themselves as intelligent, organized, and caring creatures. Meanwhile, Neville has been **kidnapping** them to experiment on.

   Instead, the movie adaptation ends with Neville sacrificing himself and killing a group of vampires before they can rescue their kidnapped member. The original moral of the story is lost, but audiences preferred the change.

   ### '28 Days Later'

   Danny Boyle's cult classic movie '28 Days Later' was never predicted to earn such a popular following. But despite having a **measly** $8 million budget, according to the Internet Movie Database, the movie attracted so much attention that producers followed up with a **sequel**. That may be because the original ending was changed.

   "28 Days Later" follows Jim, a delivery man who fell into a coma after a bike accident. During his time in the hospital, Great Britain spiraled into zombie **mayhem**. When Jim awakens, he finds some remaining survivors and they leave the city in search of others.

   At the climax of both movies, the original one and the sequel, Jim is shot in the stomach while escaping from an army compound with two of his surviving female friends. In the original version, the two frantically try to revive Jim but fail. They're left to confront the zombie **wasteland** alone.

   Test audiences got the impression that the two women were **doomed** after Jim's death, so the movie was given a brighter new ending. Jim is successfully revived after escaping the compound and the movie picks up with him waking up the same way he did in the hospital at the beginning. However, now the three survivors have successfully outlived most of the undead, who are now dying of **starvation**. The movie ends with the three catching the attention of a passing fighter jet.

   Your opinion has a lot of power. It can be used to change your favorite products for the better with paid surveys, or it can even save characters from a zombie wasteland.

   Adapted from www.opinionoutpost.com/en/blog/2-postapocalyptic-movie-endings-that-were-changed-by-audience-opinions#.W6w1NmhKjlU. Accessed on October 1, 2018.

Unit 5

2. Scan the text. What does this information relate to? *Scanning*

   a. 2007: _____
   b. Will Smith: _____
   c. New York City: _____
   d. Richard Matheson: _____
   e. $8 million: _____
   f. Great Britain: _____

3. Look at the title of the text on page 120 again. Do you agree with changing movie endings according to the audience's opinion? Justify.

_____
_____
_____

4. Read the text again and decide if the sentences are true (T) or false (F). *Understanding details*

   a. ( ) The movie industry doesn't usually use test audiences to change movies from their original plot.
   b. ( ) The movie industry was comfortable with the original endings of these movies.
   c. ( ) Many movies are adaptations based on novels. These two movies are an example of this.
   d. ( ) Neville kills himself at the end of *I Am Legend*.
   e. ( ) Test audiences wanted Jim to be killed at the end of *28 Days Later*.
   f. ( ) The viewer's opinion doesn't have any impact on the movie industry.

5. Read these extracts from the text, paying special attention to the homographs in bold. Then check (✓) the correct meaning in context.

   a. "[...] he's frantically working to concoct a cure using his natural immunity and vampire test **subjects** he abducts."

   ( ) the thing you are talking about or considering in a conversation, discussion, book, movie, etc.
   ( ) a person or animal that is used in a test or experiment
   ( ) an area of knowledge that you study at a school or university

   b. "They're **left** to confront the zombie wasteland alone."

   ( ) the side of your body that contains your heart
   ( ) the opposite direction of right
   ( ) the past tense and past participle of leave

   c. "The original cut of the movie and the **book** end with Neville realizing that he is the monster preying on the misunderstood vampires."

   ( ) to make arrangements to stay in a place, eat in a restaurant, go to a theater, etc. at a particular time in the future
   ( ) to put someone's name officially in police records, along with the charge made against them
   ( ) a set of printed pages that are held together in a cover so that you can read them

   Adapted from www.ldoceonline.com. Accessed on October 2, 2018.

6. Which of the words in activity 5 can be pronounced in two different ways? Underline the stressed syllable in each of the cases. Use a dictionary if necessary.

_____

7. Use the third conditional to complete the statements related to the text.

   a. If the producers of *I Am Legend* _____ (keep) the original ending, Neville _____ (be) kidnapping creatures to experiment on them forever.

   b. If the producers of *28 Days Later* _____ (stick) to the original ending from the book, Jim's gunshot wound _____ (kill) him.

8. **Complete the sentences so that they are true for you. Use the third conditional.**

   a. If I had gone to bed earlier, _____
   _____.

   b. If I'd known that _____
   _____.

   c. If I'd studied _____
   _____.

   d. I would have been on time _____
   _____.

   e. Last year, I would have gotten better grades in _____
   _____.

   f. I wouldn't have missed _____
   _____.

9. **Read the comic strip. Complete the blanks with the verbs from the box.**

   > tell   need   have   send

   Panel 1: I WISH I ____ A SECRET ADMIRER…
   Panel 2: SOMEONE WHO WOULD ____ ME FLOWERS AND LITTLE NOTES AND THINGS LIKE THAT…
   Panel 3: AND THEN, ALL OF A SUDDEN, HE WOULD ____ ME WHO HE WAS…
   Panel 4: THEN YOU'D ____ ANOTHER SECRET ADMIRER

   Adapted from www.gocomics.com/peanuts/2003/06/20. Accessed on September 1, 2018.

10. **Read the situations below. Then check (✓) the best past regret for them.**

    a. I stayed up late watching a movie last night. I'm so tired today.
       (   ) I wish I had watched one more movie last night.
       (   ) I wish I hadn't watched that movie last night.

    b. I went to Suzy's house on Sunday and I missed the latest episode of *The Walking Dead*. Now my friends are all giving spoilers.
       (   ) I wish I had stayed at home on Sunday.
       (   ) I wish I had gone to Suzy's house.

    c. I woke up late this morning and missed my bus.
       (   ) I wish I had slept in today.
       (   ) I wish I had set my alarm clock.

    d. We went to the movies on Friday to watch a horror movie. I had horrible nightmares that night.
       (   ) I wish I had seen a comedy instead.
       (   ) I wish I had seen that horror movie twice.

Unit 5

11. Look at the pictures. Guess what these people are wishing for and complete the blanks.

a.

I wish _____ _____ to Paris.

b.

We wish _____ _____ that beautiful car.

c.

They wish _____ _____ famous singers.

d.

She wishes _____ _____ more money to pay for her studies.

AN EYE ON VESTIBULAR

VESTIBULAR DE VERÃO PUC SP 2017 – Prova V
1ª fase – Questão 40

The Heyday of the Silents
GEOFFREY NOWELL-SMITH

By the middle of the 1920s the cinema had reached a peak of splendour which in certain respects it would never again surpass. It is true that there was not synchronized sound, nor Technicolor, except at a very experimental stage. Synchronized sound was to be introduced at the end of the decade, while Technicolor came into use only in the mid-1930s and beyond. Nor, except in isolated cases like Abel Gance's Napoléon (1927), was there anything approaching the wide screen that audiences were to be accustomed to from the 1950s onwards. It is also the case that viewing conditions in many parts of the world, particularly in rural areas, remained makeshift and primitive.

Source: The Oxford History of World Cinema EDITED BY GEOFFREY NOWELL-SMITH OXFORD UNIVERSITY PRESS 1996

De acordo com o texto,

a. no início da década de 20, a indústria cinematográfica não contava com som nem com tecnicolor.
b. de acordo com Nowell-Smith, recursos cinematográficos como som sincronizado e tecnicolor foram introduzidos no final da década de 20.
c. a leitura do texto permite inferir que a palavra "heyday", encontrada no título, representa algo positivo.
d. o esplendor da indústria cinematográfica, atingido na década de 20, só se repetiu com a introdução de efeitos especiais, principalmente em algumas partes do mundo.

Unit 6 — Uncovering Blockchain and the Dark Web

1. Look at the text in activity 2. What is the genre of the text? Who wrote it?   *Identifying the genre and the author of the text*

_____

2. Read the text that follows and answer the questions.   *Reading for specific information*

   a. What sells on the dark web for just $5.20? _____
   b. What is described as "the shadowy corner of the Internet"? _____
   c. What is Fractl? _____
   d. What's the number of Facebook users hacked by the dark web? _____
   e. Name a special network used by the dark web. _____
   f. What are vampire apps? _____

---

www.dailymail.co.uk/sciencetech/article-5533871/How-Facebook-data-worth-Hackers-sell-dollars.html

How much is YOUR data worth? In wake of Facebook's massive privacy scandal, experts say login details sell for just $5.20 on the dark web

- A study of dark web marketplaces show that Facebook logins sell for just $5.20
- By comparison, hacked financial details are in high demand from **scammers**
- The price of user privacy has been in focus in the wake of Facebook's massive data scandal, which led to 50 million users' data being compromised

By ANNIE PALMER FOR DAILYMAIL.COM
PUBLISHED: 22:25 BST, 22 March 2018 | UPDATED: 22:59 BST, 22 March 2018

If most people were asked how much their privacy is worth, they'd likely say it's priceless.

Unfortunately, hackers and identity thieves aren't so generous.

User logins for many of the most popular apps sell for next to nothing on the dark web, a shadowy corner of the Internet that's frequented by criminals, drug users, arms dealers and is often the grounds for all kinds of illicit activities.

Now, a recent report from content marketing agency Fractl has **found out** just how much your data is worth on the dark web.

The price of user privacy has been cast into the spotlight in the wake of Facebook's massive data scandal, which led to 50 million users' data being **harvested** without their knowledge.

Facebook has since announced that it would notify all users whose data was misused by British research firm Cambridge Analytica or any app developers who are found to have mismanaged users' personal information.

This addresses the issue of user information being sold to advertisers, research firms and the like, but it doesn't **touch upon** one of the Internet's busiest marketplaces – the dark web.

For the study, Fractl **scoured** all the fraud-related listings on the three biggest dark web marketplaces – Dream, Point, and Wall Street Market – last month, according to MarketWatch.

[…]

To do this, they downloaded a Tor client, or a network that **grants** anonymity to Internet browsers, which is required in order to access the dark web.

There, they discovered that Facebook logins are sold for just $5.20 each.

Obtaining someone's Facebook **credentials** can serve as a gateway into hundreds of other apps they've also granted access.

That's because Facebook allows thousands of third-party 'vampire apps' to **plug in** to its social network and **siphon off** data from its users.

This means anything from popular services like Airbnb and Spotify, to dodgy quiz apps or online games like Farmville.

Many users may use their Facebook account to **log in** to these apps, which means that if a hacker has your credentials for the social media platform, they can easily get into many other accounts.

Meanwhile, credentials for other popular services like Gmail, Uber, and Grubhub are just as cheap.

Your Gmail username and password is a bargain at just $1, while Uber account logins go for $7 and Grubhub logins sell for $9.

By comparison, the most expensive logins are for PayPal, which can demand up to $247, according to Fractl.

According to experts, the reason why some credentials sell for cheap is because hackers can so easily obtain it nowadays. It's a classic case of supply and demand: With so much data available on the Internet, hackers can easily obtain it, sell it and **move on**.

Similarly, a separate study by security research firm Top 10 VPN revealed that your entire online identity can be sold for approximately $1,200.

Top 10 VPN also found that Facebook logins would sell for $5.20 on the dark web.

Extracted from www.dailymail.co.uk/sciencetech/article-5533871/How-Facebook-data-worth-Hackers-sell-dollars.html. Accessed on September 03, 2018.

3. Read the text on page 124 again. Check (✔) all the alternatives that apply. The author's tone is... *Identifying the author's tone*

    a. ( ) optimistic.
    b. ( ) factual.
    c. ( ) entertaining.
    d. ( ) frank.
    e. ( ) supportive.
    f. ( ) critical.

4. Read the text on page 124 again and find the phrasal verbs in bold to fit each definition below.

    a. _____ : to dishonestly take money or goods from a business, account, etc. to use it for a purpose for which it was not intended.
    b. _____ : to connect a piece of electrical equipment to the main supply of electricity, or to another piece of electrical equipment.
    c. _____ : to get information after trying to discover it or by chance.
    d. _____ : to do the necessary actions on a computer system that will allow you to begin using it.
    e. _____ : to leave your present job, class, or activity and start doing another one.
    f. _____ : to mention a particular subject when talking or writing.

Adapted from www.ldoceonline.com. Accessed on September 04, 2018.

5. Complete the sentences below using the phrasal verbs from activity 4 in the correct form.

    a. The FBI _____ that Facebook's logins were stolen by people on the dark web.
    b. The report _____ the issue of the anonymity of dark web users.
    c. You need to _____ the cord before turning the computer on.
    d. They illegally _____ secret information from other people's bank accounts.
    e. It's time for a change, let's _____ .
    f. Don't forget to _____ to your new account to change your password.

6. Read these two extracts from the text on page 124. Check (✔) all the information that describes the uses of *some* and *any* in the sentences.

"According to experts, the reason why **some** credentials sell for cheap is because hackers can so easily obtain it nowadays."
"Facebook has since announced that it would notify all users whose data was misused by British research firm Cambridge Analytica or **any** app developers who are found to have mismanaged users' personal information."

    ( ) These determiners are being used before a noun.
    ( ) *Some* is being used with an exact quantity or number.
    ( ) *Any* refers to specific app developers.
    ( ) *Some* and *any* refer to unspecified quantities or numbers.

7. Complete the sentences below with *some*, *any*, *no*, or *every*.

    a. _____ of the information we find online is not reliable.
    b. She said that she would appreciate _____ tip she could get to learn about how she could benefit from buying bitcoin, even the basic ones.
    c. Have you ever read _____ articles about cryptocurrency?
    d. We have _____ words to express how much we appreciate your help.
    e. I really have _____ desire whatsoever to access the dark web. I think I will never want to know it.

8. Read the text below about the use of bitcoin in the UK. Then answer the question: Who did the journalist talk to in order to obtain the information for this news report?

Time to regulate bitcoin, says Treasury committee report
MPs in U.K. say 'wild west' cryptocurrency industry is leaving investors vulnerable

Bitcoin and other cryptocurrencies are "wild west" **assets** that expose investors to a **litany** of risks and are in urgent need of regulation, MPs on the Treasury select committee have said.

5 The committee said in a report that consumers were left unprotected from an unregulated industry that **aided** money laundering, while the government and regulators "bumble along" and fail to take action.

The Conservative MP Nicky Morgan, the chair of the committee, said the current situation was unsustainable.

"Bitcoin and other crypto-assets exist in the wild west industry of crypto-assets. This unregulated industry leaves investors facing numerous risks," Morgan said. "Given the high price **volatility**, the hacking vulnerability of exchanges, and the

10 potential role in money laundering, the Treasury committee strongly believes that regulation should be introduced."

Crypto-assets are not covered by the City regulator, the Financial Conduct Authority (FCA), and there are no formal mechanisms for consumer **redress** or investor compensation.

The committee argues in the report that at a minimum, regulation should be introduced to add consumer protection and counter money laundering.

15 It said that as things stood, the price of crypto-assets was so volatile that while potential gains were large, so too were potential losses. "Accordingly, investors should be prepared to lose all their money," the committee said.

The FCA said: "The FCA agrees with the committee's conclusion that bitcoin and similar crypto-assets are ill-suited to retail investors, and as we have warned in the past, investors in this type of crypto-asset should be prepared to lose all their money."

20 [...]

In 2017, the price of a bitcoin soared by more than 900%, hitting a peak of almost $20,000 in December. Its popularity has since waned, with one bitcoin now priced at around $6,270.

The digital currency emerged after the financial crisis. It allows people to bypass banks and usual payment processes to pay for goods and services.

25 [...]

The Treasury committee said cryptocurrency exchanges were at increased risk of cyber-attacks, and some retail investors who lost their passwords had found themselves locked out of their accounts permanently. However, it said that if regulated and dealt with properly, the industry could be an opportunity for Britain.

[...]

Extracted from www.theguardian.com/technology/2018/sep/19/time-to-regulate-bitcoin-says-treasury-committee-report. Accessed on September 03, 2018.

---

9. Read the extracts from the text above and decide if they are direct speech (D) or indirect speech (I).

a. ( ) "The committee said in a report that consumers were left unprotected from an unregulated industry that aided money laundering [...]."

b. ( ) "He said: 'The currency isn't going to work. [...]'."

c. ( ) "'As an industry we have been calling for the introduction of proportionate regulation to improve standards and encourage growth,' said Iqbal Gandham, the chair of CryptoUK."

d. ( ) "The committee argues in the report that at a minimum, regulation should be introduced to add consumer protection and counter money laundering."

10. Rewrite the direct speech sentences from activity 9 into indirect speech.

11. Read the pairs of sentences below and circle all the mistakes you can find in the second sentence, considering that they are not true in the present. Then rewrite the sentences.

a. "Cryptocurrency exchanges are at high risk of cyber-attacks", said the experts.

The experts said that cryptocurrency exchanges are at high risk of cyber-attacks.

_____

_____

b. "I've invested a lot of money in Bitcoin," said Marie.

Marie said that I had invested a lot of money in Bitcoin.

_____

_____

c. The president said, "we need regulation, so the money laundering can stop."

The president said that we needed regulation, so the money laundering can stop.

_____

_____

d. "John must stop throwing his money around" said his mother.

John's mother said that she must stop throwing his money around.

_____

_____

AN EYE ON ENEM

ENEM 2012 - 2º dia - Prova Amarela
Questão 93

Cartuns são produzidos com o intuito de satirizar comportamentos humanos e assim oportunizam a reflexão sobre nossos próprios comportamentos e atitudes. Nesse cartum, a linguagem utilizada pelos personagens em uma conversa em inglês evidencia a

a. predominância do uso da linguagem informal sobre a língua padrão.
b. dificuldade de reconhecer a existência de diferentes usos da linguagem.
c. aceitação dos regionalismos utilizados por pessoas de diferentes lugares.
d. necessidade de estudo da língua inglesa por parte dos personagens.

Unit 7 — Digital Influencing

1. Read the text. Then read the titles below and check (✓) the one that best fits the text. *Selecting a good title*

a. ( ) The Top 10 Digital Influencers
b. ( ) Good Influence in Digital Social Media
c. ( ) How to Spot the Fakers in Social Media Influencing
d. ( ) The Top 5 Worst Influencers In Digital Media

---

www.collabary.com/blog/bad-influence-how-to-spot-the-fakers-in-social-media-influencing

Bad influence – _____

Team Collabary | 4 August 2017

( ) Beyond the filter

Being a social media influencer, unlike being an Olympic sprinter or an astronaut, is worryingly easy to fake.

From being **sneaky** with the stuff you show in your pictures, to artificially inflating your follower count, there are plenty of ways to make you look more influential than you actually are.

Or at least, that's what these Insta-fakers tell themselves. The reality is that giving a false impression about your real social influence is a) amazingly easy to see through and b) will kill off any hopes you had about making a living from influencer marketing.

Some of the more obvious tricks are about creating a picture of your amazing, inspiring life that simply isn't true. For example, if a travel blogger constantly shares pictures of themselves in amazing hotels – but only ever shows public spaces, like the lobby – the chances are they're really staying in a caravan down the road.

More sinister than this is the outright **theft** of someone else's creativity. Weirdly, even some of the biggest (so-called) influencers out there are just as guilty as the **wannabes**.

[...]

( ) Never trust a bot

Much worse (and much stupider) is the practice of buying Instagram followers or automating interactions.

Hootsuite recently did a fabulous study into the benefits (there were none) of each of these shady social media practices.

In a **nutshell**, they created a dummy account and clicked one of those **ubiquitous** 'get followers now!!' buttons. The results were a definite **increase** in followers – **albeit** ones that didn't offer a single engagement to any post.

Their test for automatic interaction is even more revealing (and funnier). Signing up for a bot to automatically target selected hashtags with generic comments like 'great job!' or 'love this!', Hootsuite's experimenter quickly realized auto-commenting this way is, at best, a bit pointless and at worst can make you look weird, irrelevant, and **creepy**.

( ) Keep it real

But if we now know a bit more about how these people fake their credentials as content creators, it's still hard to understand *why* they do it.

Admittedly, some platform users (and even some brands) still regard someone's follower number as a **measure** of their authority. But, given how simple it is to determine **whether** someone's following is filled with fake accounts and **smutty** bots, that first impression of authority can be quickly and irrevocably broken.

We can't deny that some of the methods above are a cheap way to inflate your audience numbers – you can probably buy around 100 new 'followers' for just a few dollars.

But given that any brand who is serious about social media influencing would sooner give their Twitter password to a monkey than work with someone so shifty, you've potentially lost way more money than you've saved.

The reassuring truth is that there are guaranteed ways to boost your audience numbers and interactions – but these don't come from being sneaky about who you really are. They come from truly knowing and engaging with an audience and from being a specialist, who shares what you know generously and creatively.

Adapted from www.collabary.com/blog/bad-influence-how-to-spot-the-fakers-in-social-media-influencing. Accessed on October 6, 2018.

Unit 7

2. Read the subtitles of the blog post on page 128 and mark the boxes according to the content below. *Skimming*

   a. How to guarantee ways of raising your audience number without lying about who you are.
   b. How fake social media influencers give false impressions to their audiences.
   c. How the research in getting followers was conducted and its results.

3. A blog is a webpage containing information or opinions from a particular person or about a particular subject. People who read a blog can add their opinion about what it contains. Add your own opinion about the blog you just read. *Giving opinion*

_____
_____
_____
_____

4. The words in the box below were taken from the text on page 128. Match them with their definitions.

> sneaky   outright   fake   dummy   bot   share <

   a. _____ : a computer program that performs the same operation many times in a row, for example one that searches for information on the Internet as part of a search engine
   b. _____ : doing things in a secret and often dishonest or unfair way
   c. _____ : to have or use something with other people
   d. _____ : clear and direct
   e. _____ : a product made to look like a real one and is used for tests, getting people's opinions, etc.
   f. _____ : someone who is not what they claim to be or does not have the skills they say they have

   Adapted from www.ldoceonline.com. Accessed on October 6, 2018.

5. Look at the extracts taken from the text on page 128 and check (✓) the alternatives that best apply.

   a. "Some of the more obvious tricks are about creating a picture of your **amazing**, **inspiring** life that simply isn't true."
       ( ) The adjectives in bold are used to describe the characteristics of something.
       ( ) The adjectives in bold are used to describe the way someone feels.
   b. "The **reassuring** truth is that there are guaranteed ways to boost your audience numbers and interactions – but these don't come from being sneaky about who you really are."
       ( ) The adjective in bold is used to describe the characteristics of something.
       ( ) The adjective in bold is used to describe the way someone feels.

6. Now read the quote below and pay close attention to the adjectives in bold. Then check (✓) the alternative that best applies.

> "No matter how **frustrated**, **disappointed** and **discouraged** we may feel in the face of our failures, it's only temporary. And the faster you can stop wallowing in guilt, blame or resentment, the faster you can put it behind you." – Fabrizio Moreira

Extracted from www.brainyquote.com. Accessed on October 11, 2018.

   a. ( ) The adjectives in bold are used to describe the characteristics of something.
   b. ( ) The adjectives in bold are used to describe the way someone feels.

7. Read the sentences below and circle the correct alternative.
   a. Some influencers live very **exciting** / **excited** lives.
   b. They worked hard all weekend long. They must be **tiring** / **tired**.
   c. Some of the comments I read on the blog were quite **insulting** / **insulted**.
   d. My sister loves your blog! She is absolutely **thrilling** / **thrilled**!
   e. That YouTuber is so **boring** / **bored**! I can't watch her videos without falling asleep.
   f. His methods to expand his audience numbers are definitely **confusing** / **confused**.

8. Read the quotes of some top media influencers of 2018 according to cbsnews.com. Then read the sentences and underline *must* or *can't*.
   a. He **must** / **can't** be a very skilled and methodical actor and comedian.

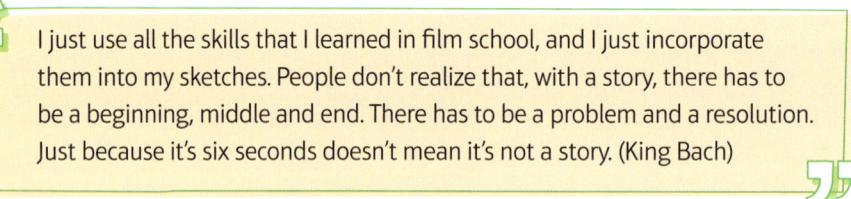

   > I just use all the skills that I learned in film school, and I just incorporate them into my sketches. People don't realize that, with a story, there has to be a beginning, middle and end. There has to be a problem and a resolution. Just because it's six seconds doesn't mean it's not a story. (King Bach)

   b. She **must** / **can't** be very worried about what people think of her.

   > I went to high school, and I started getting bullied because I was very weird. I mean, freshman year I went to school in a pirate suit – I just didn't care. I'm not like the cool girls – I'm the other girl. The one that's basically a nerd, but proud of that. (Lele Pons)

   c. He **must** / **can't** have made mistakes when he was younger.

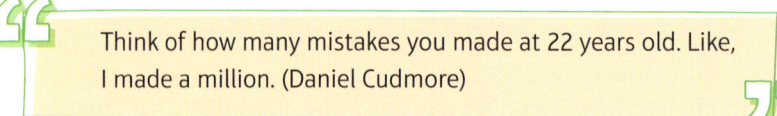

   > Think of how many mistakes you made at 22 years old. Like, I made a million. (Daniel Cudmore)

   d. She **must** / **can't** have been through difficult moments in her life.

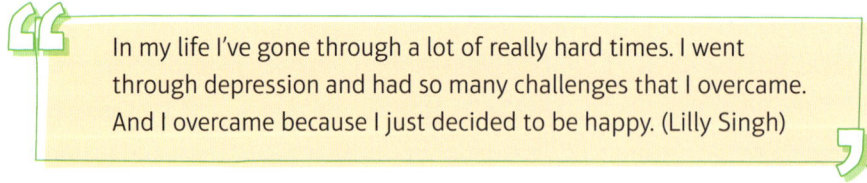

   > In my life I've gone through a lot of really hard times. I went through depression and had so many challenges that I overcame. And I overcame because I just decided to be happy. (Lilly Singh)

   Extracted from www.brainyquote.com. Accessed on October 6, 2018.

9. Read an extract from the text on page 128. Circle the correct alternatives about the rules for the passive voice.

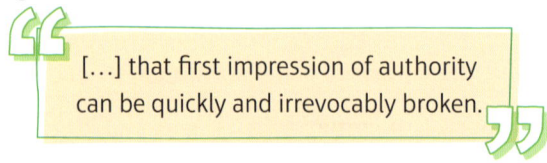

   > […] that first impression of authority can be quickly and irrevocably broken.

   a. We form the passive voice using the verb *be* + past participle.
   b. We use the passive voice using the verb *be* + the infinitive.
   c. We form the passive voice with modal verbs using a modal verb + *be* + past participle.
   d. We always use *to* after a modal verb.

10. Rewrite the sentences using passive voice. Add *by* when necessary.

a. They should organize the event in the park.
_____

b. The researchers handed in the reports about the bad influencers.
_____

c. Claire has washed John's car three times this month.
_____

d. You must read the blog messages before she gets here.
_____

e. Cameron Dallas may produce a new movie soon.
_____

f. They are going to build a new factory in my neighborhood.
_____

AN EYE ON VESTIBULAR

VESTIBULAR UNESP - 2017

Questão 29

"One never builds something finished": the brilliance of architect Paulo Mendes da Rocha

Oliver Wainwright
February 4, 2017

"All space is public," says Paulo Mendes da Rocha. "The only private space that you can imagine is in the human mind." It is an optimistic statement from the 88-year-old Brazilian architect, given he is a resident of São Paulo, a city where the triumph of the private realm over the public could not be more **stark**. The sprawling megalopolis is a place of such marked inequality that its superrich hop between their rooftop helipads because they are too scared of street crime to come down from the clouds.

But for Mendes da Rocha, who received the 2017 gold medal from the Royal Institute of British Architects this week – an accolade previously bestowed on such luminaries as Le Corbusier and Frank Lloyd Wright – the ground is everything. He has spent his 60-year career lifting his massive concrete buildings up, in gravity-defying balancing acts, or else burying them below ground in an attempt to liberate the Earth's surface as a continuous democratic public realm. "The city has to be for everybody," he says, "not just for the very few."

(www.theguardian.com. Adaptado.)

No trecho do primeiro parágrafo "the triumph of the private realm over the public could not be more stark", o termo em destaque tem sentido equivalente, em português, a

a. gritante.
b. purificado.
c. vazio.
d. simples.
e. disfarçado.

Unit 8 The End of a Journey

1. Look at the article. What do you think are some new jobs that graduates will be doing from 2026? Read the article and check your predictions. *Predicting and skimming*

---

10 jobs graduates **will be applying / will have applied** for from 2026

Rachael Pells @rachaelpells | Tuesday 9 August 2016 00:12

Tomorrow's graduates **will be applying / will have applied** for jobs working in virtual worlds and outer space, experts claim, following the release of a new report predicting career trends for the next ten years. [...]

The report highlights that 65 per cent of school students in university today will take up jobs that don't exist yet. [...]

Ten jobs of the future

1) Virtual Habitat Designer

Required skills/qualifications: _____, editing, psychology

Researchers predict tens of millions of us **will be spending / will have spent** hours each day working and learning in virtual reality environments by the year 2026. The role of a Virtual Habitat Designer will be to design these worlds, creating suitable environments for virtual meetings to take place, or VR galleries for artists to display their work.

2) Ethical Technology Advocate

Required skills/qualifications: _____, philosophy, ethics

An Ethical Technology Advocate will act as a go-between for humans, robots and AI, setting the moral and ethical rules under which the machines operate and exist. [...]

3) Digital Cultural Commentator

Required skills/qualifications: _____, business studies, PR and marketing

In ten years' time, visual communication will dominate social media. [...]

Frances Morris, director of Tate Modern, believes skilled workers such as digital culture commentators will be key to enabling art institutes such as her own to attract visitor spending power and guarantee future commercial success.

4) Freelance Biohacker

Required skills/qualifications: Biosciences, medical methodology, _____

Science has long been dominated by professional teams working in universities, corporate research and development departments – but the rise of open source software platforms will democratise this sector, say researchers.

Freelance **biohackers** will work remotely on open-source software platforms along with thousands of others in virtual teams connected online. [...]

5) IoT (Internet of Things) Data Creative

Required skills/qualifications: Engineering, problem solving, _____ and entrepreneurship

IoT Data Creatives will **sift** through the waves of data being generated each day by devices in our clothes, our homes, our cars and our offices and find meaningful and useful ways to tell us what all that information is saying. [...]

6) Space Tour Guide

Already on the horizon thanks to the likes of Virgin Galactic, Earth orbit will become the new frontier for adventurous travellers by 2026.

7) Personal Content Curator

By the late 2020s, software-brain interfaces, pioneered by teams of neuroscientists, **will be starting / will have started** to enter the mainstream, allowing mass audiences to read and capture thoughts, memories, and dreams. [...]

8) Rewilding Strategist

By 2025, the planet will struggle to cope with nine billion humans and the resources they require, and traditional conservation won't be enough. [...]

9) Sustainable Power Innovator

By the mid-2020s, resource **depletion** will mean a shift to sustainable energy. The main struggle here **will be storing / will have stored** power for the days when the wind doesn't blow or the sun doesn't shine. [...]

10) Human Body Designer

Engineering advances will extend the average healthy human life as the growth of replacement tissues and organs becomes an everyday and affordable proposition.

Adapted from www.independent.co.uk/news/education/education-news/10-jobs-graduates-will-be-applying-for-from-2026-a7179316.html. Accessed on October 9, 2018.

Unit 8

2. Read the first five jobs of the future in the article on page 132. Then complete the required skills / qualifications of these with the words from the box below. *Understanding main ideas*

> communications   data analytics
> architectural design
> art history   communications

3. Look at the article on page 132 again and pay close attention to the sentences using future perfect and future continuous. Then underline the correct alternative.

4. What do you think you will be doing ten years from now? Write your answer using future continuous.

_____
_____
_____

5. Look at these two extracts taken from the article. You will see two phrasal verbs using *take*. Check (✓) the correct meaning for each one.

   a. "The report highlights that 65 per cent of school students in university today will **take up** jobs that don't exist yet."
   ( ) to fill a particular amount of time or space
   ( ) to start something new or have a new responsibility
   ( ) to make a piece of clothing shorter
   ( ) to do something about an idea or suggestion that you have been considering

   b. "[…] creating suitable environments for virtual meetings to **take place**, or VR galleries for artists to display their work."
   ( ) to suddenly start being successful
   ( ) to let people know the true facts about a bad or shocking situation
   ( ) to make something better, stronger, etc.
   ( ) to happen, especially after being planned or arranged

Adapted from www.ldoceonline.com. Accessed on October 10, 2018.

6. Look at the words in the box below. Circle the words that collocate with *take* and underline the words that collocate with *have*.

> the lead   a dream   a plan
> responsibility   action   questions
> a rest   a chance   notes   a bus

7. Use some collocations from activity 6 to complete the sentences below. Make sure to use the correct form of the verb.

   a. We need to write a report. Did you _____ during the seminar?
   b. Today you _____ to talk to her about your problems.
   c. That's not fair. You must do something about it. Let's _____!
   d. Our country _____ in the environmental discussions last week.
   e. Sarah has been working a lot to solve that problem. I'm sure she _____.
   f. If you _____ any _____, just ask your teacher for some help.

133

8. Read an excerpt from a blog post and complete it with the verbs from the box in the form indicated in parentheses.

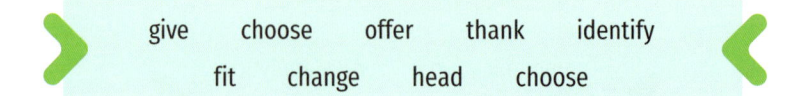

> give   choose   offer   thank   identify
> fit   change   head   choose

https://zety.com/blog/how-to-choose-a-major

HOW TO CHOOSE A MAJOR - A COMPLETE GUIDE

By Christian Eilers – Resumé expert at Zety

There are literally thousands of majors to choose from, and each university and college program will vary on their offerings. You need to pick one that your future self _____ (future simple) you for.
[…]
As with relationships and the latest **billboard** hits, you may decide that the major you _____ (past simple) is not right for you anymore.
Don't worry about this – you're not alone. According to the NY Times, a **whopping** 61% of the students at the University of Florida _____ (simple present) their minds about their major by the end of their sophomore year. So, you'd be in the minority if you *didn't* second-guess yourself.
One thing to keep in mind is to make sure that you don't just pick the easiest program out there. Choose a path that _____ (simple future) you a degree that you'll be proud of and that at least fits somewhat with the idea of the direction you _____ (present continuous).
One quick thing to mention before we end – the reality check. Before pulling the trigger on the major of your choice, ask yourself:

1. What kind of job is right for me in the future as a career?
2. Will this major _____ (present perfect) help me with this?
3. What college is right for me for my undergraduate studies?
4. _____ this college _____ (simple present) a great program for my chosen major?
5. _____ my chosen major _____ (simple present) my abilities, values, interests, and passions?
6. _____ I _____ (present perfect) all the downsides and disadvantages of my chosen major?

Adapted from https://zety.com/blog/how-to-choose-a-major. Accessed on October 9, 2018.

9. Read the six questions at the end of the post in activity 8 again. How would you answer these questions?

1. _____
2. _____
3. _____
4. _____
5. _____
6. _____

10. Reorder the words to form sentences.

a. take / will / a year off / choosing / before / a major / I / .

_____

b. last train / the / will / arriving / be / soon / .

_____

c. already / has / Samantha / several / vocational tests / taken / .

_____

d. working / really / is / hard / his final / Kevin / exams / to pass / .

_____

e. already / gone over / three first pages / the / when arrived / she had / we / .

_____

f. been / preparing / have / we / all week / for / test / this / .

_____

g. before / graduated / will / I / have / Christmas / .

_____

AN EYE ON VESTIBULAR

VESTIBULAR PUC-SP 2017-1

Questão 43

COMMENTS (4) (Please sing in to comment)

> **orinoco womble said**, _22 days ago_
> Good things. Living in the dorms, far from parental supervision, you can get up to all sorts of trouble and they won't know if you don't tell 'em. Pizza parlours and takeaways occupy a whole street near campus. You could eat pizza every night and your parents couldn't say a word (I realize I'm showing my age, I'm before the junkfood generation).
> You get to make your own mistakes. No helicopter parents around. Some of those mistakes are a lot of fun at the time! Everyone around you likes your music or something even crazier. You can experiment with life.
> _http://www.gocomics.com/JustinBoyed_
> _Acessado em 22/08/2016_

O comentário [...] foi postado após um artigo sobre

a. o uso de helicópteros por pais para supervisionar jovens adultos que moram em universidades.
b. algumas das novas experiências que a vida no campus universitário propicia.
c. o saudável controle dos pais sobre a vida universitária dos filhos.
d. o crescimento do comércio ao redor dos campi universitários.

AUDIO SCRIPTS

Unit 1

Track 02 – Activity 2

Jennifer Siebel Newsom wasn't even planning to direct her documentary, Miss Representation. She first approached some established female directors to take on her film about how women are portrayed in the mainstream media, but every one declined to do it, saying nobody would hire them afterwards – a stark illustration of who runs the entertainment industry even before you get to the hard-hitting statistics and appalling examples of sexism in her film.

Extracted from www.theguardian.com/lifeandstyle/2014/mar/03/feminist-film-maker-taking-on-hollywood. Accessed on October 4, 2018.

Track 03 – Activity 3

Her film was originally shown at Sundance and broadcast in the US in 2011. It features an impressive line-up of powerful women, including Nancy Pelosi, Condoleezza Rice, Katie Couric, and Gloria Steinem, as well as academics and activists who all flesh out the idea that the demeaning and stereotypical representation of women in the media is a significant contributor in holding women back from positions of power. This, in turn, affects the lives of all women, from the gender pay gap and career opportunities after motherhood, to mental health issues and the rise of cosmetic surgery.

[...]

Extracted from www.theguardian.com/lifeandstyle/2014/mar/03/feminist-film-maker-taking-on-hollywood. Accessed on October 4, 2018.

Unit 2

Track 04 – Activity 2

REPORTER: Their team name is Ctrl Alt Delete, and they know a lot about robots.

STUDENT: It's really nice how you can program them to do whatever you want.

REPORTER: The ten students from Berwick Lodge, Glendal, and Mount View primary schools won the National Robotics Championships in Sydney with this creation – the HotSpot Spotter robot. Fitted with a heat sensor, the robot can identify trees which don't appear burned, but are likely to explode in coming weeks. Currently, firefighters do the checks manually with handheld detectors. It's unsafe and inefficient.

STUDENT 2: It senses the obstacles in its path, so all the trees, and it looks at each of them one by one, and then whichever one of the trees have combustion, it sends the coordinates back to base, so the CFA can adjust the tree and take it down.

Extracted from http://education.abc.net.au/home#!/media/1453656/hotspot-spotter-wins-top-robot-prize. Accessed on August 13, 2018.

Track 05 – Activity 3

REPORTER: Their team name is Ctrl Alt Delete, and they know a lot about robots.

STUDENT: It's really nice how you can program them to do whatever you want.

REPORTER: The ten students from Berwick Lodge, Glendal, and Mount View primary schools won the National Robotics Championships in Sydney with this creation—the HotSpot Spotter robot. Fitted with a heat sensor, the robot can identify trees which don't appear burned, but are likely to explode in coming weeks. Currently, firefighters do the checks manually with handheld detectors. It's unsafe and inefficient.

STUDENT 2: It senses the obstacles in its path, so all the trees, and it looks at each of them one by one, and then whichever one of the trees have combustion, it sends the coordinates back to base, so the CFA can adjust the tree and take it down.

REPORTER: Robotics is slowly gaining popularity, but many schools still put it in the too-hard-and-too expensive basket.

TEACHER: Look, education's about many things. One of them is preparing children for the workforce of the future. Robotics in Asia, America, Europe is big. In Australia, we use robots, but it's undertaught in our schools.

REPORTER: And there's also the gender imbalance to address.

STUDENT 3: It's nice to have another girl, Zoe, on our team. It would be cool to have maybe, like, one or two more girls.

REPORTER: The team wants to compete at World Robotics Championships in Spain next year, but they need a sponsor. Their teachers say they're a good investment. There's no way they could have come up with the HotSpot Spotter.

TEACHER 2: Oh, no.

TEACHER 3: I'm not that clever, no.

TEACHER 2: No, it's the children's…

TEACHER 3: It's the children's idea.

REPORTER: The teachers say the CFA and the Royal Fire Service have given it the thumbs up, and have encouraged the kids to explore commercial opportunities. Kerri Ritchie, ABC News, Melbourne.

Extracted from http://education.abc.net.au/home#!/media/1453656/hotspot-spotter-wins-top-robot-prize. Accessed on August 13, 2018.

Unit 3

Track 06 – Activity 2

[...]

When we think about threats to the environment, we tend to picture cars and smokestacks, not dinner. But the truth is, our need for food poses one of the biggest dangers to the planet.

Agriculture is among the greatest contributors to global warming, emitting more greenhouse gases than all our cars, trucks, trains, and airplanes combined—largely from methane released by cattle and rice farms, nitrous oxide from fertilized fields, and carbon dioxide from the cutting of rain forests to grow crops or raise livestock. Farming is the thirstiest user of our precious water supplies and a major polluter, as runoff from fertilizers and manure disrupts fragile lakes, rivers, and coastal ecosystems across the globe. Agriculture also accelerates the loss of biodiversity. As we've cleared areas of grassland and forest for farms, we've lost crucial habitat, making agriculture a major driver of wildlife extinction.

The environmental challenges posed by agriculture are huge, and they'll only become more pressing as we try to meet the growing need for food worldwide. We'll likely have two billion more mouths to feed by mid-century—more than nine billion people. But sheer population growth isn't the only reason we'll need more food. The spread of prosperity across the world, especially in China and India, is driving an increased demand for meat, eggs, and dairy, boosting pressure to grow more corn and soybeans to feed more cattle, pigs, and chickens. If these trends continue, the double whammy of population growth and richer diets will require us to roughly double the amount of crops we grow by 2050.

Unfortunately, the debate over how to address the global food challenge has become polarized, pitting conventional agriculture and global commerce against local food systems and organic farms. The arguments can be fierce, and like our politics, we seem to be getting more divided rather than finding common ground. Those who favor conventional agriculture talk about how modern mechanization, irrigation, fertilizers, and improved genetics can increase yields to help meet demand. And they're right. Meanwhile proponents of local and organic farms counter that the world's small farmers could increase yields plenty—and help themselves out of poverty—by adopting techniques that improve fertility without synthetic fertilizers and pesticides. They're right too.

[...]

Extracted from www.nationalgeographic.com/foodfeatures/feeding-9-billion/>. Accessed on August 21, 2018.

Track 07 – Activity 3

[...] We need to find a balance between producing more food and sustaining the planet for future generations.

This is a pivotal moment when we face unprecedented challenges to food security and the preservation of our global environment. The good news is that we already know what we have to do; we just need to figure out how to do it. Addressing our global food challenges demands that all of us become more thoughtful about the food we put on our plates. We need to make connections between our food and the farmers who grow it, and between our food and the land, watersheds, and climate that sustain us. As we steer our grocery carts down the aisles of our supermarkets, the choices we make will help decide the future.

Extracted from www.nationalgeographic.com/foodfeatures/feeding-9-billion/. Accessed on August 21, 2018.

Unit 4

Track 08 – Activity 2

[...]

I was 14 when I asked a friend's stepdad where Mount Everest was. We were on a hill-walking trip and the sense of achievement at scaling those Lake District crags awakened a thirst for adventure. Bullied mercilessly at school, I suffered attacks of anxiety and was reluctant to be away from home. But once the idea struck, there was no stopping me – having asked where to find the world's highest peak, it would be only four years until I first set foot on it.

[...]

At 18, I would have been the youngest British climber ever to reach the top of Everest on the south route, but it was not to be. After weeks of trekking, my team arrived at base camp on 19 April 2014, the day after an avalanche killed 16 Sherpa guides. It was, at that time, the worst human tragedy in Everest's history, and all climbing on the mountain was abandoned for the rest of the season.

[...]

Extracted from www.theguardian.com/lifeandstyle/2016/may/13/experience-caught-in-avalanche-everest. Accessed on August 28, 2018.

Track 09 – Activity 3

[...]

I was 14 when I asked a friend's stepdad where Mount Everest was. We were on a hill-walking trip and the sense of achievement at scaling those Lake District crags awakened a thirst for adventure. Bullied mercilessly at school, I suffered attacks of anxiety and was reluctant to be away from home. But once the idea struck, there was no stopping me – having asked where to find the world's highest peak, it would be only four years until I first set foot on it.

[...]

At 18, I would have been the youngest British climber ever to reach the top of Everest on the south route, but it was not to be. After weeks of trekking, my team arrived at base camp on 19 April 2014, the day after an avalanche killed 16 Sherpa guides. It was, at that time, the worst human tragedy in Everest's history, and all climbing on the mountain was abandoned for the rest of the season.

It would be 12 months until I was able to venture back. An extra year's training left me feeling much more prepared and I started to feel excited about the prospect of some real climbing. The morning we set out to climb to camp one from base camp was grim, stormy, and turbulent. [...]

We passed towering columns, crumbling ledges, and yawning crevasses; but as thick fog obscured the route, I kept my head down, focusing on one step at a time. After several tough hours, I was past the most technical section of the climb, on some big, open ice blocks. I was close to camp one but completely alone – Tim, the team leader, and Ellis, another climber, were perhaps 20 minutes behind me. Most other members were already at the camp when the earthquake struck.

I'll never forget the cracking noise that echoed through the valley. I looked up, startled, knowing it was ice breaking away from the mountain, but was unable to see more than a few meters ahead. There was nowhere to run; I barely had time to wonder whether I'd be better off unclipping myself from my climbing rope before the avalanche hit me like an express train.

It just kept coming, forcing snow into my nose and mouth. [...] I thought of my family back home and imagined the headlines announcing my death – I had no expectation of surviving.

Abruptly, the wind subsided and the mountain fell silent. I'd only been hit by powder snow and had escaped the worst of the avalanche, but knew a further collapse could be on the way. There was no response when I tried to radio ahead, and I wondered if everyone above and below me had been swept away: was I the only team member left alive? Crying, I pressed on, eventually reuniting with Tim, Ellis, and two more members of the team; alive, but overwhelmed. [...]

When we radioed base camp, we realized how lucky we'd been. The whole area had been hit by a much bigger avalanche and completely destroyed. It was two days before we could be helicoptered down, and the camp still looked like the site of a plane crash. [...]

Nearly 9,000 people were killed by that earthquake. Since then, I've focused on raising funds to help rebuild Nepal. I plan to return to Everest for a third attempt one day. Like the bullying at school, it's something I need to overcome before I can move on.

Adapted from www.theguardian.com/lifeandstyle/2016/may/13/experience-caught-in-avalanche-everest. Accessed on August 28, 2018.

Unit 5

Track 10 – Activity 2

Cancel your Netflix session: Binge watching TV makes it LESS enjoyable as you're more likely to forget plot details.

Binge watching television series like Game of Thrones could make it significantly less enjoyable than watching it on a weekly basis.

New research found watching too much television in one go diminishes the quality of the show with viewers getting 'significantly less' enjoyment than those who paced themselves.

Research led by the University of Melbourne found how people watch television significantly affects how much enjoyment they get out of it.

'Binge watching via video-on-demand services is now considered the new 'normal' way to consume television programs', researchers wrote in their paper in peer-reviewed journal First Monday.

[...]

Researchers found that 'although binge watching leads to strong memory formation immediately following program viewing, these memories decay more rapidly than memories formed after daily or weekly episode viewing schedules.'

[...]

Extracted from www.dailymail.co.uk/sciencetech/article-4861672/Binge-watching-TV-makes-enjoyable-study-claims.html. Accessed on December 11, 2018.

Track 11 – Activity 3

The team took 51 students from the university and split them into groups of 17 to watch the BBC Cold War drama The Game over different periods of time.

One group watched one-hour weekly another watched it daily and the other group watched the whole season (six hours) in one sitting [...].

No participants had previously watched the show and they all watched it in the lab.

Any time a character lit a cigarette or poured a drink they had to press a keyboard to prove that they were concentrating.

They filled out a questionnaire straight after finishing the show, then 24 hours later, and then twice a week until 140 days had passed.

Questions included things like 'In episode four, what was delivered to Arkady's secret mailbox?'

People who binge-watched had the best memory the day after the show but this declined sharply from then on.

People who viewed the show weekly remembered the least after 24 hours but then could retain the most information over time.

Weekly viewers also reported enjoying the show more than any of the other groups.

[...]

Extracted from www.dailymail.co.uk/sciencetech/article-4861672/Binge-watching-TV-makes-enjoyable-study-claims.html. Accessed on December 11, 2018.

Unit 6

Track 12 – Activity 2

The Illicit World of Bitcoin and the Dark Web

Two words will be indelibly etched on the minds of many people following bitcoin: Silk Road. This was the original dark market, and it became notorious for enabling people to sell drugs and other illegal items online. But, what is a dark market, and how does one work?

By themselves, dark markets aren't necessarily illegal. They are simply digital marketplaces, created using the same kinds of technologies that typically underpin bitcoin. At the very least, they will accept bitcoin as a method of payment because of its quasi-anonymous characteristics.

Having said that, most dark markets quickly become illegal because of the kinds of products that they allow vendors to sell. As soon as a digital marketplace allows for the trafficking of drugs, weapons, or other illegal items, then it is breaking the law, and law enforcement officials will quickly get interested.

[...]

Extracted from www.thebalance.com/what-is-a-dark-market-391289. Accessed on September 11, 2018.

Track 13 – Activity 3

[...]

Silk Road

That's what happened to Silk Road, which was one of the first – if not the first – dark markets on the web. Created by Ross

Ulbricht, it was a digital marketplace that connected vendors of illegal drugs with potential buyers. Vendors would advertise their wares on listings maintained by Silk Road, which was similar to the kinds of listings you might find on any legitimate e-commerce marketplace.

When someone decided to buy drugs via the website, they generally wouldn't want to send money directly to that person. Drug peddling isn't exactly a trustworthy business, and everyone who advertised and purchased using Silk Road was anonymous. This would have made it very easy for crooks to make off with customers' money without sending any goods in return.

To solve this problem, Silk Road provided an escrow service. Customers buying drugs from vendors who listed on Silk Road would send their funds to Silk Road, instead of the vendor. The website would then hold these funds until the customer confirmed that they had received what they had ordered. Then, Silk Road would release the funds to the vendor.

The funds were always sent in bitcoin, rather than fiat currency, because when used correctly, the network can provide a great degree of anonymity.

[...]

Silk Road wasn't a decentralized marketplace, though. It ran on a computer controlled by Ulbricht. It was protected, though, because it ran on Tor, which is a communications protocol designed to offer anonymity to those who use it. Originally developed by the U.S. Navy, Tor has become popular among those wanting to protect their identities online.

The FBI eventually arrested Ulbricht by piecing together clues that they gathered from various places outside the Tor network. Now, though, many more dark markets have sprung up, most of them dealing with drugs.

[...]

Extracted from www.thebalance.com/what-is-a-dark-market-391289. Accessed on September 11, 2018.

Track 14 – Activity 4

Dark Markets Under Attack

Aside from the fact that they are breaking the law, one of the biggest concerns around dark markets is trustworthiness. In several cases, dark markets have suddenly vanished with millions of dollars in escrow funds, leaving customers robbed of their funds. Law enforcement is also getting better at targeting these dark markets and taking them down. In November 2014, Operation Onymous, an international law enforcement operation, seized over 400 dark web domains. Dark markets including CannabisRoad, Blue Sky, and Hydra have been taken down.

Law enforcement says that it has found a way to target sites using Tor, although has refused to reveal how.

Dark markets continue to operate, and law enforcement continues to take them down in a continuous game of cat and mouse. Anyone considering engaging in illegal activities through these marketplaces should be aware of the risks.

Extracted from www.thebalance.com/what-is-a-dark-market-391289. Accessed on September 11, 2018.

Unit 7

Track 15 – Activity 2

Next time you see someone calling themselves an influencer, next time you see a list of influencers on a very credible article think to yourself: how was this made? Influencers are everywhere, everyone's calling themselves an influencer, even I'm guilty of calling myself an influencer when I was featured as an influencer last year. But what actually makes a real influencer? What makes a fake influencer? Should you be calling yourself an influencer? Should I be calling myself an influencer? These are all questions I've been thinking a lot about lately and in this short talk I wanna share with you some of my thoughts and I wanna hear from you.

Transcribed from www.youtube.com/watch?time_continue=10&v=bN5HYYZd_Fk. Accessed on September 20, 2018.

Track 16 – Activity 3

Next time you see someone calling themselves an influencer, next time you see a list of influencers on a very credible article think to yourself: how was this made? Influencers are everywhere, everyone's calling themselves an influencer, even I'm guilty of calling myself an influencer when I was featured as an influencer last year. But what actually makes a real influencer? What makes a fake influencer? Should you be calling yourself an influencer? Should I be calling myself an influencer? These are all questions I've been thinking a lot about lately and in this short talk I wanna share with you some of my thoughts and I wanna hear from you.

Just before we start, I wanna just say that this isn't about calling anyone out, this isn't like I've seen something, I've got annoyed, and I want to dig someone out, this is literally me trying to shed some light on the whole influence of space for you and share some of the insights that I've found that I was quite shocked by, and just to kind of, put us all on a level playing field when it comes to understanding what an influencer is and how these influences are being identified. One of the main points that this talk is all about is about lists of influencers. I'm sure you've all seen on very credible articles, "The top 20 snapchatters of 2017", "The top 10 social media experts", "The top 10 LinkedIn experts". We've all seen these lists, I've been named on a few of them as well myself, but what actually is the methodology behind creating those lists? What is the data backed up to actually identify those people and those featured influencers as the most influential in that space? In a lot of cases there's no data, there's literally like no data to back this stuff up. It's all the opinions of the contributor who's writing that article. It's just someone's opinions. It's literally someone's opinions on who they think the top influencers are in that certain field and people are pulling the wool over your eyes! Every time you read these articles... Why are they choosing these people as the top 20? Why are they choosing them? I honestly think one of the big things they're doing it for is to do favors for people they wanna do favors for. [...]

So what I want you all to think about next time you see

someone calling themselves an influencer, next time you see a list of influencers on a very credible article, think to yourself: how was this made? And it will change the way you think about things. [...]

Transcribed from www.youtube.com/watch?time_continue=10&v=bN5HYYZd_Fk. Accessed on September 20, 2018.

Unit 8

Track 17 – Activity 2

You know, I've never understood how, um, imagining the audience naked was supposed to make you less nervous. Honestly, I'm just uncomfortable right now. Especially with Mr. Wardle. Um, okay. To ensure clear communication with this "social media generation", hashtags and pop-culture references will be used. #you'rewelcome. Good afternoon, ladies and gentlemen. Today is an exciting day: today I'm gonna give you a speech. Now, graduates, I don't know if you know me, but I'm Chase. We went to High School together. That was good times, follow me on Twitter.

And I want to give a big congratulations to everyone --including myself-- for being here today. The world we live in is plagued with dangers: Ebola, ISIS, Global Warming, facial acne. And despite all the odds, we still managed to graduate, so let's give us a big round of applause.

[Applause]

It was only three years ago that we came to the labyrinth known as Weber High. As young, timid sophomores we found ourselves lost in its halls like they were the changing staircases of Hogwarts.

[...]

Transcribed from www.youtube.com/watch?v=DRiV4KZBoIY. Accessed on September 25, 2018.

Track 18 – Activity 3

And now, here we are: done with high school!

As Charles Dickens put it, "It was the best of times, it was the worst of times."

[...]

Now, at the end of our careers as students, we have an opportunity: now is our time to take on the world, and to find and pursue our passions; to quote unquote, "Leave a Legacy." William Shakespeare, and also Channing Tatum, once said, "Some are born great, some achieve greatness, and some have greatness thrust upon them." In life, we can't always count on being born great, or having greatness thrust upon us, but always, always remember that the opportunity to achieve greatness is within our grasp. Keep in mind that many of our social and political leaders and heroes started their lives as an average person; as just one of you and me. Despite the failures and mistakes we will make, and although we may be "average", we find that the average can achieve greatness, whether recognized by the world or just a few. Greatness comes from our friends reaching out to us, those who go out of their way to be thoughtful; the "unsung heroes".

If there's anything you take from today, remember that to "leave a legacy" and to "achieve greatness" is not to get money and recognition, it's to leave those with whom you cross paths with a little more happiness and hope. Our time here together as a senior class will not be remembered by grades, popularity, likes, or favorites, but by our relationships. The kind of person you were. These are legacies, the kind we must leave.

Class of 2015, it's been a #splendid three years with you, and from the bottom of my heart, I wish you all the very, very, very best. Thank you.

[Applause]

Transcribed from www.youtube.com/watch?v=DRiV4KZBoIY. Accessed on September 25, 2018.

NOTES

NOTES

NOTES

STICKERS

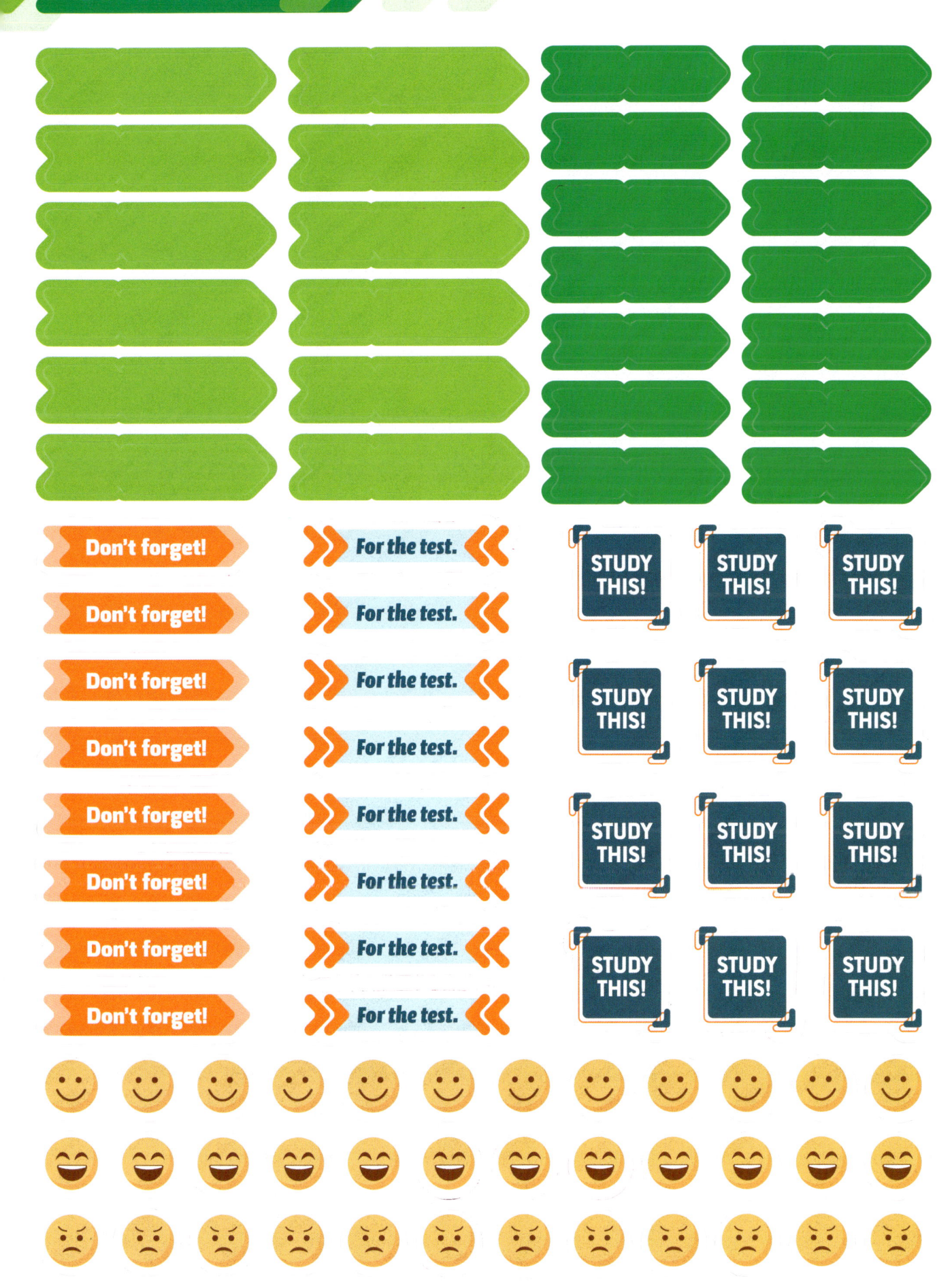

Don't forget!
Don't forget!
Don't forget!
Don't forget!
Don't forget!
Don't forget!
Don't forget!
Don't forget!

For the test.
For the test.
For the test.
For the test.
For the test.
For the test.
For the test.
For the test.

STUDY THIS!
STUDY THIS!
STUDY THIS!
STUDY THIS!
STUDY THIS!
STUDY THIS!
STUDY THIS!
STUDY THIS!
STUDY THIS!
STUDY THIS!
STUDY THIS!
STUDY THIS!